Peter Fleming, the brother of Ian Fleming, was a great
explorer before the Second World War. NEWS FROM
TARTARY was first published in 1936 and this is its
nineteenth edition.

D0259662

Peter Fleming

News From Tartary

A Journey from Peking to Kashmir

Futura
Macdonald & Co
London & Sydney

A Futura/Jade Book

First published in Great Britain in 1936
by Jonathan Cape Limited

First Futura edition 1980
Reprinted 1983

ISBN 1 7088 1919 2

Filmset, printed and bound in Great Britain by
Hazell Watson & Viney Limited,
Member of the BPCC Group,
Aylesbury, Bucks

Futura Publications
A Division of
Macdonald & Co (Publishers) Ltd
Maxwell House
74 Worship Street
London EC2A 2EN

A BPCC plc Company

CONTENTS

5

PART FOUR

NO MAN'S LAND

PART FIVE

NO PICNIC

PART SIX

THE DESERT ROAD

PART SEVEN

THE ROOF OF THE WORLD

To V. F.
Killed in Action
May 20th, 1917

FOREWORD

THERE is not much to say about this book by way of
introduction. It describes an undeservedly successful
attempt to travel overland from Peking in China to Kashmir
in India. The journey took seven months and covered about
3500 miles.

Anyone familiar, even vicariously, with the regions
which we traversed will recognize the inadequacy of my
description of them. For much of the time we were in
country very little known – country where even the collated
wisdom represented by our maps was sometimes at fault
and seldom comprehensive; and although at almost no
point on our route could we have regarded ourselves as
pioneers, there was hardly a stretch of it which did not
offer great opportunities to specialists – opportunities to
amplify, confirm, or contradict the findings of their rare
and distinguished predecessors.

We did not avail ourselves of these opportunities; we
were no specialists. The world's stock of knowledge –
geographical, ethnological, meteorological, what you will
– gained nothing from our journey. Nor did we mean that
it should. Much as we should have liked to justify our
existence by bringing back material which would have set
the hive of learned men buzzing with confusion or complacency, we were not qualified to do so. We measured no
skulls, we took no readings; we would not have known
how. We travelled for two reasons only.

One is implicit in the title of this book. We wanted (it
was part of our job, even if it had not been part of our
natures) to find out what was happening in Sinkiang, or
Chinese Turkistan. It was eight years since a traveller had
crossed this remote and turbulent province and reached
India across country from Peking. In the interim a civil

11

war had flared up and had (at least we hoped that it had) burnt itself out. There were dark rumours that a Foreign Power was making this area, the size of France, its own. Nobody could get in. Nobody could get out. In 1935 Sinkiang, if you substitute political for physical difficulties, shared with the peak of Everest the blue riband of inaccessibility.

The trouble about journeys nowadays is that they are easy to make but difficult to justify. The earth, which once danced and spun before us as alluringly as a celluloid ball on top of a fountain in a rifle-range, is now a dull and vulnerable target; nor do we get, for hitting it in the right place, the manicure set or the packet of Edinburgh rock which formerly rewarded good marksmanship. All along the line we have been forestalled, and forestalled by better men than we. Only the born tourist – happy, goggling ruminant – can follow in their tracks with the conviction that he is not wasting his time.

But Sinkiang was, in 1935, a special case; and the seemingly impossible journey through it could, at a pinch, qualify as political if not as geographical exploration. To the outside world the situation in the Province was as dark as Darkest Africa in the days when that Victorian superlative was current. So, although we brought back only News from Tartary when we might have brought back Knowledge, we at least had some excuse for going there; our selfishness was in part disguised, our amateurishness in part condoned.

Our selfishness was of course the operative factor. I have said that we travelled for two reasons only, and I have tried to explain one of them. The second, which was far more cogent than the first, was because we wanted to travel – because we believed, in the light of previous experience, that we should enjoy it. It turned out that we were right. We enjoyed it very much indeed.

There is only one other thing. You will find in this book, if you stay the course, a good many statements which – had they not reference to a part of Asia which is almost as remote from the headlines as it is from the sea – would be

12

classed as 'revelations'. The majority of these show the Government of the Soviet Union in what will probably seem to most a discreditable light. All these statements are based on what is, at its flimsiest, good second-hand evidence – i.e. the evidence of reliable people who have themselves witnessed the events or tendencies recorded. I should perhaps add that these statements are made objectively. I know nothing, and care less, about political theory; knavery, oppression and ineptitude, as perpetrated by governments, interest me only in their concrete manifestations, in their impact on mankind: not in their nebulous doctrinal origins.

I have travelled fairly widely in 'Communist' Russia (where they supplied me with the inverted commas): and I have seen a good deal of Japanese Imperialism on the Asiatic mainland. I like the Russians and the Japanese enormously; and I have been equally rude to both. I say this because I know that to read a propagandist, a man with vested intellectual interests, is as dull as dining with a vegetarian.

I have never admired, and very seldom liked, anything that I have written; and I can only hope that this book will commend itself more to you than it does to me. But it is at least honest in intention. I really have done my best – and it was difficult, because we led such a queer, remote, specialized kind of life – to describe the journey without even involuntary falsification, to tell what it felt like at the time, to give a true picture of a monotonous, unheroic, but strange existence. On paper it was a spectacular journey, but I have tried to reduce it to its true dimensions. The difficulties were potentially enormous, but in the event they never amounted to very much. We were never ill, never in immediate danger, and never seriously short of food. We had, by the only standards worth applying, an easy time of it.

Of the people who helped us, some are thanked in the pages that follow. But there were others, and I should like to take this opportunity of expressing my gratitude to Erik Norin for invaluable assistance in Peking; to Nancy and

13

Harold Caccia, under whose hospitable roof in the Legation my preparations, such as they were, were made; to Owen and Eleanor Lattimore, for inspiration, advice, and a tin of saddle-soap which we never used; to Sir Eric Teichman, for the loan of the ·44; to John and Tony Keswick, who got the rook rifle for me; and to Geoffrey Dawson, who gave me the run of Asia.

Finally, I should like to thank Kini Maillart. It is customary for the members of an expedition to pay each other elaborate compliments in print, though they may have done the opposite in the field; but ours was more of an escapade than an expedition, and in this as in other respects I have not too closely followed precedent. Explicit praise of her courage, her endurance, her good-humour and her discretion would – were it adequate – strike at the opening of this prosaic and informal narrative a note at once too conventional and too flamboyant. Here and there in the text I have paid tributes to her which could not be withheld; but for the most part I have left you to form your own opinions of a girl who travelled for many hundreds of miles through country where no white woman has ever been before. I can hardly doubt that you will find her, as I did, a gallant traveller and a good companion.

PETER FLEMING

London
May 1936

NOTE

TARTARY is not strictly a geographical term, any more than Christendom is. Tartary is where the Tartars came from, to harry Europe and Asia; and there were so many different kinds of Tartars that the name has at one time or another held good for almost all the lands outside the Great Wall, from the Caspian to Korea. But it has come nowadays to be applied, if it is applied at all, chiefly to Sinkiang (or Chinese Turkistan) and the highlands bordering it; and that is where the journey took us.

PART ONE

HEADING FOR TROUBLE

CHAPTER I

ZERO HOUR

MOST journeys begin less abruptly than they end, and to fix the true beginning of this one in either time or space is a task which I do not care to undertake. I find it easier to open my account of it at the moment when I first realized, with a small shock of pleasure and surprise, that it had actually begun.

I was sitting by myself in a dining-car on the Peking-Hankow Railway in the late afternoon of February 16th, 1935. We were running south through Hopei, not very fast. Outside, in the clear, mild sunlight, a brown plain, chequered into little fields, stretched far away to a jagged rim of hills. Although the fields were naked and the rare trees bare, a faint green patina of spring lay along the ground; there was no ice anywhere. High up in the blue sky skeins of geese were flying east. Here and there a peasant, wadded and bulbous in his winter clothes, was breaking the ground behind a team of ponies woolly and blunt-headed like puppies. Carts on huge solid wheels lurched along rut-scarred roads. From behind the mud walls of a farm unseen winnowers threw up a lovely rhythmic series of golden jets which spread into fine golden clouds, then settled slowly. A cluster of dark trees on a mound embossed with graves sheltered the tired dust of generations. Ancient and symmetrical walls enclosed a little city. 'Sifflez!' said a notice-board (unavailingly) as we approached a bend; the Peking-Hankow Railway was built by French engineers. The sun, stooping towards the horizon, began to set in a diffuse yellow haze.

In this moment, which I remember very clearly, I as it were woke up. The eleventh hour preparations which had for long absorbed not only my energies but my imagination were either finished or for ever shelved. The eleventh hour was over. We were off.

It was time to take stock of the situation, and this, with a kind of luxurious incredulity, I did. It was a sufficiently improbable situation. I found myself the leader of a party of four people who had left Peking the night before with the undisclosed intention of proceeding overland to India (a distance of some three or four thousand miles) by way of North Tibet and Sinkiang. For the latter province, which had until recently been rent by civil war and which was virtually closed to foreign travellers, we had no passports. Apart from a rook rifle, six bottles of brandy, and Macaulay's *History of England*, we had no equipment or supplies worth mentioning. Two of us were women; and our only common language was Russian. I felt extremely cheerful, nevertheless.

Neither I nor any of us thought we had one chance in twenty of getting through; but for a year I had been wanting to try this journey, and to be starting on it was all that I asked. For the sake of starting on it I had come out, for the third time, from England to China; and for the sake of starting on it with a clear conscience I had come out by a route sufficiently circuitous to enable me to discharge my obligations to *The Times* (for whom I was acting as Special Correspondent) before embarking on a forlorn hope which only success could justify from a journalistic point of view.

I had been travelling for six months already. Crèches in the Ukraine and wild boars in the Caucasus; the blue-tiled tomb of Tamerlane in Samarkand, and the legendary, dilatory Turksib Railway; forced labour gangs behind the Amur frontier gazing hungrily up at the train windows, and the garrison-town squalor of Vladivostock; the smell of opium in Manchurian inns; Japanese soldiers firing at unseen bandits between the wheels of a train; little horses and great frosts in Mongolia; a Christmas shooting snipe on the Yangtse, and squash in the Embassy at Tokyo . . . There had been a long prelude to this comic expedition, but it had yielded a sufficiency of far-fetched generaliz-

20

ations couched in three-pile, fire-proof, Printing House Square prose to satisfy the gaping maw of *The Times*'s middle page; and I felt free to fail.

Then there had been the brief – the much too brief – period of actual preparation. A confused period. Seeing dentists, scrounging gun oil, sending (our one lapse into optimism) luggage home, parrying curiosity about our plans, buying films, buying medicine, buying maps . . . For me, the scrambled memory of those days, full of large decisions and small deeds, encounters and evasions, is dominated by the silent figures of three old men. They were thin, wrinkled, resigned old men; beggars by profession. They sat on three hard chairs in a small room opening off a laboratory and full of guinea-pigs in cages. Their ragged trousers were rolled up above their knees and to the dwindled calves of each were clamped a number of little shallow boxes. The sides of the boxes which pressed against the flesh were made of gauze, or something like it; and each box contained 500 lice. For two hours every day, and for the wage of twelve Chinese dollars a month, the three old men pastured, between them, some 18,000 lice.

Why? For our especial safety. The lice, thus nobly nourished, supplied an anti-typhus serum; and on each of the three occasions that we visited the old men we came away injected with the essence of no less than thirty of the little creatures. Humble, impassive, not even perplexed – hired for petty martyrdom in a cause beyond their comprehension – the old men stood enigmatically at the gateway of our enterprise. Their lacklustre and unregarding eyes reflected the indifference of a continent: the continent that we had now to cross.

Peking had seen us off in fancy dress; Peking – in this, as in several other ways, curiously resembling Oxford – can usually be relied upon to be characteristic. Half a dozen pierrettes and apaches, in fur coats and burnt cork, suitably fantasticated our unserious departure on the midnight train. A fellow-journalist, renowned for his collection of portraits of missionaries in stations likely to be bandited, took our photographs in an unmistakably ghoulish manner;

and against the heavy, writhing clouds of magnesium smoke the not improbable captions seemed to dance . . . *'The last photograph taken . . . this foolhardy enterprise . . . In the light of the Provincial Governor's report . . . hope must now be definitely abandoned . . . further efforts towards recovery of the bodies . . .'*

But the smoke dissolved quite quickly.

'Good luck!'

'We need it.'

'Good-bye! Good-bye and good luck . . .'

The train rumbled dubiously off into the night. The lit faces, the friendly known voices, slid away and were lost. To at least one of us it occurred, as though for the first time, that it was really a very long way to India.

CHAPTER II

HEROINE

NIGHT had fallen. Electric lights, wan and uncertain, lit the interior of the dining-car. A fat general, who looked like a Moslem from the North-west, was supping very audibly with two of his staff. A young Pekinese, with Y.M.C.A. stamped all over his European clothes, was eating foreign food unhappily; his unsuccessfully overweening manner had earned the contempt of the waiter. An English couple were deploring the length and discomforts of the journey to Hankow. 'Well, there's only another twenty-four hours.' 'Darling, I don't *think* I should eat that fish if I were you. It's much safer to stick to boiled food on these trains. You know what happened to Elsie . . .' 'Very well, dear. Boy!'

The door behind me opened and Kini came in.

'I've slept for eighteen hours,' she said. 'Let's eat.'

I had first met Kini during the previous summer in London. The guests of a distinguished Orientalist, we found ourselves drinking beer together in a night club, 'How do I get into the Soviet Republic in South China?' asked Kini. 'You don't,' I said, and told her why; at that time I used to pose as an authority on the Chinese Communists. We parted with the migrant's casual formula, which men forget but fate sometimes remembers. 'See you in China, probably?' 'Yes. See you in China.' Kini went off with a strong dislike for me. I thought her nice, and suspected her of being effective.

Our next encounter was less commonplace. It took place in Harbin, on an evening of early November.

The office of the Chief of the Railway Police was uncomfortably crowded. Three foreigners in fur coats, including one consular official, sat on a wooden bench. I, more shabbily attired, leant against the wall beside it. Opposite us, behind a large and littered desk, were grouped two uniformed White Russians and a Chinese, wearing the coloured star of Manchukuo in their fur hats; a Japanese subaltern, who looked surly and sucked his teeth; and a black clad Japanese civilian, a member of the most conspicuous of all Secret Police Services. In the no-man's-land between us – across which, growing momentarily more nearly palpable, flowed electric currents of racial animosity – stood the plaintiff and her chief witness, a Russian sleeping-car attendant with a frightened face.

Kini – tall, rather good-looking, with a brown face and fair hair – was less well dressed than she had been in the night club; but she seemed more at home. The Railway Police were taking down her statement. She spoke quietly in fair Russian, eked out with pantomime which betrayed a sense of humour and a sense of the theatre.

'Name?'

'Ella Maillart.'

'Nationality?'

'Swiss.'

'Home?'

'Geneva.'

'Age?'

'Thirty-one. But all these details are on my passport. . . .'

'Yes, yes. Of course. Occupation?'

'Journalist. I'm the Special Correspondent of a Paris newspaper.'

'When did you arrive in Harbin?'

'But you know that. On the train that got in ten minutes ago.'

'Coming from where?'

'From Hailin.'

'How did you get to Hailin?'

'I travelled down the Harbin-Lafa line to the Korean frontier. Then I came north up the uncompleted railway to Ninguta.'

'Yes?'

'This morning I got on the train at Hailin. It was about

24

eight o'clock. I had been living in small inns for over a week, and you can understand that I was hungry. I asked the *provodnik* . . . this man here . . . where the dining-car was. He told me. I left my compartment and went along the train. Between my compartment and the dining-car there was a coach full of Japanese soldiers. At the door of it I was stopped. I can't speak Japanese, but I smiled and pointed to my mouth and showed them that I wanted to go on to the dining-car. The soldiers at the door pushed me back. At that time they were quite cheerful and laughing: only rather rude.

'I went back to my compartment and found the provodnik. He came along with me, and the soldiers at the door let us through. I got about a third of the way along their coach. There were a lot more soldiers in the corridor, and they suddenly started pushing me back and shouting. They got very angry. I didn't know what it was all about, but I tried to go on to the dining-car, because I didn't see why I shouldn't.

'Then they all seemed to go mad. They hit me in the face and one of them kicked me in the stomach. The provodnik was behind me, and they started hitting him too. I had to give way. I protected myself as well as I could, but when I got to the door I was kicked twice in the back, hard. That made me furious; I hit backwards . . . like this . . . and I knocked one of their caps off on to the line. Then I saw one of them drawing his bayonet, and that frightened me; I jumped across to the entrance of my compartment and shut the door . . . That's all.'

The atmosphere had grown somewhat tense. The fur coats beside me bristled with just wrath. The White Russians looked worried and the Chinese shocked; the Japanese conferred in some agitation; the provodnik's hands, I now saw, were trembling. The only person who appeared not only unruffled but definitely amused was Kini.

The situation had, as a matter of fact, its amusing side, though few women (or men) in Kini's position would have seen it at the time. The conduct of the Japanese soldiery in

25

Manchukuo was, at the period of which I write, rarely endearing. The conscripts – raw, very young, and ridiculously susceptible to alcohol – were becoming increasingly truculent to foreigners, increasingly brutal to the Chinese. (I do not say that all, or even most, gave way to impulses which I believe were common to almost all; but incidents were frequent.)

But here, for once, the Japanese had made a false step. The soldiers on the train had, pardonably enough, mistaken Kini – carrying her own kit-bag, wearing hob-nailed boots – for a White Russian; and you can beat White Russians up till you are blue in the face, because they are people without a status in the world, citizens of nowhere. But Kini, it now awkwardly appeared, belonged, not to a dead Empire, but to a live Republic; she had consulates behind her, and a Foreign Office behind them. Worse still, she was a journalist. No wonder that there was whispering and embarrassment behind the desk; or that our side of the room metaphorically and vindictively licked its lips.

It was now officialdom's move, but officialdom was plainly in a stew. Kini cut short their tentative apologies ('A mistake had evidently been made ... The matter would be reported to the proper quarters ...') by asking for an explanation. Manchukuo, she said, was in many respects a puzzling country, and she was new to it. It wasn't so much that she minded being kicked by private soldiers; but she minded being kicked by private soldiers without knowing why. Couldn't they tell her?

The Japanese subaltern stopped sucking his teeth and clanked out in search of the commandant of the anti-bandit guard on the train. They were back quite quickly. The commandant seemed disconcerted. He was sorry for what had occurred, he said; two men, suspected of being the agents of bandits, had been arrested on the train at the station before Hailin, and he had given orders (he didn't say why) that no passengers were to be allowed to pass along the corridor.

'Why had those orders not been transmitted to the passengers, or even to the staff of the train?' – Through two layers of interpreters, the commandant repeated that he was sorry for what had occurred.

'Let's leave it at that,' said Kini. 'I'm hungry.'

We – the back-benchers and I – were still seething with righteous and primitive indignation in the taxi which was to drop Kini at her hotel.

'Blackmail them,' in effect we said. 'Lodge a protest with your Consul. Write an article about it and send a copy to the Foreign Office at Hsinking; they're hardly on speaking terms with Headquarters as it is, and there'll be hell to pay. Get your own back.'

Kini was wiser. She said that she had to spend another two months in Manchuria; she wasn't going to start a vendetta which might jeopardize her chances of seeing what she wanted to see, going where she wanted to go. She regarded the incident as closed.

It was clear that she was a person not easily rattled.

CHAPTER III

TWO'S COMPANY?

SEVERAL times during the next two months Kini and I found ourselves hunting Manchuria in couples. Armoured against the cold with cumbrous furs and high felt boots of a Bensonian cut, we did two or three short, easy, but fairly uncomfortable journeys together. In smoke-acrid yurts[1] near the Outer Mongolian frontier we watched Mongol reserve stalemating the clumsy, pseudo-altruistic advances of the Japanese; we followed the bed of a new strategic railway into the frosty, pheasant-haunted heart of the Hsingan Mountains; we toured Jehol by embryonic bus-routes. Winter – cloudless and windless – gripped the yellow land, laced here and there with silver by a frozen river. Smoke rose with great deliberation in the sparkling air. At night footsteps fell with a curious and sullen emphasis upon the frosty ground. We lived in inns for a few pence a day and came, almost unconsciously, to know a very little of the country.

We got on well together, though we both paraded our conviction, which was perhaps not wholly justified, that we should have got on better by ourselves. I had had no previous experience of a woman traveller, but Kini was the antithesis of the popular conception of that alarming species. She had, it is true, and in a marked degree, the qualities which distinguish these creatures in the books they write about themselves. She had courage and enterprise and resource; in endurance she excelled most men. She was also what is known as 'good with the natives', and knew, when dealing with a proud but simple

---

[1] A yurt is a round tent with a roof shaped like a flattened cone. The walls and roof are of felts, superimposed on a collapsible wooden framework.

people whose language she did not speak, where to be formal and silent, and where to be mildly the buffoon. She could eat anything and sleep anywhere. The only chink in her armour was her very keen sense of smell; here alone I, who have none, could count myself the better equipped.

Differing widely in character and temperament, we had one thing in common, and that was our attitude to our profession (or vocation, or whatever you like to call it). We were united by an abhorrence of the false values placed – whether by its exponents or by the world at large – on what can most conveniently be referred to by its trade-name of Adventure. From an aesthetic rather than from an ethical point of view, we were repelled by the modern tendency to exaggerate, romanticize, and at last cheapen out of recognition the ends of the earth and the deeds done in their vicinity. It was almost the only thing we ever agreed about.

Kini had had an unusual life. In her late teens the depression drove her from Geneva to teach French in a school in Wales, a task which can hardly have been facilitated by her (then) complete ignorance of English. Other jobs followed, an inconsequent series. She was an expert sailor, and had at a very early age attained the abstruse distinction of sailing for Switzerland in the Olympic Games; on the strength of this she got various jobs navigating other people's yachts for them. She acted in a play in Paris. She captained the Swiss Ladies at hockey. She did odd bits of journalism. She was a ski-ing international, and covered the important races for a Swiss paper. At a time when Fank's *White Hell of Pitz Palu* looked like creating a vogue, she played lead in a ski-ing film. She made a rather considerable voyage round the Mediterranean in a very small boat with a crew of three girls. She helped with excavations in Crete.

Then – penniless as ever – she went to Berlin for a year; learnt German, taught French, played small parts in the film studios, and lived mostly on one meal a day. Somebody lent her fifty dollars, so she went on to Russia.

She lived in Moscow for five months, studying film-production, and rowing in what she described as 'the Alimentation Workers' Eight'. After that she joined a Russian expedition and walked across the Caucasus from north to south, by way of Svanetia; she was badly bitten by a dog half way across, but finished the course, recuperated in the Crimea, and went home for the skiing.

She published a book on that journey, which flopped, and in 1932 went back to Moscow and on into Russian Turkistan. She wanted to get across country to China through Sinkiang, but the Soviet frontier-guards in the passes of the Celestial Mountains did not see eye to eye with her in this matter; so she went back to the plains and knocked about Samarkand, Tashkent, and Bokhara, ending up a roughish journey by riding a camel across the Kizil Kum Desert in December, alone save for guides whose language she could not speak.

The book she wrote this time was not a flop. Kini stood as much lionizing in Paris as she could (it wasn't much), then left for China with enough contracts for articles to cover her expenses. She hated writing and was not a born journalist. But she had tried a lot of things, and journalism alone of them gave her the chance of doing what she wanted to do; so she accepted, with a certain amusement, the role of Special Correspondent.

Quite early on we discovered that we had both come out to China with the same idea – to travel back to India overland. The discovery created a certain embarrassment. We were quite content to potter about the comparatively civilized backwoods of Manchuria together; but neither of us – and we both hastened to make this clear – wanted to commit himself or herself to the other's society on a journey which was not only very long and allegedly dangerous but which had for each of us (I think) a curious kind of personal importance.

The situation eased, however, when we made the further discovery that, whereas Kini contemplated a route which would lead her up through Szechwan into

Eastern Tibet and thence as God might provide, I was aiming at Urumchi and Kashgar via Mongolia. Thenceforward we discussed the little we knew about our respective routes with complete tranquillity. We were not to know that they were both, for the moment, impossible.

CHAPTER IV

THE FORBIDDEN PROVINCE

WE knew it when we got to Peking.

When we got to Peking it was at once apparent that the chances of reaching India overland were infinitesimal. Kini's projected route was certainly out of the question; the Red Armies, dislodged from Southern Kiangsi, were operating in Szechwan and elsewhere (but chiefly in Szechwan), moving up and down the country with astonishing rapidity, making legendary night marches, sustaining defeat only in the columns of the press. That way was barred.

On my route the prospects were hardly brighter. For most travellers, and all merchants, the road from China into India lies, as it has lain for centuries, through Sinkiang[1] along that ancient 'Silk Road' which is the most romantic and culturally the most important trade route in the history of the world. The Silk Road takes – or used to take – you through Sinkiang to Kashgar and the Himalayan passes by one of two alternative routes; the first (a road now practicable for wheeled traffic) running along the line of oases which fringe the Takla Makan on the north, below the foothills of the Tien Shan or Celestial Mountains; the second (sandier and less well watered) skirting the Takla Makan on the south and backed by the Kuen Lun Mountains, behind which mass the 20,000 foot escarpments of the Tibetan plateau.

The first and more northerly of these routes is best approached by one or other of the Mongolian caravan

[1] The correct romanization of the two Chinese characters which mean 'The New Dominion' (the official designation of the Province of Chinese or Eastern Turkistan) is Hsin Chiang. But in this book, which does not purport to be any more serious than the journey which it describes, proper names will appear in whichever of their various forms seems to me the most widely current and therefore the most easily recognizable outside China.

trails; Owen Lattimore, at that time the last traveller to have reached India from China, went this way in 1926–27, and so – later in 1935 – did Sir Eric Teichman. (The journeys of both these travellers belong to an order far above ours.) The southern route through Sinkiang, of which Tunghwang and the Cave of a Thousand Buddhas may be called the eastern terminus, is most conveniently joined by following the old Imperial Highway which runs up through Kansu to Hami.

In the spring of 1935, however, to have attempted to enter Sinkiang by either of these routes would have been most inadvisable. The bloody civil war, or succession of civil wars, which had ravaged the province in 1933 and 1934 was indeed believed to be in abeyance. The capital, Urumchi, and with it the cause of the self-appointed provincial government, had been saved from the invading Tungan rebels in January 1934 by Soviet troops and aeroplanes operating – inadmissably and unavowedly – on Chinese soil; and the redoubtable Tungan army – the best fighters, bar the Communists, in China – was thought to be confined in that string of oases through which the southern road across the province runs, and of which the centre is Khotan. But the provincial government, although its authority had been more or less firmly re-established over the greater part of its territories, was not at home to visitors. The Governor, General Sheng Shih-tsai, though professing allegiance to, and indeed – *faute de mieux* – confirmed in office by, Nanking, rarely answered, and never demurred to, the Central Government's telegraphic protests at his Russian affiliations. His real masters were the Soviet civil and military 'advisers'; the destinies of the province were being worked out by methods, and towards ends, which their manipulators were the reverse of anxious to advertise.

Peking was full of rumours, but for two years Sinkiang had been virtually cut off from the rest of China, and the few reliable scraps of information obtainable were at least several months out of date. Such news as there was was bad. Two Germans – the last representatives, save for a few missionaries, of the non-Russian foreign community in Urumchi – had been causelessly imprisoned there for over a year without being tried or even charged; one of them had been kept in chains throughout a bad attack of typhus. A Swede, who had also seen more than was healthy, was being detained under open arrest. The Eurasia Air Line (one of the Germans was their local manager) had since 1933 been obliged to abandon indefinitely their service to Urumchi. In the spring of 1934 Mrs. Thomson-Glover, the wife of the British Consul-General in Kashgar, had been shot through the shoulder while standing on the terrace of the consulate, and a doctor attached to the consulate had been killed. None of this was reassuring.

Of the few foreigners who had attempted to enter Sinkiang since 1933 a young German of good family, travelling for adventure, had disappeared in the neighbourhood of Hami; from information that we gathered on the road, it is pretty certain that he was murdered. An Italian, featured by the press as 'The Second Marco Polo', had got into the province through Mongolia, only to be arrested and sent out again. Even Dr. Sven Hedin, who had just – on the eve of his seventieth birthday – concluded a road-surveying mission in Sinkiang on behalf of the Central Government, had, in spite of his personal prestige and his semi-official status, been treated roughly by the Tungans and suspiciously by the provincial authorities.

From our point of view it looked as if, with Russian influence astride both the recognized routes through Sinkiang to India, we should be lucky if we got into the province at all; and luckier, perhaps, if we got out.

In the circumstances, the obvious thing to do was to find a route not generally recognized as such, and to take the province in the flank at a point where the influence of the provincial government – Soviet-dominated and prudently exclusionist – might be expected to be weak. The map showed that our best, in fact our only chance of doing this was to go to Lanchow and thence – instead of following the Imperial Highway north-west to Hami, where we should have been either arrested, sent back, or got rid of in some even more humiliating and final way – to continue due west across (not to be technical) the top right-hand corner of the Tibetan plateau. This route would take us through the remoter and not more than nominally Chinese parts of the Province of Chinghai, through the mountains round the lake called Koko Nor and across the basin of the Tsaidam marsh, 9000 feet above sea-level, until we reached the eastern ranges of the Kuen Lun. These, if our prospects were locally considered good, we should by some means cross, dropping down into one or other of the oases on the south of the Takla Makan, where we should find ourselves within Sinkiang and well on the main road to Kashgar. This strategy, if all went well and if the rumours that we heard were true, would give us our first contact with Sinkiang at a point where the rebel Tungan armies – anti-Soviet, anti- (by reputation) -everyone – were in control; where travellers were not expected and whence travellers could hardly be sent back; where the lack of a passport from the Central Government might be anything but a handicap; where, in a word, it all boiled down to bluff.

But of course this plan, so pat and smug on paper, was not vouchsafed in a vision, or even evolved by abstract poring over maps. It was built in a ramshackle way on circumstance by opportunism and a little imagination. Briefly, what happened was this:

Kini met Dr. Norin, the geologist of the Sven Hedin Expedition. So, a little later, did I. Norin, at the outbreak of the civil war in Sinkiang in 1933, had escaped from the province by way of the Tsaidam. In the Tsaidam he had met a White Russian couple called Smigunov, who were also on the run, and the three of them travelled back to civilization together. He spoke highly of them. They had lived in the Tsaidam for several years, trading with the Mongols. They talked Mongol, Turki, and a little Chinese, knew the country well, and were liked and respected by the people. At present they were in Tientsin, where the husband worked as a waiter in the Russian Club. But they wanted to go back to the Tsaidam. If anyone (said Norin) wanted to get to India by what seemed the only potentially practicable route, they couldn't do better than take the Smigunovs as guides.

Thus, gradually, the plan and the party took shape. I was only intermittently in Peking between trips to Shanghai, Tokyo, and Mongolia; and Kini, who had been the first to hear of the Smigunovs, had first claim on their services. We still felt a perhaps unreasoned aversion from the idea of travelling together; but this sentiment was as nothing to our not less unreasoned desire to do the journey somehow. And at last – reluctantly, rather suspiciously – we found ourselves joining forces.

It was against our principles. Kini's last book had been called *Turkistan Solo*; my last book had been called *One's Company*. If we felt foolish starting together, what would we be made to feel when we came back?

CHAPTER V

EXILES AND ARMAMENTS

THE Smigunovs, brought up from Tientsin by train, accepted our proposals with alacrity. For the last two years their life, like the life of nine-tenths of the White Russian community in China, had been hard and drab; but not quite hopeless. Unlike most of their compatriots, whose nostalgia reached back to places they would never see again, to a life that no longer existed, the Smigunovs dreamed of a Utopia that was not irrevocably off the map. In the Tsaidam (of which, I must say, they drew a somewhat over-idyllic picture) they had a tent and a few animals and a primitive but profitable business; and friends, and prestige, and the chance of living as they liked to live. In Tientsin they were strangers and doubly exiles; and in Tientsin life was more squalid and more precarious than it had ever been on the Central Asian uplands. We offered them what they wanted above all else: their travelling expenses back to the Tsaidam. They were as pleased and excited as children.

They were indeed children in almost everything. Stepan Ivanovitch had commanded a poison-gas company on the Western Front during the war, and after the Revolution had drifted into China with the broken remnants of one of the White Armies. He was a tall, burly man, with a florid face, a black moustache, and a fierce expression which, in dealing with the Chinese, was too seldom qualified by a smile. Like almost all Russians, he was an optimist; but his optimism had guts and initiative behind it.

His wife was even more of an optimist. Nina was always sure that everything would be all right in the end. The daughter of a much-respected doctor in Urumchi, she had had, for a girl in her early twenties, an unusually outlandish life. It had bred in her resource and a complete indifference to discomfort. She was calmer and shrewder in her judgment – especially of people – than Smigunov; and though she quite often got excited, she never got excited to no purpose. In appearance she was plump and pretty; but the most attractive thing about her was her spirit – her refusal to accept, or even to admit the possibility of, defeat. You felt that she was a person who deserved to be lucky. She wasn't lucky, though.

The Smigunovs had undertaken to guide us to the western extremity of the Tsaidam and thereafter as far along the road to India as political conditions permitted. We started, as I have said, with the minimum of equipment and supplies, believing – rightly, as the event proved – that the paraphernalia and accoutrements which contribute to the comfort and efficiency of a proper expedition would have been the death of ours. Except for a very few friends in Peking, nobody in China knew what we were going to try to do; the most we admitted to was a passion for sport and photography, which we hoped to indulge in the course of a short trip round the Koko Nor. Passports for Sinkiang could only be obtained from the Central Government, which really meant that they could not be obtained at all; Nanking could hardly be expected to issue passports for a part of her territories where she was neither able to take responsibility for a traveller's safety nor likely to gain credit from a traveller's observations. Moreover, it seemed, as I have said, doubtful whether – relations between Nanking, Urumchi, and the Tungans being what they were – a passport from the Central Government would prove the best of recommendations to the officials in Sinkiang. So we carried papers which would take us as far as the Province of Kansu, and hoped for the best thereafter.

Both Kini and I preferred, on principle and from previous experience, to travel light. Moreover, in view of the very limited scope of our ostensible itinerary, large quantities of baggage, stores, and tents would have stimulated the curiosity of officials to a dangerous degree (to say nothing of their cupidity); and as it turned out we should often have found it impossible to get animals to carry the stuff. Our staple foodstuffs we knew that we could buy as we went along, and tents and sleeping-bags could be made for us in Sining, on the edge of the Tibetan plateau. So apart from old clothes, a few books, two compasses and two portable typewriters, we took with us from Peking only the following supplies: 2 lb. of marmalade, 4 tins of cocoa, 6 bottles of brandy, 1 bottle of Worcester sauce, 1 lb. of coffee, 3 small packets of chocolate, some soap, and a good deal of tobacco, besides a small store of knives, beads, toys, etc., by way of presents, and a rather scratch assortment of medicines. There may have been a few other oddments which I have forgotten, but these were the chief items.

Our clothes were a random collection and call for little comment. We would have cut very unprofessional figures by the side of a properly caparisoned expedition, but our wardrobes stood up to the journey well enough. We had with us only two garments of an unexpected nature. One was a Russian cavalry overcoat which I had bought in Samarkand and whose long skirts made it invaluable both for riding and sleeping in cold weather; the other was a pair of white flannel trousers which Smigunov brought with him because he had no place in which he could leave them behind. Kini dressed very much as I did, only rather better.

She and I both had Leica cameras; in fact she had two. She is by way of being an expert photographer, knows the difference between Isochrome and Superpan and other mysterious things, and holds exhibitions in Paris from time to time. The Leicas turned out very satisfactorily. From our point of view one of their great virtues was that they can be handled with one hand; a large proportion of the photographs we took were taken from the saddle; and it made a lot of difference being able to hold your horse in with one hand while you focused the camera with the other.

Then there was the question of armaments: a question quaintly destined to assume, in the winter of 1935, an almost national importance throughout Great Britain. In the first of an interminable series of articles describing this journey, which *The Times* published on my return to England, I wrote: 'Our armaments consisted of one ·44 Winchester rifle, with 300 rounds of pre-war ammunition of a poorish vintage, which was not worth firing; and a second-hand ·22 rook rifle, which surpassed itself by keeping us in meat throughout the three months during which there was anything to shoot.'

On the day following the appearance of this article a gentleman wrote a very good-natured letter to the Editor, saying that he could not help feeling 'slightly annoyed at my inefficiency' at setting out to cross Central Asia with such a poor selection of weapons, and recalling that in Central Asia, as in Brazil, 'only a rook rifle had stood between Mr. Fleming and an untimely death'.

For some reason I was irritated by the last sentence, with its implication that in remote parts of the world one carried weapons with a view to shooting oneself out of tight corners. I have never been in a tight corner myself; but my instincts and my common sense tell me that there are two possible explanations for finding yourself in a position in which you feel that you have got to use firearms in self-defence. Either you have been foolish or you have been unlucky; and the chances are that if you do shoot you will be committing more folly or incurring more bad luck. The methods of melodrama may serve for an ugly scene. But when the ugly scene is over you are still a long way from the rescue party and the third act curtain and 'God Save the King'; and if you are (as we rapidly became) entirely dependent for your food, your guides, your transport – in a word, for your continued existence – on the goodwill of the local inhabitants, it is as well not to decimate the latter. Even if by holding your fire you rather tamely lose your life, you can in most cases congratulate yourself, as you look down from heaven on the unkind wastes that you had still to cross, on having chosen wisely between a quick death and a slow one.

My critic, at any rate, I answered with what – writing in some haste – I imagined at the time to be an eminently reasonable defence of my choice of weapons (on the grounds that they were the best I could get) and an urbane but whimsical exposure of the fallacy underlying the words 'untimely death'. When *The Times* printed it, unfortunately, it turned out to be about as urbane and whimsical as an adder; and I was distressed to find that I had poured upon the good-natured gentleman a flood of intemperate and overweening scorn. I was ashamed of myself, and I should prefer to forget the whole incident were it not that, *post* and *propter hoc*, there forthwith opened in the columns of *The Times* a controversy so long, so fiercely and so curiously waged, that I should be offending a minority – but, as then appeared, a formidably articulate minority – of my readers if I omitted all mention of it in this context.

Of the letters that were printed, some were for me, some were against me, and almost all had, in contrast to the prominence given them, a superb, Olympian irrelevance. Someone drew a deep breath and called me 'hybristical'; someone else charmingly described a primitive weapon of precision much in vogue at the private school at which we had both been educated; a third adduced, in support of me, his own experience when hunting for the pot in the Arctic; a fourth retorted with contradictory evidence from the same region. But the letter I liked best was from a lady. She wrote: 'In Mr. Peter Fleming's narrative he speaks of the crawling of a woman between the fore and hind legs of a strong camel, believing' (me believing, or the camel believing?) 'it would impart vigour to her offspring. I myself saw a child passed beneath an elephant's body to cure it of stomach trouble. This was near Kandy but years before, on the outskirts of Cork, I remember a child being passed backwards and forwards beneath a donkey as a cure for whooping cough.' Nobody will deny that that is an interesting letter; but for me the most interesting thing about it is that not only did I never see a woman crawling between the legs of a camel, either a strong camel or any other sort of camel, but I never even said I'd seen it. That letter made me feel as if I'd done the rope trick.

I took no further part in the controversy about my

weapons, though for weeks the sort of people (they are bad enough anyway) who slap you on the back in bookshops and ask you where you are off to next found a god-sent conversational standby in my rook rifle; so that at last I began to wear a hunted look, and to know what it feels like to have to duck a joke, like a father of quadruplets. But in his original letter my critic had suggested that *The Times* should present me with a good sporting rifle, and I and several of my supporters had seconded his suggestion. So that when, just before Christmas, I got married to someone fairly firmly fixed in the public eye without the public knowing anything about it, *The Times*, in an announcement which was also a scoop, revealed that the directors were giving us a rifle as a wedding present. A generous stranger weighed in with a hundred rounds of ammunition, and a family near Bristol sent us half a crown to buy the fire-arms licence with. So it all ended happily.

To revert (briefly) to the weapons which were to prove a kind of journalistic Jenkins' Ear:

I would have liked, had it been possible, to have with me one good high-velocity sporting rifle and one ·22; the former for the yaks, bears, and other big game which we had been told we should encounter in profusion, the latter for wild geese, duck, and whatever small game should present itself. If I had had to choose between them, I should have chosen the smaller rifle without hesitation. My experience, limited as it was, in Brazil had taught me the pot-hunting potentialities of a ·22 in country where human beings are so rare that the wild life does not regard them as a serious menace. With a big rifle, you run the risk of scaring the game for some distance round, of spoiling the meat of wild-fowl or ground game, and of arousing the unwelcome curiosity of the local inhabitants. A shot-gun is open to the first and last of these criticisms, while the weight and bulk of the necessary ammunition are an additional drawback. And, anyhow, in the wilds a ·22 is almost always more fun to use than a shot-gun.

Events were to justify my theories. Sporting rifles and ammunition are practically unprocurable in China, and

Smigunov and I scoured Peking for one without success. Then Sir Eric Teichman, the Counsellor of the British Legation (as it then was), most kindly offered me the unconditional loan of a little ·44 Winchester which had seen honourable service in Eastern Tibet fifteen years before. (He did not know either that I was starting for India overland, or that in a few months he would be doing the same thing himself). There were 300 rounds of ammunition, past its prime a decade ago, with the ·44; I tested it on the Legation Guard's range, and found it fairly accurate at fifty yards, but no good over that. Still, any rifle was better than none, and the ·44 looked all right; I took it with me largely for reasons of 'face'.

The rook rifle market in Peking was sluggish to the point of stagnation, and at the eleventh hour I wired, in despair, to a resourceful friend in Shanghai, who undermined the coastal defences of the Chinese Republic by buying the indispensable weapon from a lighthouse-keeper. It was put on the train for Peking; but the train for Peking left the rails at Tsinan, and it was only on the very eve of our departure that the expedition finally acquired what was to prove perhaps the most important item in its equipment.

So much for armaments.

CHAPTER VI

NIGHTMARE TRAIN

At Chengchow the Peking-Hankow 'express' was due to make connection with a train, similarly miscalled, on the Lunghai Railway. We had been warned that it was a point of honour on the former line to miss this connection by a matter of a very few minutes, and found this tradition faithfully observed.

Midnight saw us stamping and cursing on an ill-lit platform. The coolies who had seized and shouldered our luggage assured us that the train for Sian had left already. This was not true, and we might have caught it with a few seconds in hand; but by the time we had discovered that it was not true, and deduced that the coolies were lying because they were employed as touts by the innkeepers of Chengchow, it was too late; the train had really left. 'Sleep here to-night,' said the coolies, grinning.

We were determined not to; we were loth to lose, so early on, the *élan* of departure in a day's delay. Diligent inquiry revealed that a slow train, with third class accommodation only, was due in an hour or two. We decided to go on to Sian in that.

At about half-past one the slow train dragged itself wearily into the station – a long string of trucks, of the type whose cubic capacity is usually assessed at *hommes 40, chevaux 8*, and from which the doors, like so many of the detachable portions of public property in China, had been removed. But we were too tired and too resolute to criticize so low an estimate of the third class passenger's deserts; our trouble was that the train was full to bursting point. As we ranged desperately up and down it in the darkness I came on a black-clad policeman making great play with an electric torch. Hearing himself addressed by an excessively respectful term, and seeing (as he thought) a solitary foreigner, he kicked his way into an already crowded truck and made a place for me in a corner.

How it was done, save that it was done ruthlessly, I do not know; but ten minutes later the two feet of bare bench allotted to me had been expanded into a large island of suit-cases and kitbags against which the four of us leant, panting. Our arrival brought the total number of passengers in the truck up to seventy-two; all of them had been woken up, half of them had been seriously inconvenienced, and several of them had been trodden on. We were not popular, but we had caught the train. At two o'clock it started. For the first time we were heading due west.

And for the first time we were tasting discomfort. There were no lights in the truck, and in the absence of its doors, which left a third of each side open to the frosty air, the small moribund stove in the middle of the floor did not appreciably affect the mean temperature. Our former train had been overheated, and we were not dressed for what amounted to a night in the open; nor were our warm clothes readily accessible. We lay – numb, and growing more numb – in contorted attitudes while the train banged, lurching, on its way. At frequent intervals it entered tunnels, so that for a time the truck was filled with the pungent, gritty smoke of bad coal. A baby cried incessantly. . . .

As soon as it was light enough to see we emerged without reluctance from that not more than semi-oblivious stupor in which such nights are passed, and fumbled eagerly for sweaters in our kit. Presently the sun rose. The baby stopped crying. At a little station we bought bowls of queer grey gruel, with peanuts in it; they revived us considerably.

We were passing through country which, according to the learned men, is the original home of the Chinese race. A yellow country, streaked here and there with red. Everywhere startlingly terraced hills of loess, grotesquer than the most outlandish ant-hills, reared silhouettes which had enough of symmetry in them to suggest the artificial. The ochre earth had, for so ancient a place, a strangely brittle air, and was in fact most easily eroded. The smallest

45

stream had eaten out for itself an incommensurate gully; and on the roads the wheels had found their task no harder than the water's, so that every well-frequented highway was a little cañon, often proclaiming itself to us by no more than a dancing whiplash or the dark blue elephant-back of a Peking cart's hood.

There was a kind of prehistoric look about this land, through which the train snorted laboriously, like an ante-diluvian monster. There were few houses, but many habitations. The terraces above us and the gullies below were riddled intermittently with man-made caves – caves with doors and tattered paper windows, above which a black tapering smear commemorated on the yellow sandstone the house-fires of many generations. The men and women who came out from these catacombs to watch us pass were mostly thin and ragged; sun and smoke had made their faces black and they seemed strangely un-Chinese, mopping and mowing on those narrow ledges.

There was nothing un-Chinese about our fellow-passengers. They all had that gift (which the Chinese need and have, which the Russians need and lack) for making one cubic foot into two and turning the Black Hole of Calcutta into an only slightly overcrowded debating hall. Sixty-eight of the seventy-two people present were impervious to the lack of elbow-room, and except in our corner the intricate pattern of humanity had a surface as smooth and harmonious as a completed jigsaw puzzle. Sleeping, eating, talking, nursing their babies, hunting lice in their padded winter clothes, they accepted the prospect of the day's journey with complete equanimity; the day would be a long one, the night had been cold and almost sleepless, the air was thick with dust, the train was slow – these considerations, which meant in a small and nagging way so much to us, had no effective impact on their minds at all. To-day was to-day; no disaster threatened, no responsibility had to be incurred; to-day was to-day.

The train carried a good many soldiers, who were being drafted up to join units engaged in anti-Communist operations on the southern boundaries of Shensi and Kansu. At one station, walking up the train, I came on a big soldier, with a comically disagreeable face, dressed only in a smart suit of foreign-made underwear and vigorously engaged in cleaning his teeth in the open door of a truck. Struck by such conspicuous devotion to the laws of personal hygiene, I took a photograph of him. Somebody laughed. He looked up, saw what was happening, swore, and very pardonably (I should have done the same myself) threw the contents of his tooth-mug at me.

I smiled (he had missed) and said 'That kind of conduct is *extremely* not good to look at', which was the best I could do towards saving my face. But I am afraid I lost it. I deserved to.

The day wore on. We ate scraps of food, and slept in fits and starts. Incident was provided only by a succession of very small, very ragged little boys who periodically jumped the train and clung to the couplings between the trucks until they were discovered and turned off by a train guard with a Mauser automatic and an uncompromising manner. One of them was a master of his craft. The first time he was caught he grinned in a disarming and apologetic way and made the guard believe that he was only trying it on as a joke. They turned him off at the next station, but an hour later found that he was still with us. The guard, having lost face, had to put up a tremendous performance of a man being angry. The little boy countered with a still better performance of a destitute waif with sorrowing relations just a little further west; he wept, fell on his knees, and clasped the puttee'd legs of officialdom. To no avail; they turned him off again. But he had crossed half a province without capital outlay before he was detected, for the third time, on the roof of our truck. What happened to him after that I do not know; he was a singularly self-reliant little boy.

Night fell. The studied, familiar faces of our nearest neighbours slipped, though we had not parted, down the first stage towards oblivion. It grew cold again. At ten o'clock, two hours behind time, the train stopped outside the walled city of Tungkuan. Ruefully reflecting that had we not missed that connection we should have been in Sian (still half a day's journey away) several hours ago, we got stiffly out, found a stationmaster who spoke French, saw our luggage locked up in his office, and took rickshaws into the city, where the China Travel Bureau maintains a small hotel, equipped with the anomalous luxury of beds.

We washed a little and slept a lot.

CHAPTER VII

RAILHEAD

At least, the others slept a lot.

I got up, with a very bad grace, at dawn, walked to the station, and caught the early train to Sian. It was a slow, uncomfortable train, like the one yesterday, and it only reached Sian two or three hours before the 'express', which left Tungkuan in the middle of the day and boasted a dining-car and the accommodation to which our tickets entitled us. But I carried a letter of introduction to two of the English missionaries in the Baptist Mission Hospital in Sian, and I felt it was hardly fair to present this letter – thereby virtually soliciting hospitality – without any warning at all; not everyone, either inside or outside missionary circles, would care to be taken unawares by a party so uncouth in appearance, so internationally and unconventionally constituted, as ours. So I caught the early train.

I got a seat in the guard's van, which I shared with an officer and half a dozen of his men. We had a sunny, dawdling journey through flatter country. Snow showed on mountains to the south and in the sky geese were still flying east. Lunch and breakfast were grey gruel.

In the middle of the afternoon the train stopped beneath the massy walls of Sian, the capital of Shensi and at that time the terminus of the Lunghai Railway. It was very evident that the Communist threat to the south of the province was being taken seriously. Barbed wire entanglements surrounded not only the isolated station but the entire circumference of the city walls. The great gates had a strong guard on them and were kept ajar, so that not more than one person could pass through at a time; nobody could enter or leave the city without a pass of some kind. Inside the walls Central

Government troops, well armed and disciplined, drilled and skirmished on a stretch of waste land with unwonted seriousness and unwonted efficiency. The railway had conferred on Sian the mixed blessing of strategic importance.

I took a rickshaw and set off through wide, somehow characterless streets in quest of the Baptist Mission Hospital. I knew the Chinese for 'the Protestant Mission' and 'the Catholic Mission', but the Baptists were beyond me; and we were going, as it turned out, in the wrong direction when we met two foreigners on foot. They were both Germans, the agents in Sian of various foreign companies; as they were on their way to the hospital I paid off my rickshaw and joined them. They cheered me up by saying that we should have no difficulty in getting a lorry to take us to Lanchow.

The missionaries were charming, they said they could easily put two of us up, and the other two could go to an inn. Armed with a special pass (for passport regulations at the gate became still more stringent after dusk) I walked back to the station to meet the express.

The express was on time. As our flotilla of rickshaws jigged back to the hospital through darkness periodically cleft by the headlights of military lorries, Kini said:

'I wonder where we shall see our next railway?'

'God knows,' I said, not wanting to provoke the fates by pitching our hopes too high, and secretly thinking that it would be here, in Sian, on our frustrated and dejected way back to Peking.

The next railway we saw was in Lahore.

We spent the next day in Sian, and things seemed to be going well. It is true that the maximum of four days which, we had been assured in Peking, sufficed for the journey by road to Lanchow had almost imperceptibly altered to a minimum of five; but I was a sufficiently hardened traveller to feel that it would have been unnatural, almost ominous, if this had not occurred. Moreover, an expected delay of three or four days in

Sian was not materializing. Smigunov and I began at an early hour to scour the city for Lanchow-bound lorries, and before noon had found a convoy of three which was due to leave next day. They did not look as if they would leave next day; they did not look as if they would ever move again. Their loads were mountainous already, and a substantial number of passengers, with luggage, were expected; in corners of the yard in which they stood the more indispensable parts of their engines were being hammered on, blown through, and bound with wire by the drivers and by relations of the drivers.

Nevertheless, discreet and circuitous inquiry revealed that the proprietor of the convoy really did intend to leave to-morrow. For 140 dollars (Mex.), or about £10 (half to be paid in advance), we booked what for lack of a better word may be called accommodation, securing at the same time a very special kind of contract guaranteeing that we should be delivered in Lanchow within six days. This document was of course entirely worthless, but in the wrangling days to come it occasionally gave us a slight tactical advantage in dispute, and it was satisfactory to have fixed things up so quickly.

In the afternoon, under the auspices of the kindly missionaries, Kini and I had the honour of being received by the Provincial Governor. General Shao Li-tze's yamen is part of the once palatial premises to which the Empress Dowager fled from the vengeance of Foreign Powers after the Boxer rebellion and the siege of the Legations. General Shao, an elderly but vivacious little man with stubbly grey hair and beautiful manners, welcomed us in the innermost of many courtyards with cakes and fruit and tea. With him was his young and attractive wife, formerly a Moscow-trained Communist, whom marriage (it is said) saved at the eleventh hour from execution. With one of the missionaries interpreting, we had a long talk, asking the sort of questions (and getting the sort of answers) that are the life-blood of interviews with officials in China. But somehow this interview was less anaemic than most; the Governor and his wife had so much charm, were so merry and hospitable and intelligent, that we enjoyed what might have been a formal and empty occasion as you enjoy a good party. When we asked if any special kind of pass was necessary for the journey to Lanchow, General Shao broke all records of Oriental bureaucracy by having one made out for us in ten minutes; and when we took our leave he and his wife accompanied us to the outermost gate of all, a very signal honour which so greatly enhanced our prestige with the waiting rickshaw coolies that we had to tip them a munificence appropriate to our new status.

We called also on the Germans, and here we heard rumours of Sinkiang. Sven Hedin and Joe Soderböm, fresh from Urumchi, had passed through Sian a few days ago on their way down to the coast, and though neither of them had been disposed to talk we were able to supplement a little the gossip of Peking. Dark tales of methods used to strengthen Soviet influence at Urumchi we heard with keen but academic interest; news of the Tungan rebels touched us more nearly, for we were headed for their territory. They had held up Hedin's party; had for several weeks used their two lorries for military purposes, forcing Soderböm and another Swede to act as chauffeurs; were now in the south of the province, planning to rise once more in revolt when the summer came; Ma Chung-ying, their leader, reported interned across the Russian frontier, was back in Kashgar.

We listened with resignation rather than dismay. It was, on paper, the worst of news (if it was true); but Sinkiang seemed much farther away even than it had in Peking, and we had already become like a hen with its beak to a chalk line, hypnotized by the next step, blind to all beyond it. It was far too early to start talking destinations.

General Chiang Kai-shek and his wife, adding to the responsibilities of High Command the self-imposed duty of socially regenerating China through the New Life

Movement, had recently visited Sian by air. Their doctrines had not fallen on barren ground. As I walked back to the hospital I was reprimanded by a policeman, for the second time that day, for smoking a pipe in the street.

That night I wrote in my diary: 'We start at 8 tomorrow, I don't think.'

CHAPTER VIII

FITS AND STARTS

'I DON'T think' was right.

At an early hour, it is true, our lorry – one of the convoy of three – turned up and added to its already colossal load our own effects. We said good-bye to the missionaries, who had been the most charming of hosts. My own position under their roof had been slightly embarrassing, for one of them, I had heard, knew me by repute as 'the young man who goes round being funny about missionaries', and the more innocuous and agreeable I tried to make myself appear, the more (it seemed to me) did I acquire the hall-marks of a viper in the bosom. Still, they concealed their misgivings; and I hope I concealed mine.

Soon after 8 o'clock Kini took her place beside the driver, the Russians and I climbed on top of the freight, and we moved incredulously off. This manoeuvre was repeated, at lengthening intervals, throughout the morning. We went to some kind of control bureau to get a permit; we went somewhere else to get some petrol; we went to the house of the proprietor of the lorries; we went to an inn to pick up passengers; we went to a restaurant where the driver had some food; we went to a place which was nowhere in particular and just stayed there. Then, at some imprecise moment, we suddenly discovered that everyone had vanished – the driver, the proprietor, the proprietor's friend who usually knew where he was, and all the passengers except ourselves.

We split up and started a desultory search; but Sian is a big city and the quest was hopeless from the start. Occasionally one of the other passengers reappeared, announced that we were starting at once, and disappeared. I began to get angry.

The day before I had met a young man from Nanking,

who had 'Powers A. Lay, Reconstruction Commissioner' on his card and clearly wielded, as a direct representative of the Central Government, a certain amount of influence: a sad-looking young man, with a bow tie and American education, few illusions, and (I suspected) considerable ability. I got in touch with him; he brought official pressure to bear; and in the tail end of a trying afternoon we started, eight hours late. The reason for the delay we traced to the creditors of a man who had a consignment of goods on one of the lorries; they refused to let the lorry leave until he gave them something on account.

On paper it was a barren victory for me, for there was hardly any daylight left and we might just as well (on paper) have postponed departure till the next morning. But I knew how swiftly the beanstalk of procrastination grows in the soil of Asia, and how easily another day, or two or three more days, could lose themselves in the intricate Chinese labyrinth of delay. So I was very glad to be lurching, however tardily, through the streets leading to the West Gate; and the Russians were delighted, for they had seen a black bear being led along on a chain and thereby knew infallibly that luck was with us.

We ran out of the city and on through flat fields which looked dank and dingy in the twilight. At this stage there were only seven passengers on top of the freight; Kini shared the seat beside the driver with a mysterious little Cantonese, who wore spats and smoked a pipe but spoke no word of any foreign language. He said that he was a friend of the Governor of Sinkiang and was going to fly up to Urumchi from Lanchow, then go on to Moscow and afterwards to London. At first the only question in our minds was not whether he was a secret agent or not, but whose secret agent he was; but gradually he showed himself to be such a silly, ineffectual little man that we were not in the least surprised that he never got farther than Lanchow. He had a camp bed with him, which was more than we had.

We were only twenty miles nearer India when we stopped for the night in a very small and miserable village. There was no inn and no eating house. The four of us secured, and held against all comers, a mud-walled cell some 10 feet square, with a *k'ang* to sleep on. It was very cold. We made tea and chatted to an anti-bandit patrol which turned up, valiantly flashing torches. Then we slept.

We were up at dawn, but there was – as there was always to be – a maddening and motiveless delay before the convoy started. The skies were cheerless, and so was the country. We walked behind the lorries over a precarious bridge whose architecture seemed to be an affair of mud and mass-hypnotism. One of the lorries was having engine trouble and we waited for it a long time outside a little village. I remember very clearly the angry despair, the feeling that we should *never* get on, that settled on my impatient soul as twenty-five minutes became half an hour, and half an hour three quarters; and then the light-headed and not less irrational exhilaration which surged up in me as the last lorry came lurching and sputtering into view. These emotional transformation scenes were very common in the next few days.

We began to climb into naked, terraced hills. The Russians chattered happily and interminably of the delights that the Tsaidam would offer. Occasionally we exchanged elementary badinage with the Chinese. We stopped to snatch a meal at an inn and then drove on until, well after dark, we reached the village of Pinchow. Quantitatively, it had been a good day's run.

The inn yard was deep in mud. We were stiff and cold, and when we tried to heat our tiny room by putting a charcoal fire underneath the k'ang we were nearly asphyxiated. Before the fumes had cleared away we received a visit from a Catholic Father, an Italian, whose order maintained a mission in Pinchow. We had some choking conversation with him in a variety of languages, and he very kindly gave us a tin of butter, prepared by the Sisters of a convent in Honan. As we were going to sleep the man in charge of the convoy, a disagreeable person in an overcoat with a velvet collar, called to inform us that a particularly early start was to be made on the morrow.

56

A raw grey dawn found us ready, but one of the engines had frozen up and it was not till three hours later that we took the road. It led us almost immediately into a ford, where blocks of dirty ice danced on the water and our lorry sustained a puncture; the convoy was immobilized again. Kini and I walked on ahead to keep warm, following the zigzag cutting which carried the road up a low range of loess hills. Big partridges, like a kind of chikkor, clucked dubiously at us on the terraces, and little flocks of rock-pigeons swept down on shining wings towards the fields below. Occasionally we stopped and looked back. The lorries – scarce so gross as beetles, and their crews like ants – still stood far beneath us at the ford; it was an hour and a half before they caught us up.

After that for a time there was good going across a plateau, and we were childishly delighted when we passed through a big walled village which marked the boundary between Shensi and Kansu. At first there seemed little enough to choose between the two provinces; but presently we dropped down into a river valley and realized that Kansu was the muddier. Much the muddier. The lorries plunged and lurched wildly, and one of the less likable of our companions, losing his grip on the bucking freight, shot like a cannon-ball into the morass.

This spectacular and pleasing incident was the only bright spot in a black afternoon. One after another the lorries – two of which were very badly driven – stuck fast. They were unloaded; we dug and pushed and pulled; the engines roared; mud flew up; the lorries jerked forward several yards and stuck again. It began to rain.

At last we got through the worst bit and at 3.30 reached the little village of Chingchow where (for no Chinese will ever do anything while it is raining) it was decided, to our fury, that we should stop till next day. Once more we had a cold, cramped night on a k'ang, but this time it was varied pleasantly by supper with an old Norwegian missionary and his wife, who told us tragi-comic tales of banditry and fed us like kings.

The next morning was not much fun. Velvet Collar, the

man in charge, had to pay *likin* on his goods, and this lengthy process, which he had promised to complete the night before, was far from being finished. Kites hung moodily in the slate-grey sky. A semi-circle of scrofulous children screamed with delight outside a butcher's shop where a sheep was having its throat cut. On the summit of a cliff overlooking the village a small and presumably devout party beat enigmatically and monotonously upon a gong. Rumours began to run about that we should not leave until the next day.

But at last the *likin* was paid (it came, we learnt with pleasure to the considerable sum of 360 dollars, and Velvet Collar had a hangdog look). We took our places and the lorries slithered down the steep streets and turned westward once more. We forded another river, ran the gauntlet of a rain of rocks dislodged by blasting on the hill-side above us, and passed a cliff which bore the superstructure of a temple and within which a Buddha – forty-five feet high, according to Rockhill – is hewn in the sandstone. There were several soft patches on the road, but it was a puncture which finally held us up. Once more Kini and I walked on, until we came to a tiny and attractive village, where we sat under a tree and ate prodigious quantities of bread and thought how depressing it would be if we had to come back along this road.

Presently the lorries caught us up, but one of them, through sheer bad driving, stuck in a quagmire at the village gates and was only extracted by the exertions of the entire population. We were bogged three or four more times before we reached, after dark, the large but dilapidated market town of Pinliang, our hearts full of wrath against Velvet Collar and his drivers.

By comparison with the last few days, the inn at Pinliang provided luxurious accommodation: wooden k'angs with fires underneath them and paper windows and chairs and tables and illumination of a sort. But there were sinister rumours abroad and Velvet Collar, when asked what time we were starting to-morrow, was ominously evasive.

CHAPTER IX

A LORRY AND THE LIU PAN SHAN

NEXT day, sure enough, our worst fears were confirmed. One of the lorries needed repairs, another had to wait for a spare tyre from Sian; the convoy would remain in Pinliang for two or three days, perhaps more. Furious, we bearded Velvet Collar, but got nothing but a worthless promise that we should start the next day. Our contract, that ironic document, besides guaranteeing us delivery in Lanchow in the now impossible time of six days, provided that, should one or even two of the lorries break down, the third would not be thereby delayed; this clause being now extremely relevant, Smigunov and I set off to find the city magistrate.

Pinliang is a very long, very narrow town, and we had walked for over a mile before we found the magistrate's yamen. The magistrate was out. As we stalked, glowering, back to the inn, snow began to fall heavily. The worst part of the road, including the 10,000 foot passes of the Liu Pan Shan, lay ahead of us; and if it went on snowing like this the road would be blocked. India, indeed!

As we arrived at the inn, the building next to it – an eating-house where we had breakfasted – quietly and rather sadly collapsed, crumbling into rubble in a cloud of dust. It was one of those days.

It was maddening to have lost a day, and to face the prospect of losing more and the possibility of being held up indefinitely by snow. Kini and I, in search of distraction for our troubled minds, set out once more along the interminable main street. The 61st Division – a reorganized version of Tsai Ting-kai's 19th Route Army which did so well against the Japanese at Shanghai – was billeted in Pinliang pending transfer to the anti-Communist front in southern

Kansu and Shensi. The town was full of grey uniforms and the queer-sounding speech of the South.

We had a good day and almost forgot our anxiety and annoyance. We found an American missionary near the West Gate, a sorrowful man who cheered up only when he spoke of the probability of the Liu Pan Shan passes being closed. From him, by some roundabout way that I have forgotten, we went to visit a little Chinese doctor who spoke French and who, after giving Kini some medicine that she needed for an ailment in her nose, took us to see the Catholic Fathers. The Catholic Fathers gave us a riotous reception. They were nine enormous Spaniards, of whom the younger ones looked, in their large new beards and medieval habit, like supers in a Shakespearean production. They gave us cakes and chocolate and roared with laughter at everything we said. A good time was being had by all when an orderly arrived with a request that we should call on General Yang Pu-fei, the commander of the 61st Division.

At headquarters we had a not less friendly welcome. The General and his Chief of Staff – the little doctor interpreting – talked with unusual frankness about troop movements in the anti-Communist campaign. Everything they said confirmed the impression, which we had began to get at Sian, that the operations in West and North-west China were being carried on with great seriousness, and that Nanking's authority – if only by virtue of the presence of her troops, her currency, and some of her civil officials – was being notably strengthened in regions which, but for the Communists, she would not have bothered very actively about.

As we came back in the evening to the inn snow was no longer falling; but we did not dare to hope that some miracle would have made it possible to go on to-morrow. It had, however. The Smigunovs, beaming triumphantly, announced that another lorry had just come in – a good lorry, with a splendid driver; they had arranged for us to transfer to that; we should start at dawn and perhaps reach Lanchow in three days. This was no time for the scepticism which Russo-Chinese forecasts must normally inspire, and

Kini and I were jubilant. We gloated over Velvet Collar, who had lost his face and half his dollars; we gloated over the mysterious Cantonese, who had paid the full fare in advance and could not bring himself to sacrifice it by a transfer; we were elated beyond measure by this trivial increase in our chances of success.

By half-past nine the next morning all this elation had ebbed. Our new lorry was, as the others had always been, immobile without discoverable cause; and Velvet Collar's convoy, as though to spite us, had gathered itself together and self-righteously gone. The gravest misgivings assailed us as we cooled our heels.

But suddenly everything was all right; the signal for departure was given. It had struck me as odd that a large crowd had gathered to see us off. I now realized that they were not seeing us off; they were coming too. We had twenty-seven souls on board when we started. Their baggage, and ours, made a load no whit less mountainous than Velvet Collar's loads, and it was early apparent that accommodation came under the heading of footholds rather than of seats. But we were off, and that was all that mattered.

The sun was shining. We bumped out of the West Gate and across a greasy stretch of plain; then we began to climb. The engine ran well and there was a feeling of spring in the air. Pheasants strutted imperturbably by the roadside. We were in the foothills of the Liu Pan Shan. One by one the three cars of Velvet Collar's convoy were passed, and the sunshine seemed brighter and warmer than ever. (We never saw any of those three lorries again. One left the road and rolled down a steep slope to destruction; no one was killed. The others finished the course in nine and twelve days respectively.)

In the middle of the morning we began the ascent of the principal pass, the top of which is over 9,000 feet above sea-level. The road swept this way and that in huge zigzags, but the gradient was stiff. At first we momentarily expected the familiar cry of 'Hsia! Hsia!' which means that the passengers have got to get down and walk, and probably push as well. But the engine was indomitable and we came smoothly up to the summit, from which we could see the dun-backed, empty hills, ribbed horizontally with terraces, rolling for miles and miles.

The descent was less placidly accomplished. There could be no doubt that our driver was a very good driver; and there could be no doubt that this was lucky. The lorry hurled itself into the valley, swinging round the hairpin bends, skidding sickeningly in soft patches on the straight. Our speed, in view of the precipitous nature of our immediate surroundings, would have been uncomfortable in normal conditions; but seeing that at least half the twenty-seven of us had considerable difficulty in keeping our places when our vehicle was proceeding along a level surface, the giddy and headlong gyrations of descent were more than disconcerting. It was not long before the man next to me was sick. I did not blame him.

The foreign engineers responsible for the construction of the Sian-Lanchow road had impressed on their Chinese subordinates the desirability of marking difficult or dangerous passages with the traffic signs current in Europe: such as an 'S' for a double bend. The Chinese, however, either ignorant of or impatient with the orthodox sign-vocabulary, declined on their notice-boards to commit themselves to the exact nature of the peril in wait for the motorist, and merely painted a bold and arresting exclamation mark. As we hurtled downwards the recurrent '!' atoned for its inadequacy as a warning by its charming aptness as a comment.

When at last, rather breathless, we reached the foot of the pass the back wheels of the lorry fell through a small erection which was masquerading as a bridge, and we were glad enough to stretch our shaking limbs while the driver attached to the axle ropes with which eventually we pulled it out. At four o'clock we reached Tsingningchow, a small place but a pretty one, where we scraped some of the dust off our faces, ate a heavy meal, and spent the night.

The next day we really did start at dawn. Our numbers had increased to twenty-eight, and we had a somewhat wearing drive. The sun still shone but dust rose in clouds, and the clouds, thanks to a light following wind, were not easily left behind. Everyone clung or squatted or sprawled in the closest possible proximity; the slightest change of position affected half a dozen neighbours. Nothing more vividly brought home to me the degree of overcrowding to which we were subject than the sight of a large louse, some four inches from my nose, crawling majestically up the back of a minor official. The minor official was far too tightly wedged to reach it; my only disengaged arm was fully employed in keeping me from falling off the lorry; and an outsider, a man from another pudding of humanity altogether, had to be called in to arrest the louse's progress and destroy it.

A woman was sick with extraordinary persistency all day; and my neighbour of the Liu Pan Shan was not always able to contain himself. We looked forward with longing to the infrequent halts; but when they were over a brisk hand-to-hand engagement had to be fought before everyone was once more settled in their places. During one of these struggles tempers ran high, and the minor official came to blows with an oafish little soldier, whose nose bled with regrettable profusion. Hostilities were never formally suspended, and the vendetta kept on breaking out again all through that day, to everyone's discomfort and annoyance.

In the evening we stopped, thankfully, at an inn outside a little walled town. It was dusk, and when we walked up to the town gates in quest of an eating place soldiers denied us admittance; then, seeing that we were foreigners, began to implore us to exercise on one of their number that skill in dentistry which nothing would persuade them we did not possess. We peered sympathetically into a large, pathetic mouth which had very recently been eating garlic, told its owner that he would feel better to-morrow, and went back to eat at a place near the inn. We were pretty tired, and Smigunov had lost his voice.

But ordeal by lorry was almost over and we were due in Lanchow next day. Again we started at dawn, climbing on to a long hog's back among the drab and indistinguishable hills. It began to snow hard, which suited us because it laid the dust. At a cluster of wretched houses a small and excitable posse of militiamen, armed with rifles of a kind, stopped us to say that there was a gang of bandits astride the road ahead; our driver, a man not less sceptical than resolute, ignored this warning and we went on, the passengers betraying for the first time a lively interest in the landscape. The bandits failed to materialize (in my experience they always do) and presently we dropped down into a long valley where the snow stopped and the sun came out. We had a hurried but delicious meal of rice and eggs in a little village where an east-bound camel caravan floundered past us in the slush and where a bandit in chains, his eyes full of anger and fear, was riding, perhaps for the last time, on a donkey, attended by two soldiers.

The sun was warm and the air was clean and tingling. We were full of excitement, imagining Lanchow as a haven of security and comfort after the jolting, irksome squalor of the last few days. At three o'clock, debouching from a gully on to the floor of the Yellow River valley, we saw before us the pagodas and machicolations of a great walled city. We passed an air-field; were delayed briefly by a consignment of Windsor chairs which fell off the stern of the lorry into the road; and at last went waltzing down greasy streets into the heart of the provincial capital.

It was February 27th. The journey from Sian had taken eight days. So far, we thought, so good.

We little knew what was coming to us.

CHAPTER X

OPEN ARREST

WE got an inkling of it almost at once.

'Fuss about passports on arrival,' notes my diary, altogether too casually; but the entry for the day closes: 'We are going to have a difficult time.'

Bureaucracy all over the world is apt to be both mystifying and undramatic in its methods, and the 'fuss about passports' hardly lends itself to narrative. So I will skip the hours immediately following our arrival at Lanchow (only recording that they filled us with perplexity and alarm) and pass on to the moment, shortly after nightfall, when we found ourselves walking down a narrow lane towards the headquarters of the China Inland Mission under an armed guard of six soldiers: our belongings, loaded on two Peking carts, preceded us, and a policeman with a paper lantern preceded them. We walked in silence save for the screaming of the axles.

Mr. Keeble, the local secretary of the Mission, had already sought us out and offered us his hospitality; and when we reached the Mission his diplomacy and his prestige did much to mitigate the thoroughness with which the soldiers searched our effects.

'You mustn't bother about this,' he said, as they rummaged rather half-heartedly in our gear. 'There's pretty well martial law here as far as foreigners are concerned. You've come at a bad time.'

'But what are they looking for?'

'Communist literature. They think you're Bolshevik agents. They caught one here the other day, and now all strangers are suspect. Especially Russians,' he added, glancing at the Smigunovs.

Over supper he developed his thesis. The south of the province was seriously threatened by the Red Armies from

Szechwan; to the north-west Soviet Russian influence was paramount in Sinkiang. The abstract theory, on which one had so often dined out in Peking, that the Communist forces might be heading for the nearest Marxist haven in Chinese Turkistan had suddenly become a concrete obstacle to our designs. There had been several shady characters knocking about Lanchow of late (one of them, the one they caught, was a genuine Soviet agent from Shanghai; he had been mixed up with the Christian General in the days when Feng was being run from Russia); and three months ago Nanking had sent a circular telegram to the Provincial Governments of Kansu, Chinghai, and Ninghsia charging them to allow no foreigners to proceed towards the north-west. Two Poles and several White Russians – all perfectly harmless and respectable people – had recently been sent down from Lanchow to the coast under open arrest. Things looked black for our party.

For half of it very black. The Smigunovs had, like many other White Russians, adopted Chinese nationality. Both their passports were about ten years old; Nina's had been issued – a suspicious circumstance – in Urumchi, and her husband's had been visaed there. They could both have got new passports in Peking, and I blamed myself for not looking into this before we started; but Smigunov had travelled this road before without having any trouble, and neither of us could have foreseen that Kansu would suddenly have gone so very *Morning Post*. It was certain that we were in for a delay of several days, and probable that we should get no nearer India than Lanchow. We retired to the unaccustomed luxury of beds in a gloomy frame of mind.

Six days dragged by. After the first rapture of not having a number of Chinese sitting on our legs all day had worn off, life in Lanchow had little to recommend it, in spite of the kindness of Mr. and Mrs. Keeble. On the unwarranted assumption that we should eventually get permission to proceed, we began inquiring about lorries for the next stage of the journey, which should take us to Sining, the capital of Chinghai. There were several lorries going up, and they were all (they said) on the very point of starting; we gave up imploring them to wait for us when we learnt that they had been on the very point of starting for several weeks. Snow and rain had virtually closed the motor road to traffic, and though it meant six days' journey instead of one and a half it would be better to take mules. We were sick of lorries anyhow.

The streets of Lanchow are romantic. The women hobble round the puddles on bound feet, their sleek heads shining like the shards of beetles. The faces of the Moslems – very influential, here as in Sian, though they form only ten per cent of the population – are swarthy and fierce and almost hawk-like; most of them wear white caps or turbans. Occasionally you see a Turki from Sinkiang, a bearded, booted figure in a long *chapan*, with features so Aryan and un-Mongoloid that he might almost have come from the Caucasus. Very few of the Chinese wear European clothes. There is a bazaar much nearer in atmosphere to the bazaars of Central Asia than to the markets of Peking. It is all very different from the China you see from the Treaty Ports; you have the feeling that you are on the frontiers of another land, that you have come almost to the edge of China. As indeed you have.

But Lanchow might have been Leeds for all the joy we had from its romantic atmosphere. We could not love a place that was like to see the shipwreck of our darling plans. The police had taken away our passports and we were told that they were being submitted to the Provincial Governor with an application for visas that would authorize us to travel to Chinghai. (We still, of course, described our motives as sporting and our goal as the Koko Nor.) On the impressive note-paper of *The Times* Foreign and Imperial Department I wrote a flowery letter to the Governor, emphasizing the honourable nature of our intentions and asking for an interview; at least two members of his entourage could, it was said, read English, but I never got an answer. Inquiries made in person at his yamen, where we called and left our cards, were politely side-tracked. All this was very uncharacteristic of a country where the unpleasantness of your fate at the hands of officialdom is usually in direct ratio to officialdom's affability.

The more obvious it became that there was nothing we could do to improve our chances the more anxious we grew to learn what our chances were. The Minister of Education called and said airily that he was sure it would be all right; he was much distressed at the small appropriation allotted to his Department in the Provincial Budget and I angled for his help at court with an assurance that I would ventilate his grievance in *The Times* if ever opportunity offered. The Minister of Communications agreed to see us but was ominously absent when we called. A Mr. Wang, of the Police, had once been cured of an illness by Nina's father in Urumchi and guaranteed, several times, that we should have our passports within twenty-four hours. Another Mr. Wang, of the Department of Foreign Affairs (a very conciliatory man), said that the Governor had forwarded our application to Nanking and it was only a question of waiting a few more days for a reply. A third Mr. Wang, whose official status I forget but who had a name for being in the know, told Smigunov in confidence that he and his wife were to be refused passports and that, although Kini and I would be allowed to go on, telegraphic instructions had been sent to the Chinghai frontier to have us arrested there. The situation was further complicated by a succession of public holidays during which no official business could be transacted.

We strode irritably about the streets in pursuit of these conflicting rumours. Kini picked up some mail at the office of the Eurasia Air Line and read me extracts from the letter of an office-bound friend who thought it must be wonderful to travel and be free. Free, indeed! To pass the time we visited the German Catholic Fathers, who have a palatial establishment outside the city gates. We called at the Baptist Hospital. We went to a party at which practically the whole of the secular foreign community was gathered; it consisted of a resilient young German, his Russian wife, an Armenian, and a Czech. We noted with interest that, thanks to the wireless, a speech of Sir John

Simon's could be quoted in the local Kuomintang organ only a day after he made it. We took obscure comfort in the sight of a parrot hanging outside a shop because it might conceivably have come from India. But most of the time we were bored and very anxious, fearing the worst.

On the sixth day the worst happened. Or almost the worst. We were notified that the Governor had given permission for Ma and Fu (which meant Kini and me) to proceed to Chinghai; but that the Russian persons were to be sent back to Tientsin, under open arrest.

I went round to Police Headquarters in a rage, taking Smigunov with me. The Chief of Police was a tough, slick, antipathetic Moslem called Pai. He had both power and personality and his subordinates were frightened of him. The only one of them who spoke English was very unwilling to interpret and trembled all over during the interview. It was, as a matter of fact, an indecorously stormy interview. I was very angry and, quite apart from the mess that Kini and I were going to be in, I felt responsible for the Smigunovs, for whom defeat was a serious and bitter matter. I pressed Pai as far as I dared. What charge was preferred against the Russians? Were they not perfectly respectable people? Had not the Governor of Shensi issued a passport to us? In what respect were any of our papers out of order? I had travelled in almost all the Provinces of China and had never been treated like this before; when I wrote of my journey in *The Times* it would be impossible to suppress all mention of the discourtesy and injustice I had met with in Kansu.

All this, and much more, was to no purpose. But I had the empty satisfaction of seeing that I had (slightly) rattled Pai, so that in the end he was driven to ringing up the Governor and getting him to confirm his verdict in our hearing. We parted frigidly.

The expedition was crippled, if not paralysed. But what did the expedition matter? I saw suddenly how absurd and trivial it all was, this irresponsible assault on the heart of a continent, this escapade in Tartary. We had known all along that we were going to fail, and the fact that the loss of the Russians multiplied our chances of failing by ten was really, when you came to think of it, a matter of the greatest unimportance.

But for the Smigunovs it was very different. They had staked so much on reaching the Tsaidam. The thought of it had been almost meat and drink to them. If the inn was dirty or the lorry stuck or fuel was scarce, 'Ah,' Nina would cry, 'it won't be like that in the Tsaidam', and her eyes would shine like a happy child's. All day long on the lorries they had discussed what they would do when they got there, whether they would move their tent and what their Mongol friends would say when they saw them and how much yaks' tails fetched this year. Now the bright vision was broken. They were going back to the dreary uncertainty of Tientsin (where Smigunov had thrown up his job); and they were going back under open arrest. I felt terribly sorry for them.

It was bad luck, too, on Kini and me. Looked at dispassionately and in the light of reason, the early, ignominious failure of our plans was nothing beside the Smigunovs' misfortune; but it was difficult, at this stage, to be dispassionate and the light of reason had never shone very steadily on our enterprise. Without the Smigunovs we could hardly hope to get much further. Three languages at least were needed to get us into Sinkiang – Chinese, Mongol, and Turki (Tibetan would also have been useful); of these I spoke only a few words of Chinese. We did not know the road or the people or the customs. In the unlikely event of our getting past the officials in Sining, we had only the vaguest idea how to set about organizing a caravan, what animals were best or what supplies were necessary or what kind of currency to take. We were heading for fiasco.

Still, it would have been unthinkable to turn back, if only because the officials were hoping that we would. We sent round to an inn to order three mules for the next morning, and began to pack.

At ten o'clock (the date was March 6th) we started. A man with a humble, dog-like face loaded our belongings (they looked ridiculously few) on to the mules; his name. to nobody's surprise, was Wang. The Russians and Mr. Keeble said they would come with us as far as the West Gate. We followed the animals past the familiar, hated gates of the Governor's yamen (how long would it be before we saw those stone heraldic lions again, and the stacked rifles of the guard?) and on through the noisy sunlit streets towards the Yellow River. As we passed under the Drum Tower a small troop of cavalry came jingling towards us through the press of people. They were armed with carbines and executioners' swords, and their huge black fur hats gave them a demoniacal look. In their midst, hunched in his saddle, rode a prisoner, a burly European with a fair beard. As they passed us he raised his eyes; they were far from philosophical. 'Caput!' he said with a grimace, and went clattering out of our ken.

I wondered how soon we should have to echo him.

PART TWO

THE SKIN OF OUR TEETH

CHAPTER I

THE MOUNTAIN ROAD

WE were alone. The mules plodded in a small fine cloud of dust along the track which followed the crumbling bank of the Yellow River. A merganser was fishing the shallow water near the shore. Before us, to the west, the bare and jagged hills sprawled interminably, red and yellow under a bright blue sky. Wang – possibly wondering at the queer company he had fallen in with, more probably meditating on his last meal or his next – trudged beside the animals; he wore on his head a dark blue turban which he sometimes used as a sash to keep his trousers up, and he sang a harsh song quietly. Kini rode on top of one of the loads. I walked. The sun shone but it was not very hot.

We both agreed that it felt odd to be alone. From the first the Russians had been such an integral part of our plans ('Smigunov says . . . Smigunov will know . . .') and for the last three weeks we had lived at such very close quarters with them that it was hard to believe that they had really dropped out of the picture, that they were no longer a factor in the present and the future, that we should probably never see them again. They had been cheerful and courageous and effective; it was sad to have parted from them.

But sadder for them than for us. We were still going on, were still headed for India; we had postponed, however temporarily, the admission of defeat and – partly because of that, partly because we had put an end to an exasperating period of anxiety and enforced stagnation – we were full of a kind of wild elation. We were on our own; the odds against us had lengthened fantastically, but from now on, every stage, every ruse, every guess that helped us towards the west would be a very personal triumph. And the mere fact that the odds against us had lengthened gave us a feeling of freedom, a perverse, light-headed conviction that we were irresistible. Luck had always been the chief of the factors that could get us through; now that it was the only factor the journey had lost what little seriousness it ever had. By way of a gesture to celebrate the occasion, we told Wang that we proposed to do the six stages to Sining in five days.

We did, too. They were good days. On the first we halted for lunch beneath a temple, of more than usually fairy-like appearance, built into the side of a hill. Lunch, and indeed every meal until we reached Sining, consisted of *kua mien*, which is a kind of spaghetti violently flavoured with red pepper and obtainable *passim* at the wayside; I, who have no palate, found it delicious, but it palled on Kini after a bit. Wang fell into conversation with a carter who was taking a very elaborately decorated coffin up the road, and for part of the afternoon we travelled behind this gaudy and impressive object, in company with a little boy riding on a donkey and carrying a white rabbit in his arms. It was all rather like some sort of fable.

Because we had started late, we did not reach our inn till after dark. It got cold as soon as the sun went down (we were over 6000 feet above sea-level) and in order to keep our spirits up we sang the Swiss national anthem on the march; it goes (a very extraordinary thing) to the tune of *Rule Britannia*. Invisible but clamorous dogs charged from the shadows as we rode into a little village where the cooking fires were all out, so that the tea and mien off which we dined were tepid. We had done about twenty miles, and neither the rugged surface of the k'ang nor the yelling of a sick child could keep us awake.

We woke before dawn to the stately and deliberate (yet somehow urgent) sound of camel bells; some caravan was doing a night-march. It was bitterly cold until the sun reached the bottom of the valley. With a boat-load of other travellers we crossed the Yellow River in a big flat-bottomed ferry, the animals jibbing and squealing as they were dragged on board. Then we struck up the gorges of the Sining Ho. Most of the rare fields were covered with round stones from the river-bed, to prevent the soil from becoming dust and being stolen by the wind; in others harrows were being dragged along with a man standing on them like a chariot-driver. A few low mud houses crouched in sparse groves of poplars; the trees were delicate, lovely and colourless. The Sining Ho ran clearer and swifter than the Yellow River, but its valley was so narrow and so little cultivated that there were no more of the huge, intricate, hundred-feet-high water-wheels that we had seen the day before and whose proprietors sell irrigation to the farmers.

A great wind sprang up when we halted to eat, and we had a hard struggle in the teeth of a dust-storm to catch the mules up afterwards. I walked all day, and indeed almost all the way to Sining, in a characteristically premature endeavour to get fit; we did a ten-hour stage before reaching a little village where the people looked even poorer and more diseased than usual. They were indeed so poor that, when we were buying eggs and one egg dropped, there was a race – won by the most respectable-looking person present – to salvage the unbroken yolk. All along this road the standard of living is pitiably low, and a substantial proportion of the population lives for (and largely on) opium. It is said that forty per cent of the children born in Kansu die before they are a year old.

The next day, and for two more days thereafter, we travelled on. Life had become a very simple, soothing affair: so soothing that we forgot our complicated ambitions and the difficulties that lay in store for us. It was enough to be crawling westwards in the bright, clean, mountain air; food and sleep were the only things that seemed important. Occasionally we passed a caravan of donkeys, tripping demurely under disproportionate loads; travellers of consequence in litters or carts drawn by the famous Kansu mules: once a fur-hatted detachment of the 100th Division – provincial troops from Sining – marching down to the anti-Communist campaigns, their officers riding Tibetan ponies, their equipment on camels, and their two superannuated cannon dragged by coolies. (Them we met in the twilight before dawn. One of their camels had

77

knelt down and refused to rise, and I tried to help by putting burning paper underneath it. The soldiers' faces, when the light of the flame showed them what a strange kind of creature I was, looked startled; I believe I could have passed myself off as a demon in that chilly and uncertain hour.) On the swift waters of the Sining Ho huge rafts, made of numerous inflated ox-hides, were poled skilfully through the rapids, carrying wool and hides on the first stage of their tremendous journey from the pastures of the Koko Nor to Tientsin. Here and there at the water's edge men squatted, washing gold; and gold, in little tiny specks, sometimes glittered in the dust beneath our feet. Through gaps in the steep walls of the river-valley snow peaks appeared to the south-west.

At first we eyed the single telegraph wire with misgiving, remembering the most sinister of the Lanchow rumours, which had predicted our arrest at the provincial frontier; and when, at the end of our third day on the road, we found ourselves winding down a zigzag path to where a roofed and brightly painted bridge, spanning the Tatung Ho, linked the two provinces of Kansu and Chinghai, we felt a little gleeful stirring of curiosity and excitement. There was no guard on the bridge. The mules' feet drummed on it hollowly; the mules' eyes (and mine) looked with longing at the lovely dark green water swirling 200 feet below. Beyond the bridge we came into Hsiangtang, the first village in Chinghai, momentarily expecting grey uniforms and old rifles and a brusque '*Nali Lai?*' and the wait while an officer is woken in an inner room. But not even the mangy dogs accosted us. There were no soldiers and no officials in the place; we breathed more freely.

The next day we did a forced march of thirteen hours. The valley widened, and there were fields and fruit trees. At dusk we came to Nienpai, a little walled city famous in those parts for its tobacco. Several camel caravans monopolized the mean inns beneath its ramparts, and owing to incomprehensible curfew regulations we were not allowed inside the gates; so we went on for an hour, to halt at a poor house where we ate half-cooked mien in the reek of opium and got a few hours' sleep. It had been a long day.

The next was even longer. We were woken at one, but did not get off till after three. Mules and men went forward stiffly in the teeth of a little searching wind; but presently the sun rose and by midday it was hot. We crossed the river by the bridge beneath which a flotilla of skin rafts was moored, and at three o'clock sighted the walls of Sining at the far end of a shallow, open valley. They were further away than they looked, and it was dusk before we reached the gates. On the bastions above them little sentries armed with stocky automatic rifles were silhouetted against the fiery west. Bugles brayed thinly. We passed like dusty ghosts through streets where rich food-smells hung on the frosty air and paper lanterns were golden in the darkness until we came to a disappointing inn which Wang said was the best.

It had only one storey. We got a room opening, as all the rooms opened, on to the long courtyard, stowed our luggage in it, and went out in quest of food (in north and west China board and lodging can seldom be obtained under the same roof). Just down the street there was a big eating-house, garish but warm and friendly, kept by Moslems; here we stuffed ourselves with delicious and contrasting dishes of chopped meat and vegetables, and made the Moslems send out for a measure of the raw local spirit, which you drink heated, a thimble-full at a time.

We were dog-tired but happy. Happy because we had done another stage – the last stage, almost, before roads and houses finished and the wilds began; happy because we had done it in five days instead of six; happy because we were not defeated yet.

It was a good moment: the last of its kind for a long time.

CHAPTER II

DEFEAT?

Dr. Johnson once compiled a list of six maxims for travellers. Number 5 is 'Get a smart sea-sickness, if you can'. Number 6 is 'Cast away all anxiety, and keep your mind easy'.

In Sining the first of these rules was no whit more impossible to observe than the second. Within twenty-four hours of reaching the city we knew, almost for certain, that we should get no further west. But not quite for certain; we dangled on a thin and fraying cord of hope above the black depths of despair, and peace of mind was as unobtainable as *pâté de foie gras*.

It was passport trouble again. In Lanchow the authorities, when they gave us back our papers, had assured us that they were in order for Chinghai. But they were not; before sending us on to Sining, Lanchow should have provided us with a special passport. By failing to do so Lanchow had neatly delegated the responsibility for stopping us to her neighbours, while at the same time increasing both the likelihood and the legality of such action on their part; it was a beautifully Chinese gambit, in the best tradition of passive resistance. It looked as if we were done for.

But in China nobody likes to give the *coup de grâce* if they can get somebody else to do it for them, and the matter, we were told after two or three days' suspense, was being referred to Nanking. (We had been told the same thing in Lanchow; but this time we knew, through a friend of a friend of the wireless operator, that it was true.) I sent a wire to Tommy Chao, who was Reuter's Correspondent at the capital and who, with his fund of stable gossip, would be sure to know the form; I asked him what chances we had of getting visas to travel in the interior of Chinghai and briefly rehearsed the more deserving aspects of our case.

The answer came next day. 'Visas doutfullest,' said Tommy Chao.

'Visas doubtfullest.' For all my incurable optimism – which was stimulated by Kini's occasional lapses into an opposite frame of mind – it was difficult to assess our chances very high. Nanking had, in that circular telegram of three months ago, specifically vetoed travel towards the north-west; and it so happened that our few predecessors in this particular part of the country had done little to enhance the prestige of foreign tourists. Several years before two Frenchmen had gone into the Tsaidam and there been murdered, a fate which they courted by their treatment of the natives. More recently, a British army officer on leave had fallen foul of the authorities in Sining and had been sent ignominiously down to Lanchow under cavalry escort. And only a year or two ago a party of English near-Buddhists, led by a very old and very indomitable lady, had arrived in lorries with the declared intention of ending their days in one or other of the neighbouring lamaseries; for various reasons they curtailed their programme and returned to Peking, but during their stay in Chinghai their presence had embarrassed, no less than it had perplexed and amused, the local officials. The more we thought about it, the less reason we saw why, either in Sining or at the capital, an exception should be made in favour of two travellers who, in addition to journeying in a style which suggested that they were insignificant persons, carried the wrong papers and appeared to be mad.

Life, in these circumstances, was an anxious, dragging, squalid business. We woke in the morning feeling stiff and cold; the k'ang, from which we were separated only by a dirty felt, was hard, and the charcoal brazier was dead. We hastily put on whatever clothes we had been rash enough to discard the night before, yelled for hot water, and sent out for bread and butter. The bread took the form of large round buns, golden in colour and rather clay-like in consistency; the butter was veined with dark green, like gorgonzola cheese, and contained a liberal admixture of hairs, both yak and human. We breakfasted with gusto off this, washing it down with mugs of milkless tea.

The principal business of the day was to collect rumours about our fate; but we knew from experience that it was a mistake to address ourselves too early to this task, thereby prematurely exhausting the day's small stock of hope and leaving us with many hours to kill. So for a time I played endless games of patience on the k'ang while Kini read or sewed or wrote up her diary. But gradually, as the glow of breakfast faded in our bellies, we became restless.

'Let's go up to Lu's.'

'Wait till I've finished this chapter.'

'How much more have you got?'

'Ten pages.'

'Hell, that's too much. Come on. I'm going now.'

'Oh, all right . . .'

So off we went, giving our by now celebrated performance of caged tigers down the long main street. The sun shone, the air was crisp. Above the house-tops the rugged yellow peaks across the river stood out very clear and tantalizing. By midday they were usually blurred or hidden by a dust-haze; it was only in the morning and the evening that they emerged to dominate the town. Around us as we walked the untiring thud and clank of the local form of bellows measured, in the opened-fronted shops, the pulse-beats of the city's life. Mountains of wool lurched down towards the East Gate on carts with screaming axles. In the inn yards camels endured with glassy hauteur an interlude of urban life.

The main street was always crowded and the crowd was always picturesque. But for us it was not the inhabitants but the people from outside who made Sining exciting with the promise of remoter places. Mongols from the Tsaidam, Tibetans from Labrang or even Lhasa, lounged at the street corners, not altogether mastering a tendency to gape. Both races dressed in the Tibetan style. Huge sheepskin robes, worn with the wool inside, were gathered round the waist by a sash, above which, and concealing it, capacious folds

82

overhung, making a kind of pocket in which all personal possessions, from the inevitable wooden bowl to a litter of mastiff puppies, were carried. Below the waist the skirts of the robe hung in pleats like a kilt, swinging outwards as gracefully as a ballet skirt when the wearer leapt on to his horse or camel. Stocky boots with upturned toes were worn on the feet, and in these was stowed the long pipe, with its tiny metal bowl and heavy jade mouthpiece. Except in the bitterest weather the robe was slipped back, leaving one brown arm and shoulder free. In Sining the whole barbaric outfit was usually crowned by a cheap Homburg hat, the first-fruits of a shopping expedition which had lasted months; the hats enhanced an air of callowness and bewilderment which clung, for all their toughness, to these country cousins. From their waists dangled a metal-shod pouch containing flint and tinder, and a cheap knife in a sheath; many of them also wore broadswords, of a Wardour Street appearance, and almost all had hanging round their necks a massive amulet enshrining a picture of Buddha. These amulets came, by way of Lhasa, from India, and we were vaguely, unwarrantably reassured by the sight of them, as we had been by the sight of the parrot in Lanchow.

CHAPTER III

CONFINED TO BARRACKS

THE middle of the morning usually found us installed in the back room of a photographer's shop not far from the Governor's yamen. The shop belonged to Lu Hwa-pu, a big bear-like man who had been, under the Empire, an official in Urumchi and who spoke thick but fluent Russian. He was a friend of the Smigunovs and he showed us the very greatest kindness.

How many hours did we spend in that dark little room, with its scrolls and spittoons and rickety chairs? Though the photographer's business apparently prospered, very little actual photography ever seemed to take place. It was only occasionally that a Mongol or Tibetan notable from the back blocks would bring his wife – half giggling, half terrified – to pose rigidly before a faded, tattered, manorial back-cloth on which segments of unimaginable architecture framed startling gouts of boskage. The ladies, their traditional finery invariably and unhappily culminating in a Homburg hat, presented first their front and then their back view to the camera: the latter in order to place on record the magnificence with which their hair, hanging in long, grease-solid plaits almost to their ankles, was decorated with chank-shells and heavy silver ornaments. The Tibetans were better-looking than the Mongols.

We drank cup after cup of tea and skimmed the gossip brought by a succession of visitors. Such and such powerful Mongols were in town and would be shortly returning to the Tsaidam. Such and such a message about us had been sent by wireless to Nanking. General Ma Bu-fang, the autocratic young Military Governor, at present absent on a hunting trip, would return in two days, in four days, would not return for a week. The old and illiterate Civil Governor wanted to send us back but could not decide anything without Ma Bu-fang. The Chief of Police was favourably disposed to us. A reply was expected from Nanking to-morrow, to-morrow or the day after, to-morrow or the day after. . . .

Thus it went on. The benign Lu Hwa-pu, his friend the red-faced sergeant of police, the jerky loud-voiced radio operator, the little hunchback with the charming smile – all these and many others came and went, planting the seeds of hope and then uprooting the premature and sickly growth. We always stayed in the shop as long as we could, partly because we had nothing else to do, partly because we found it paid to postpone as long as possible the chief meal of the day. We used hunger as a drug, to numb for a time anxiety and the anticipation of defeat. We played off the flesh against the spirit, trying to ensure that for an hour or so each day we forgot our troubles in the keen if bestial delight of looking forward to and at last consuming a meal. It was a base but effective stratagem.

Lu Hwa-pu was one of our two chief allies in Sining. The other was Lieutenant-General C. C. Ku, of the Nanking General Staff. It so happened that, by the merest chance, I carried a letter of introduction to Ku from his brother, whom I had first met in Manchuria in 1933. Ku was a young man of thirty-one, who had been educated at Cornell University and had also undergone military training in America; he was now inscrutably engaged on some kind of military intelligence work on China's North-west Frontier and had under his command some fifteen young officers who were dotted about the fringes of the Tibetan plateau. He was intelligent, charming, and rather disillusioned, and wore an extremely well-cut khaki uniform and a rakish fur hat. He knew about the Smigunovs and our troubles in Lanchow, but I think we dispelled whatever suspicions the knowledge may have given him. At any rate, though he unfortunately left Sining soon after we got there, he used his considerable influence on our behalf, sent a reassuring wireless message about us to Nanking, and gave us some useful advice.

Neither to him nor to Lu Hwa-pu did we disclose our

trans-continental ambitions. Although we were sometimes asked if we were going to Lhasa, no one up here imagined that we harboured designs on Sinkiang, for the route leading into that province from Sining is not generally known to be practicable.

We made other acquaintances in the city, though none who stood us in such good stead. First of all there was our inn-keeper, a small, courteous man with an affliction of the eyes which made them rheumy. He bore a very close resemblance to a former professor of poetry at Oxford University, and further endeared himself by his mode of address. Europeans, when talking to a foreigner who clearly understands very little of their language, usually raise their voices, shouting out simple phrases in a terrible and intimidating manner; the Chinese, in my experience, never do this. Our inn-keeper used to chant at me. Sitting on a box in our room, he would coo out slow, polite, mellifluous questions, putting great emphasis on the various tones and measuring his speech like a man engaged in some strange and holy ritual. The result was that he was easy to understand, and one day we had quite a long philosophical discussion (in descant) about the disadvantages of a Republic as compared with an Empire. He was a very old-fashioned little man.

Then there were the missionaries. The first one we met did not really belong to Sining. He was an American, maintained by some sect of which I had never heard before, in Tangar, a day's journey further west and the last village in China. Smitten by a sudden and somewhat premature fear of being cut off by the Communist armies, he had withdrawn to Sining and contemplated withdrawing to Lanchow. We did our best to allay his fears, which were at that time utterly groundless, and he professed himself reassured by our news; nevertheless, after vacillating for several days, he beat a surreptitious retreat to Lanchow and we never heard of him again. He was a large, bearded man, dressed like a sort of noncomformist lumberjack; he had a melodramatic mind and a melodramatic manner, glancing continually over his shoulder, opening doors very suddenly, and trying to persuade us that a lot more of these fellows knew English than we might think. As for our chances of getting further into the interior, he said that we should come up against a 'network of spies', but that we should be all right if we could give them the slip. He had with him an unhappy young man with toothache and two ladies who, from their basilisk glances at Kini and me, appeared to place on our association a more romantic interpretation than the facts warranted and who probably referred to Kini, in conversation, as a Jezebel.

We called at the Catholic Mission, where a cheerful, gnome-like German Father gave us coffee and good advice and where Kini prevailed on one of the sisters to put in a stopping which had come out of her teeth. They also very kindly gave her a bath, ladies not being admitted to the municipal bath, a forbidding establishment where I used to go and wallow in hot, opaque water in company with officers of the provincial forces.

Then there was a Protestant Mission, manned by English and Americans. The missionaries were charming when we met them, and one of them lent us some English papers; but though we had to call on them several times (for we had had permission to give them as our postal address), they never asked us in. We thought this odd at the time, but later heard that they had been warned from Lanchow that we were suspect to the authorities and heading for trouble. A missionary's position depends very largely on his standing with the local officials, and it would therefore have been imprudent for them to have anything to do with people whom the local officials might consider undesirable. All the same, if I had been in their place – living in the back of beyond, seeing a new face from the outside world not more than once or twice a year — I believe I should have taken a big risk and asked us to lunch.

There is not much night-life in Sining. In the evenings we used to go back to our inn, patch the fresh holes made in our paper windows by the fore-fingers of the curious, and sit reading or writing on the k'ang with the flat brazier of charcoal between us. At this time of day there was a tendency to feel forlorn and even sentimental. The worlds we knew seemed very far away and we had left them, apparently, to no purpose. We were not even to be allowed a run for our money. Anybody could get to Sining; the journey, if you took the air-line to Lanchow and if the motor-road was open, could be done in less than a week from Peking. It had taken us more than a month to struggle irritably across China; if our journey ended here in slow and painful anti-climax it would be a waste of time and money which neither of us could conveniently afford. It was small wonder that Kini sighed for the spring ski-ing, and I felt wistful and guilty, remembering the imposing and attractive job which had been offered me by cable three months before, and of which, for the sake of attempting this journey, I had airily postponed acceptance. We were sick of the suspense, sick of unprofitably collating rumours, sick of the jungle of bureaucracy in which we were benighted.

But we were not, fortunately, sick of each other; and suddenly one of us, by a preternaturally gloomy or a preternaturally silly remark, would make the other laugh. Our spacious and remorseful meditations, our regrets for things distant and foregone, would contract rapidly to consciousness of the candlelight and the embers and the kettle; life, and our venture, and ourselves would be reduced once more to their right and ridiculous proportions. What did it all matter? Things might be worse. We still had a chance. Let's make some tea.

But soon we would be obsessed again, only this time cheerfully obsessed, in scheming chimerically for success. If it came to a pinch we would bolt; go down to Kumbum (they couldn't refuse us that), jettison most of our stuff, cut across country, and pick up a caravan in the hills west of Tangar. If only we could find a guide, somebody we could trust. . . .

Thus we talked, hotly and foolishly, until the candles guttered. Then we took off our boots and wrapped ourselves in our coats and lay down on the k'ang to sleep. If there had been a wind in the middle of the day the k'ang, and everything else in the room, was covered with half an inch of fine dust.

There usually had been a wind.

CHAPTER IV

THE GREAT LAMASERY

I FORGET, now, exactly how or exactly when we heard that we were going to be granted visas. I remember only our incredulous and fearful joy. Nanking, apparently, had declined to hold the baby and was leaving the matter to the discretion of the local authorities. We had played the innocents so successfully that the local authorities saw no reason to deny us our excursion to the Koko Nor; our passports would be ready in a few days.

In a few days? I did not like the smell of that. Our holidays, I urged, were short; already we had lost more than a week in Sining. Could not the formalities be expedited, as a special favour?

They could not, it seemed, be expedited very much. But we had expressed a desire to visit Kumbum; by the time that had been gratified the passports would be ready for us. The authorities would be glad to provide transport and an escort for our protection.

The transport was a Peking cart. The escort was a spindle-shanked and defenceless dotard, a scarecrow in uniform with a face of wrinkled parchment. His fragility was alarming and we hoped sincerely that no strong wind would arise, for then we must surely lose him. He had with him a white and equally venerable pony, and on its back, wrapped in a tattered greatcoat, he rode, hunched in a coma, protecting us.

We left by the South Gate early on March 18th and bumped along a little river valley in a south-westerly direction. It should have felt wonderful to leave the city which had been our virtual prison for what seemed a very long time, but we missed a due feeling of release because of a sudden panic that some pretext would be found to withhold the passports on our return. The day was hot and the track very dusty. A Peking cart, lightly loaded, travels just too fast for the passengers to walk beside it; this I thought a pity, for it has no springs and soon becomes a Little Ease on wheels.

Still, it was exciting to pass from time to time little parties of Tibetans, their wild dark faces alive with curiosity beneath their fox-fur hats, the scabbards of their broadswords projecting horizontally athwart their saddle-bows, their shaggy ponies pacing briskly. At one o'clock, breasting a low ridge, we saw below us the great monastery of Kumbum. Its coloured roofs, the tiles of one of them plated with pure gold, crowded the steep slopes of a narrow, sparsely wooded ravine; temples on one side, low white-walled dormitories for the lamas on the other. Figures in dark red robes, diminished by the distance threaded the narrow, climbing passages between the buildings. A gong boomed lengthily.

Kumbum means 'a hundred thousand images'. Legend associates the monastery, which is one of the richest and most important in Tibet, with Tsong-k'apa, who founded the Yellow Sect of lamas (so called because their ceremonial headgear is yellow instead of red) and who thereby regenerated a priesthood fast lapsing into ways of ill repute. About the year 1360 Tsong-k'apa was born at some place not far from the present site of Kumbum. When he was seven his head was shaved, an essential preliminary to an ecclesiastical career; his mother scattered his hair upon the ground, where it took root and in the course of time grew up in the form of a white sandal-wood tree. The leaves of this tree were miraculously stamped with the image of Tsong-k'apa, and a monastery not unnaturally sprang up around it. Travellers more learned than I have reported conflictingly on these photographic leaves; the only thing that seems to have been established beyond doubt – and might indeed have been deduced without any first-hand evidence at all – is that the lamas sell them. There were no leaves when we visited Kumbum.

As we dropped down towards the gay and curious buildings I had the sudden conviction that, whatever political maps of Asia might say to the contrary, we had done at last with China. It was not so much the obvious difference in the architecture as a more elusive difference in the atmosphere. Here was something altogether more dour, more self-sufficient and aloof than pliable, conciliatory, irresponsible China; something that Time had hardly touched, that the West had not touched at all; something that had not yet faced, perhaps would never face, the necessity to prove itself adaptable, to change certain of its spots; something for better or for worse immutable. Probably it was the little that I knew about China, the little that I had read or imagined about Tibet, that gave me this feeling, or at any rate forced its growth; but certainly there was a difference there, though my preconceptions may have misled me in defining it.

The first thing you see as you approach Kumbum is a row of eight white *chortens*, which I believe commemorate eight lamas who were killed by the Chinese (perhaps during the Moslem rebellion of the '60's, when a lot of them were massacred and their temples partially sacked). We crossed a little bridge, passed the chortens, and turned left into the maze of buildings whose small trapezoid windows, wider at the top than at the bottom, seemed to frown down on us from under lowering brows. Directed by quavering injunctions from our aged escort, the cart drew up at the gateway of a large, clean, pink-walled building and we walked through it into the central courtyard. It was surrounded by a carved gallery on to which the upper rooms opened; two camels were tethered by their head-ropes in a corner. Several lamas in dark red robes, whose sly, cheerful, earthy faces hardly suggested the tremendous mysteries commonly associated with their calling, came wandering out of various doors and gave us a giggling welcome. It appears that this was one of the more secular branches of the monastery, where official business was transacted and official guests entertained.

The chief lama, an old man with a fine Roman head, led us into a small panelled room full of shadows where we all sat for some time, occasionally beaming at each other in a perfunctory way. Then tea was brought in and with it, flanked by slabs of butter, a pyramid of some drab-coloured powdery substance. In the dim light we could only guess what this was. First we thought it was sugar, then we thought it was salt; finally we decided it was very fine grey ash, of the kind you see in portable braziers in Japanese inns. Then we tasted it and agreed that it was sawdust, possibly sawdust from the holy tree. It was only gradually that it dawned on us that this was *tsamba*, or parched barley meal: *tsamba*, which was to be our staple food for months: *tsamba*, of which much more anon. We were very green.

Afterwards we were taken round the monastery. My few words of Chinese were, alas, no key to its mysteries and we were miserably conscious of moving in a fog of ignorance which hid the significance of everything we saw. All around us lamas with shaven heads, in red robes or in yellow, paced and squatted in the courtyards. Others, inside the temples, seated rank upon rank in semi-darkness, endlessly intoned their prayers, sending up waves of rhythmic, hypnotizing sound to beat upon the scarlet pillars and the hangings between which a dull gleam betrayed the smiling and gigantic god. Here, in the greatest temple, looking down from a high gallery upon the huddled chanting figures, I caught for a moment, and for the first time, something of that dark and powerful glamour with which western super-stition endows the sacred places of the East. I had been, as every traveller has, in many kinds of temples; never before in one where I had that tight, chill, tingling feeling which I suppose is something between spiritual awe and physical fear.

Outside the main temple pilgrims, outlandish in their sheepskins and fur hats, turned gleaming prayer-wheels in the sunlight or walked slowly round the building, keeping it always on their right as custom demands. Others mech-anically, almost absent-mindedly, prostrated themselves before the tall doors which hid the Buddha, sliding their bodies up and down in grooves which generations of their ancestors had worn deep in the wooden floor; these people, with their sideways glances at us, their furtively moving lips, and their unenergetic manner of throwing themselves on their faces and getting up again, suggested a physical training class of small boys carrying on in the absence of their instructor.

Then we went on into a warren of galleries and little rooms, on whose panels imps and demons, half animal and half human, dismembered or otherwise acutely incommoded the unrighteous, whose anguish was very graphically portrayed; in these frescoes the demonology was more vigorous and more dominant than in any I had seen in China. Stuffed tigers, bears, and yaks, their flanks shiny and mucous with melted butter ritually applied, goggled with painted eyes from wooden balconies. In the monastery kitchen stood three huge copper vats which are used to prepare the tea for the Butter Festival, the most important event of the year. There were many strange things at Kumbum; we saw them but we could not understand them, and the reader must forgive (here as elsewhere) my bald and superficial presentation of much that perhaps stirs his curiosity. There are no dates, no figures, hardly any facts; but we, who lacked interpreter and guide-book, must perforce strive to be truthful and objective: and leave it at that.

A short mile from Kumbum there has sprung up in comparatively recent years (before Rockhill's days, but after Huc's) the small Chinese trading-post of Lusar; and there, we had reason to believe, was to be found a rich and powerful Moslem merchant called Ma Shin-teh. Smigunov, who had done business with him and won his friendship, had strongly recommended him as the best man to advise us about our journey into the Tsaidam, where Ma had many dealings with the Mongols; he was a good and kindly man, Smigunov said, and possessed one of the most important qualifications for business success in China – that of being related by marriage to the Military Governor of the Province. So in the evening, a little limp from our sight-seeing, we walked over to Lusar, leaving behind us our unhappy escort, who was clearly on the point of collapse.

The flat mud roofs of Lusar terraced the sides of a shallow gully. Camels, brought in from pasture, were converging on the village from all sides, and this was reassuring to see, for it meant (perhaps) that a caravan was being assembled and would soon start west. At Ma Shin-teh's house a selection of his numerous progeny gave us to understand that their father was at his evening devotions, and we agreed to call again next day.

On the way back to Kumbum we saw a striking anti-imperialist poster on the wall of a shrine. It was mainly directed against Japan, who was shown as a fat and oafish fisherman on the point of transferring a fish (Mongolia) from his hook to a basket already containing the flaccid form of Manchukuo; but there was another picture in which Sinkiang, Chinghai, and Lhasa were threatened from the west by a lion (representing the Communist armies from Szechwan) and from the east by a tiger which, I learnt to my shame, personified Great Britain.[1] Although not one in fifty of the people who saw the poster could read Chinese characters or have the faintest idea what it was about, it was odd to find the symptoms of political consciousness in so remote a corner of Asia.

[1] The lion got there first. In the autumn of 1935 *The North China Herald* reported that Mongol and Tibetan troops had been in action against the Reds in the neighbourhood of Sining.

CHAPTER V

ESCAPE FROM OFFICIALDOM

NOT all lamaseries are dirty. The panelled upper room in which we slept that night was the cleanest lodging we had had for a long time, and there were carpets on the wooden k'ang. A friendly and quick-witted young acolyte served the evening meal of half-cooked mien and brought us washing water and tended the brazier. To have wind-proof, dust-proof lodging was by now a luxury, and we slept like logs.

We woke in the morning to the incongruous mixture of two sounds. In the bare trees near our window crows and little choughs made a chorus which took me, still muzzy with sleep, back to the early clamour of an Oxfordshire rookery; while through their cries came, from the hill behind the temples, the insistently barbaric notes of conches, drums, and gongs. For a moment I was in a No Man's Land, neither here nor there; then I opened my eyes and saw the great beams above me and the dun chequered oblong of the paper window, and felt the rolled-up coat beneath my head. I was here, all right.

We breakfasted clumsily off tsamba, which needs practice in the mixing and the kneading; then we walked over to Lusar, passing, near the chortens, a roadside market where motley rubbish was displayed for sale by men squatting on the ground: second-hand broadswords, rifle cartridges green with verdigris, packets of Japanese needles, beads, bits of cloth, and local medicines arranged in little baleful piles.

At Ma Shin-teh's house we sent in our visiting cards, with Smigunov's, and presently were sitting in a small ornate room containing no fewer than eight far from unanimous clocks. Ma, a typical Moslem – hook-nosed, bearded, vigorous, and velvet-capped – was charming and pressed on us tea and sugar and bread. Half a dozen of his sons, all slightly Levantine, were also present, and the whole family went into committee over my less successful efforts at Chinese. By the end of the journey I spoke as much bad Chinese as was needed for the business of the road; but at this stage my vocabulary was exiguous, and I still wonder how I managed this crucial conversation so successfully.

Our mere presence and identities took a good deal of explaining, but this could be done by a string of place-names linked by the simpler verbs of motion. The Smigunovs' fate was not much harder to convey, for by now the words for 'passport' and 'out of order' were sickeningly familiar. The real difficulty came when I had to detail our requirements and solicit assistance.

Somehow it was overcome, and with the happiest results. Ma understood our needs (though in one important respect, as will appear later, he misinterpreted my stumbling jargon) and was prepared to meet them. We gathered – and prayed that we were not mistaken – that an agent of his, one Li, was leaving for the Tsaidam with a Mongol caravan in eight or nine days' time; we could go with Li, who could cook for us, look after the animals, and generally protect our interests. Li was summoned; he was an awkward, likeable young man, with a weather-beaten face and very slit eyes. We arranged a rendezvous in Tangar for the 23rd of the Chinese month, which would be March 27th.

But Ma, though genially prepared to humour lunatics, was concerned for our safety. The road was hard, he said, and there were many bad men on the gobi. It would be *excessively* not good if . . . he drew his hand across his throat and laughed apologetically.

I laughed too, in a bluff and carefree way. We were, I untruthfully assured him, heavily armed; we had two big foreign rifles, very good ones. 'Bad men no importance,' I said.

Ma agreed. 'Big fire-arms have-got, bad men altogether no importance.' But he added: 'Small heart, day-by-day small heart!' meaning that we were to take great care all the time. I put on a vigilant sort of look and did my best to explain that we were prudent people. Then – for there had been some talk of a military escort – I said that we were people of no consequence, neither entitled to nor anxious for an escort; our safety was fully assured by the fact that we were travelling under the auspices of Ma Shin-teh. Could he not write a letter to the Governor's secretary, which we could take back to Sining with us as proof that the arrangements for our journey were complete and that no official assistance was required? All this, of course, was conveyed in a vile mixture of pidgin and pantomime; but Ma grasped my meaning and promised to write a letter and let us have it before we left Kumbum. We took leave of him in a glow of gratitude and triumph and walked back to the monastery.

After two hours' feverish guessing I felt physically exhausted. Some of the guessing had been pretty wild; I learnt later, on a second visit to Lusar, that when Ma, looking at Kini and then back to me, had asked how old she was, I had replied without a moment's hesitation: 'No. Only friends.' They must have thought us very odd indeed.

Back at Kumbum, we summoned the carter and the scarecrow bodyguard, gave the delighted lamas four silver dollars and a fountain pen, collected Ma's reassuring letter, and started for Sining. Before we went we induced the head lama to stamp our Chinese passports with the official seal of the monastery, in case the force of circumstances should drive us southwards into Tibet Proper. We had an uncomfortable journey back, for a bitter wind had sprung up; when we reached Sining after dark we were numb with cold and the grubby inn was a welcome haven.

The next day we were early at the Governor's yamen. But the secretary who was to have taken us to interview the Governor was in bed with a stomach-ache, and when he got up there was some muddle about the rendezvous; so we never saw Ma Bu-fang, who is by all accounts a tough and energetic young autocrat, and who certainly inspires a craven terror in his subordinates. Our passports, we were told, were not quite ready; we should have them at noon. At noon we were once more put off until the evening, and chill forebodings settled on my soul. It's all a hoax, I thought; we're never going to get away.

Still, we pretended to each other that we were; and in the light of this pretence we had a lot to do. There were the stores and gear that Lu Hwa-pu had provisionally ordered for us to be collected and paid for: flour and rice, and bricks of tea and coloured cloth to barter with, and a cooking pot and a utensil approximating rather remotely to a frying-pan, and a long piece of wire to use as a cleaning-rod for the rook rifle, and sugar and mien and many other things. Also there was the tent, a very small tent designed by Kini on the wind-resisting lines of one she had used in Russian Turkistan. It was made locally of cotton, cost about fifteen shillings, and when erected in Lu's backyard looked like an abstruse practical joke.

At five o'clock I returned to the yamen: past the lounging sentries, past the mural painting which showed Japan as a ventriloquist with Manchukuo a puppet on his knee, into the familiar little ante-room where guards and underlings drank tea and gossiped. My card was sent in. Minutes passed. At last a man returned. The Governor's secretary would see me.

The secretary had stomach-ache again. He looked cross and out of love with life and I feared his mood. But it was all right; he handed me a big, flimsy sheet of paper on which a rectangular scarlet seal ratified the dancing characters. I could have shouted for joy. (It was not, we discovered later, the right sort of passport; the right sort of passport should have been made out in Tibetan and Chinese, and ours was only in Chinese. But this, as things turned out, did not matter.)

That night we left the hated inn and slept at Lu Hwa-pu's, in a last-night-of-term litter of boxes and bundles. At dawn two Peking carts, provided by the authorities for the day's journey to Tangar, were loaded under the curious eyes of a large crowd, most of whom had for us – I liked to think – the ephemerally proprietorial fondness which menagerie elephants inspire, during their week's stay, in the children of a small country town. Once more an escort had been furnished; but the excellent fellow was only too glad to accept my visiting card, which, after two days of intensive opium-smoking at home, he would present to the authorities in token that his mission to Tangar had been faithfully discharged.

At last everything was ready. I slipped upstairs and left a present of silver in the little room where we had schemed so long for this moment; Lu, who had done a very great deal for us, had indignantly refused to accept anything in return. We said good-bye. Whips cracked, and the little hooded carts went lurching down the street towards the West Gate.

Very soon the walls of Sining, which for ten days had so oppressively enclosed us, were no more than a drab, horizontal, crenellated smudge stretching across the valley up which we moved slowly westwards. It was March 21st.

CHAPTER VI

THE GOOD SAMARITANS

WE reached Tangar after dusk, cold, shaken, and covered with dust. The narrow gorge, flanked by ragged, rocky hills which recalled, under a lowering sky, the Scottish Highlands, had opened at dusk to reveal a village strung out along the banks of the river and surrounded by a wall. The inn which the carters called the best was full, and it took some time, and a good deal of shouting and flashing of torches, before we were meanly installed in another further down the street. We got some food and retired for the night, using for the first time the capacious, stinking flea-bags which we had had made in Sining out of black and white sheepskins. For the first time we could have done without them; there was a fire under the k'ang and by midnight we knew just what it feels like to be fried.

We often used to talk about luck. The further west we got the more important luck became. In Sining, for instance, we had been lucky to find, in Lu Hwa-pu and General Ku, the friends and interpreters who were indispensable to our business in that place; if we had not been lucky, we should probably have met defeat in Sining. Here, in Tangar, it once more behoved us to fall on our feet. I have no great faith in elaborate plans, scrupulous preparations in advance (though it is true that the margin by which they miss fulfilment often provides the best joke of the journey); particularly for travellers as ignorant and inexperienced as we were, the only possible answer to the question 'What shall we do when we get there?' was 'Get there, and see what turns up'.

Well, we had got there. We had got to the point from which we must set out to cross 1000 miles of barren, almost untravelled country before we reached – if we were lucky – the next place where men lived in houses, where you could buy things in shops (and even that place would be no more than a small oasis, situated on the edge of the world's worst desert and held by rebel armies). Something, it was clear, would *have* to turn up; we needed a slice of luck.

I argued that we were due for one. I have a superstitious conviction that every improbable enterprise, as long as it is carried out in a sensible and modest way, has a kind of divine right to one slice of luck every so often. All the rest of your luck may be bad, dreadfully bad, but every now and then you are entitled to expect – to demand, indeed, if only you knew whom to apply to – some specific, unmistakable manifestation of good fortune, no matter on how small a scale. Since we left Peking five weeks before the luck had been against us; except for the loss of the Smigunovs fate had dealt us no smashing and sensational blows, but we had been losing on points all the time. From the moment that we missed that connection on the Lunghai Railway things had gone quietly, naggingly against us all the way. There was nothing – not even Lu Hwa-pu's assistance, for we had known in advance that he was there – to which we could point with glee and gratitude, saying 'Well, that *was* a slice of luck'. I felt that this state of affairs had prevailed long enough.

Fate, it seemed, held the same view. We were lucky in Tangar, getting help from a quarter whence we had no right to expect it: from the missionaries. They belonged to the same Protestant Mission whose representatives had wisely kept their distance in Sining. Their names were Mr. and Mrs. Marcel Urech; he was Swiss, she was Scots. We called on them on our first morning in Tangar.

We called on them partly from politeness, hoping for no more than (at the most) some friendly advice, and partly because they were, once more, our postal address. You must not think from this that we were receiving or even expecting mail, a luxury which we dispensed with for seven months; but Kini had left behind in Lanchow – whether in a fit of intrepidity or of amnesia I see no reason to disclose – an automatic pistol, together with some underclothes by which she set great store, and we had written asking that these things should be forwarded on. The automatic pistol had been obtained, on my advice, from a diplomat in Peking, and Kini claimed to have broken innumerable bottles with it in the compound of the French Legation. Whether there was anything in this boast I had no opportunity of judging, for the automatic pistol never caught us up. The authorities in Lanchow refused to allow it to be sent through the post; as a Parthian shot we thought this hardly worthy of them.

At any rate, we called, rather perfunctorily, on the missionaries. As in Sining, we found them charming; but a departure from the Sining precedent was made when they gave us tea and cakes in large quantities. Where were we staying? At an inn. Wasn't it very uncomfortable? No, it was as good as most. But why on earth didn't we come and stay at the Mission?

The invitation, which took us by surprise, was half-heartedly refused and then accepted under pressure. We would clearly be a great nuisance to them; but they were the only foreigners in the place, and it really looked as if they would be glad to see fresh faces, however travel-stained, from the outside world and to break for a time the monotony of their isolation. It was not until later that I learnt that they had received, but elected to ignore, the same confidential warning about us which had been issued to their station in Sining; they were kindly, humorous people, and saw no sense in treating us as Untouchables because of a three-weeks-old rumour.

We stayed with them for a week, eating prodigiously and finding that it already felt queer to sleep in beds. The Urechs were delightful hosts. They had in the house an article which I had once written in an American magazine, and though it was a very bad article they thought it funny and it somehow seemed to establish my *bona fides*. (There are times when this base craft, this pushing of a pencil across a piece of paper, stands suddenly justified.) As guests, our appearance was against us; we had only the roughest clothes and were already so weather-beaten that the Urechs' little son, who had seen few enough foreigners in his time, always referred to us as 'the Mongols'. The Urechs, however, were not without experience of expeditions. When they were stationed at Tatsienlu, on the borders of Tibet and Szechwan, they had had an American expedition billeted on them for some time; but that had been a pukka expedition, with camp-beds and cases of whisky and two cooks, and servants and gear galore. The contrast between the Americans and us provided material for a lot of jokes.

Much as we valued their hospitality, we valued their assistance more. To have found somebody we could trust, who understood our needs and sympathized with our ambitions, who could tell us what we wanted to know in either of our own languages, made a tremendous difference to life. We pushed on our preparations in an atmosphere of sublime self-confidence. We bought two Tibetan ponies[1]: an ungainly, gentle-mannered bay for Kini and a rufous, raw-boned animal belonging to Mr. Urech for me. With mine went a battered foreign saddle, but Kini bought, from preference, a Chinese saddle, a wooden fore-and-aft affair covered with red and blue padding.

There were many other things to buy: hobbles, spare horseshoes, copper kettles to fetch water in, soft sheepskin boots to wear in camp, a little chest for our medicines, a round iron fireplace – in short, a lot of important odds and ends. Partly from the bazaar and partly (I fear) from the Mission kitchen we supplemented our supplies of food. There was always something to do, and the days passed pleasantly.

But meanwhile there was no news from Ma Shin-teh at Lusar and no signs of a Mongol caravan. I began to get uneasy, to doubt more and more whether either he or I had

[1] These animals are referred to *passim* in this narrative as horses, which is what the Chinese and the Mongols call them, never having seen anything bigger, and what we always thought of them as. Actually they were about the same size and build as the so-called 'China pony', which comes from Mongolia; the most noticeable difference was that you saw fewer greys that you do in Mongolia, and that the heads were more nondescript and conformed less to a type. I suspect that the Tibetan ponies are the hardier.

in fact understood what the other was saying, whether the arrangements I thought we had come to had really been come to at all. So on March 25th I rode down to Lusar, taking with me one Ngan, an extremely nice and intelligent convert of the Urechs. We rode hard and did the journey in seven hours, which was quite good going. My red horse was strong, but clumsy and characterless; also I felt that he had been living too soft in the Mission compound to be ideal for the Tsaidam. As we jogged between the yellow hills in the sunlight I saw two magpies carrying up twigs into the fork of a tree. I watched them for perhaps three minutes, and the three minutes, though I did not know it at the time, held the whole of a season. Those beginnings of a magpie's nest were all I saw of spring in 1935.

We found an inn at Lusar, dismounted stiffly, and were immediately discomfited by learning that Ma Shin-teh had left that morning for Sining. But presently, while we wolfed mien at an eating place, there appeared a brother of the Li who was to be our guide and mentor; and he brought news which was mostly good. Li was leaving for Tangar to-morrow. The Mongol caravan, which belonged to the Prince of Dzün, was already assembling, as the custom is, in the open country, two or three marches to the west. It was a very big caravan.

And what about our camels? The face of Li's brother went suddenly blank: what camels? My hopes, which had been soaring, prepared to drop. There had clearly been a misunderstanding.

Ngan explained it; he was an educated man, and knew how to make my little Chinese go a long way. Ma Shin-teh had understood from me, not that we wanted four camels, but that we had four camels; but for the impatience which had driven me a second time to Lusar, Li would have arrived in Tangar (through which the caravan did not pass) expecting to find our transport arrangements complete, and it would probably have been impossible to get the animals in Tangar at the last moment. As it was, Li's brother said, it didn't matter in the least; plenty of the Prince of Dzun's camels were still in Lusar and we could hire four of them. So all was well, and before dusk I had chartered four camels for a journey of sixteen to eighteen days for about as much as it would cost you to charter four taxis from Hyde Park Corner to Hampstead and back again. In the last month we had knocked only six days' march off our itinerary; now it really looked as if we were going to get started at last.

We slept that night in the house of Li's family. I was full of contentment at the way things were going, and it was pleasant to squat beside Ngan on the principal k'ang and to catch, however fragmentarily, the atmosphere of a poor but respectable Chinese household. The wrinkled and delightful mother, very proud of her four sons; the shy, pretty daughter-in-law; the children who alternately peeped and squealed; the fresh bread specially sent out for and the hot bowls of mien; the wick floating in a tipped earthenware saucer of oil which gave us light; the whole family's pride in the youngest son, who alone of them was a 'recognizing-characters person' – i.e. literate; the laughter and compliments provoked by my Chinese; and, most characteristic of all, the eternal, untiring question: 'Mr. Fu, how much did this cost?' My boots, my breeches, my watch, my knife, my camera – I had to price them all. Then there was a short lecture by Ngan on the T'ai Wu Shih Pao, the Newspaper-for-the-Enlightened-Apprehension-of-Scholars, of which my visiting card proclaimed me the Extra Special Correspondent Officer; the youngest son, the literate one, nodded vigorously and repeated the more striking of Ngan's phrases, pretending that he knew all about it too. It was a long time before we went to sleep.

We rose at two, gulped some tea, and went out into a moonless night. We took a short cut over the ridge behind the village, and as we were leading our horses down a steep place on the further side a dog barked suddenly in the darkness. My horse bolted, spun me round as I clung to the reins, kicked me hard in the small of the back, and vanished. The girth slipped, the saddle turned round underneath his belly, and by the time we caught him again he had pounded to pieces whatever was breakable in my saddle-bags. Casualties included a flask of brandy, and when I remembered the dozens of times I had refrained, with an effort, from drinking its contents I resolved never to husband anything again.

We rode on. Presently it got light. It was a grey day, bitterly cold, and I was underclad. At the half-way halting place no food was available, and the seven-hour ride developed into something of an ordeal. But at last it ended, and I had good news to break off-handedly, and a warm room to break it in. There was not much wrong with anything just then.

That night, long after the missionaries had gone to bed, our typewriters rattled in the living-room. 'Probably last chance to post a letter . . . don't seriously expect to get through but are having a crack at it . . . odds heavily on our being turned back sooner or later . . . absolutely no danger . . . 10,000 feet above sea-level and salubrious to a degree . . . back by autumn, win or lose . . .' Farewell letters, tentatively valedictory in tone. Writing them took me back two and a half years to a place at the other end of the earth. I remembered very clearly the slung hammocks, the almost silent river, the dripping jungle, the Indians sprawled about the fire, the pencil moving stickily in the precious light of our torch. Probably I had used the very same words: 'Odds heavily on our being turned back sooner or later.' Well, it had been sooner, that time; I swore it would not be my fault if history repeated itself.

The next day, which was March 28th, followed closely many precedents. We got up very early in the morning and started rather late in the afternoon. The intervening hours were full of the usual contradictions and surmises. The stages ahead of us lengthened and shortened in popular report, the caravan swelled and dwindled. The hour of departure, the estimated weight of our gear, the number of our fellow-travellers – these and other things were established and disestablished with bewildering rapidity. But at last four camels, shaggy and supercilious, stalked into the little compound and knelt, one by one, to be loaded.

Mongols, conjured up by Li, apportioned and adjusted the loads. By three o'clock all was ready.

'You might as well stay for tea,' Mrs. Urech urged. There was something incongruous in the invitation, something still more incongruous in its refusal. 'I don't think we will, thanks awfully. We really must be going . . .' The formula, which should have ended 'We've got to dress for dinner,' echoed ridiculously across the map of Asia and the months to come.

Still, we went. We followed the camels through the narrow streets and out of the South Gate. We watered our horses in the last sea-bound river we were destined to see for four and a half months. At the bridge we said good-bye to the missionaries, wishing with all our hearts that we could express one tenth of our gratitude; they had been wonderfully kind to us.

Then, with joy and incredulity, we remounted, turned our horses' heads in the general direction of India, and cantered after the camels.

PART THREE

INTO THE BLUE

CHAPTER I

TRAVELLING LIGHT

HE who starts on a ride of two or three thousand miles may experience, at the moment of departure, a variety of emotions. He may feel excited, sentimental, anxious, carefree, heroic, roistering, picaresque, introspective, or practically anything else; but above all he must and will feel a fool. It is like sitting down to read *The Faërie Queene* right through, only worse. Not yet broken in to the stately unhurrying tempo of the caravans, not yet absorbed in the life of the road, he finds, in the contrast between the slowness of the first short stage and the hugeness of the distances before him, something keenly ridiculous. His imagination and his sense of drama reject so little a beginning to so great an enterprise. His mind is full of the immensity of his ambitions; his body, sitting on a horse, makes the first move towards their fulfilment at a pace which is often exceeded by old ladies in bath chairs. He feels a fool.

It was like that, at any rate, with me, though perhaps not with the more philosophical Kini. The Bactrian camel, loaded and marching at a normal pace, does about two and a half miles an hour. Our four, led by a silver-haired and somehow episcopal Mongol, strode with what seemed to me intolerable deliberation away from Tangar and up a narrow valley into the dark and sullen hills. A bitter wind blew in our faces. The sky was leaden. Once more – by something in the bleak outline of the hills, by the shaggy mount between my legs, by the feel of the rifle slung across my back – I was reminded of Scotland, of coming home from stalking in the back end of the season.

The camels' loads deserve analysis here. We were travelling light, and except for our personal effects and the few luxuries enumerated on page 39 the camels were carrying exactly what they would have carried if we had been Mongols or Chinese. The chief items were: Two big sacks of grain (barley) for the horses; flour; rice; mien (two kinds); tsamba; sugar; a few onions and potatoes; some little indestructible cubes of biscuit, baked to a recipe of Kini's, and serving as a substitute for bread; a certain amount of garlic; a few rather leprous dried apples; a sack of raisins from Turfan; a small keg of Chinese spirit, which smelt awful; one cooking pot, bought locally; and one diminutive tent.

One thing in this inventory, which covers all our supplies that I can remember (and the journey gave me a good memory for food), needs explaining: tsamba. Tsamba, known to travellers in North China and Mongolia as *tso mien*, is the staple food of Tibet. It is parched barley meal, and can be mistaken, even in a good light, for fine sawdust. You eat it in tea, with butter if you have got butter, or with melted mutton fat if you haven't got butter, or with neither if you have got neither. You fill your shallow wooden bowl with tea, then you let the butter melt in the tea (the butter is usually rancid and has a good cheesy flavour); then you put a handful of tsamba in. At first it floats; then, like a child's castle of sand, its foundations begin to be eaten by the liquid. You coax it with your fingers until it is more or less saturated and has become a paste; this you knead until you have a kind of doughy cake in your hand and the wooden bowl is empty and clean. Breakfast is ready.

Tsamba has much to recommend it, and if I were a poet I would write an ode to the stuff. It is sustaining, digestible, and cheap. For nearly three months we had tsamba for breakfast and tsamba for lunch, and the diet was neither as unappetizing nor as monotonous as it sounds. One of the great virtues of tsamba is that you can vary the flavour and the consistency at will. You can make it into a cake or you can make it into a porridge; and either can be flavoured with sugar, salt, pepper, vinegar, or (on special occasions, for you only had one bottle) Worcester Sauce. And, as if that were not enough, you can make it with cocoa instead of with tea. I would not go so far as to say that you never get tired of tsamba, but you would get tired of anything else much quicker.

There was another thing that the camels carried, and that was various forms of currency. The currency problem was an important one. Through that admirable institution, the Chinese Post Office, I had been able to transfer the bulk of our capital from Peking to points west by simply paying in a cheque at the Peking branch and drawing the dollars at Lanchow and Sining. But the Mexican silver dollar which they use in China is a big coin, and the country through which we were to pass had a lawless reputation; a suitcase heavy with silver could not be relied upon to remain indefinitely an asset and might indeed prove a major liability. So we carried the minimum of coin – 600 or 700 dollars secreted in different places among our gear. With the remainder of our capital – rather more than a thousand dollars – I had bought in Lanchow a 12 oz. bar of gold which, besides being easily concealed, had the advantage of being negotiable anywhere where a file and a pair of scales were available. For the remoter Mongol communities, who often have no use for gold or silver, we took with us eight bricks of tea and a good deal of cheap coloured cloth, one or the other of which is always legal tender.

Our supplies and equipment, though they would have made any respectable modern expedition sick with laughter, proved completely adequate to our needs and to conditions on the road. For this the credit goes to Kini, who ran the commissariat with unfailing foresight and whose housekeeping instincts, though perhaps rudimentary by the highest standards, were an excellent foil to my contemptuous improvidence in these matters. There was nothing that we seriously lacked, though we could have done with a Primus stove and it was certainly a pity that our failure to procure a basin reduced us to washing in the frying pan when we washed at all. But we had with us no single thing which proved itself superfluous, no single thing which, as the journey dragged on, provoked us to wonder, with growing exasperation, what the hell we had brought it along for; and this, I fancy, is a record in the history of expeditions.

That first day we did a short half-stage. Dusk caught us not more than six miles from Tangar, and we were glad enough to stop, for the cold wind had grown very cold and it was beginning to freeze. Li said that there were bandits in these parts and urged us to sleep in houses as long as the houses lasted; so we found ourselves installed, almost luxuriously, on a k'ang, while Li, a touch of swagger not entirely hiding his own secret perplexity, explained us as best he could to a half-Mongol, half-Chinese family. The walls of the room were decorated with crude, old-fashioned, highly-coloured pictures (with the captions in Russian) of the Russo-Japanese war; perhaps they had found their way down from Urumchi or from Urga in the old days. We ate bowls of mien and drank tea. Everything felt curiously unreal. It was hard to believe that we had really started, impossible to imagine what kind of strange things lay before us; the present had a dream-like quality. Kini, turning her back on Tartary, took refuge in the surer realities of an Arsène Lupin novel.

When we woke next day it was snowing. We put on more clothes, had breakfast, and as soon as the camels were loaded continued down the narrow valley, which ran a little west of south. Twice we met herds of yaks going up to Tangar; shaggy, lowering beasts, black or grey in colour, grinding their teeth reflectively as they plodded along. The Tibetan herdsmen, amorphous in their sheepskins, urged them on by whistling; every man had a musket or a matchlock slung across his back with a forked rest protruding barbarically beyond the muzzle. At noon (in order, I think, to avoid a Chinese Customs post) we left the main track and branched west up a smaller, more desolate, more romantic valley. Rock pigeons flashed and wheeled about the cliffs; there were no other signs of life. But soon, terraced upon the northern slopes, we saw the gaudy roofs of a big lamasery and learnt, with a regret considerably modified by the extreme cold, that we should go no further that day.

CHAPTER II

THE PRINCE OF DZUN

As we rode up, ahead of the camels, to the chief building of the monastery, lamas came flitting like dark red bats. Li parleyed, and we were admitted. The monks grinned, curious, child-like, and we grinned back. It was wonderful to go in out of the cold to a little panelled room, where the k'ang, beneath its carpets, was in places almost too hot to touch. They brought us tea and tsamba and mien with lots of red pepper, and we felt slack and sybaritic. On the walls there were Protestant missionary posters, advertising Christianity with Chinese texts illustrated by garish and improbable pictures; the lamas, without bothering about their ideology, thought them decorative.

The head lama was a vigorous and friendly young man. He wanted to trade a black horse that he had for my red one, and the whole afternoon was given up to bargaining, with Li as intermediary. I went out and tried the black. He was a little Tangut horse (the Tanguts, who according to the learned men are misnamed, are a shy and unruly aboriginal tribe of Tibetan stock who infest the region of the Koko Nor). He was much smaller and had a much prettier head than the average Tibetan pony, and he certainly had more pace and more spirit than mine. In the end, after ultimata had been issued and negotiations broken off for the correct number of times, after Li and the lama had repeatedly plunged their hands into each others' sleeves to convey, by pressure of the fingers, the amount of the successive bids, I got the black in exchange for my horse (which had cost eighty dollars) plus twenty-four more. We christened him Greys, after the house in Oxfordshire towards which he had to carry me. He turned out to be a demon of a horse.

Horse-coping apart, the chief topic of conversation was

the imminent arrival of the Panchen Lama, who was expected from Mongolia *en route* for Lhasa and whose camels were already accumulating at Kumbum and Lusar. The Panchen (or Tashi) Lama is the highest dignitary in Tibet after the Dalai Lama; as the latter had died the year before, and as his infant successor had not yet been chosen, the Panchen Lama's return from foreign parts was likely to have an important but unpredictable effect upon the abstruse politics of his native land. At the moment of writing the Panchen Lama is still *en route*; it was from Kumbum that he dispatched to the British Ambassador in Peking a telegram of condolence on the death of King George V.

That was our last night of luxury, the last roof (with one exception) that we slept under for two and a half months. The next day there was a lot of snow on the ground but the wind had dropped. The world was silent, and not too cold. We said good-bye and gave the head lama a mounted photograph (the far-sighted Kini had bought several from Lu Hwa-pu) of the Dalai Lama; this, judging by its reception, more than repaid the monastery's hospitality. Then we rode off across the valley and up a low pass into the white hills. The Chinese call that place Tung ku ssu.

We did a longer stage that day, though it was only six hours and not a full one. A faint broad track made by the feet of beasts led us over a succession of little passes, and in the afternoon we dropped down into a country of sand dunes and rank grass. There were a few hares about, and I missed one badly with the ·22. At three o'clock we sighted tents and about twenty camels. It was a party of Mongols bound, like us, for the Prince of Dzun's caravan, and we camped with them in a flat place by a little stream. Nearby was one of the crouching black Tibetan tents which Huc immortally compared to spiders and which at first glance are not unlike the tents of the Bedouin. The people it belonged to came with their huge mastiffs to stare shyly from a distance.

Here, for the first time, we pitched our own tent. It was roughly nine feet long, five feet wide, and four feet high, and when we had put it up it looked so small and flimsy that we had to laugh. It was made of thin stuff which could not have kept out rain for more than five minutes; but as we had only two light showers in the six and a half months between Lanchow and Kashmir this was unimportant. It was almost completely wind-proof and weighed next to nothing; the only thing you could possibly say against it was that it was rather small. But it had to be small; every day the two of us pitched it unaided, usually in half a gale, and anything substantially larger would have been unmanageable. Moreover, its smallness had compensations; if you could not light a fire in it (which was a drawback), neither could you receive more than two visitors at a time (which was an advantage, for no bearded woman ever got sicker of exhibiting her peculiarities with a good grace than we did). It was a good tent, and it never quite blew down.

That first camp was very much of a picnic. Li collected dung and made a fire, using the local bellows with great dexterity. The bellows consist of a funnel-shaped iron nozzle, to the wider end of which is fastened a sort of skin bag; this you inflate by opening and shutting the mouth with a complicated interlocking movement of your forearms. It is quite impossible to use without practice. Kini cooked and we ate by candle-light, squatting with Li in the mouth of the tent, while a mastiff in the Tibetan encampment bayed the moon and our horses munched their barley near at hand.

The next day was the last of March. We woke at dawn. The Mongols were on the move already, and we made a flurried and irritable start because the camels had to be loaded before we had finished our breakfast. It was fine but misty, and very cold at first. We rode west through yellow grasslands below a little range of hills, skirting a patch of marsh which was only partly frozen. Just before noon, breasting a ridge, we saw clustered in the hollow below us fifteen or more drab cones, the tents of the main caravan; the country for miles round seemed to be dotted with camels and horses grazing.

We forded a stream, followed Li to a clear space on the

edge of the encampment, dismounted, and waited for the camels to come up. A crowd, the wildest you could wish to see, formed quickly round us – Mongols garbed unwieldily in their great sheepskins, one shoulder bare, one hand on the hilt of a Tibetan broadsword: Chinese Moslems, more trimly dressed but still barbaric, with hard, cunning, cruel faces, the cruellest faces in the world. Li parried a Babel of questions; we looked amiable and said again and again: No, we are not missionaries. Missionaries were the only kind of foreigners they knew about.

Our stuff was still being unloaded when we received a summons from the Prince of Dzun. The Prince ought, I am conscious, to be a romantic figure, a true-blue, boot-and-saddle, hawk-on-wrist scion of the house of Chinghis Khan, with flashing eyes and a proud, distant manner and a habit of getting silhouetted on sky-lines. But God, not Metro-Goldwyn-Mayer, made the Prince, and I must tell you what I saw, not what you will be able to see for yourself when Hollywood gets loose in Tartary.

The Prince's tent, by virtue of a blue design worked on it, stood out a little from the rest; but inside magnificence was neither achieved nor attempted. Dirty felts covered the floor; bundles and boxes were stacked round the perimeter of the tent. Half a dozen men were squatting round a dung fire. They made room for us in the place of honour, which is at the left of the back of the tent as you go in.

The Prince greeted us non-committally; it would have been beneath his dignity to show surprise or curiosity. He reminded me of a cat. At first it was something about the way his eyes moved in his head, about the way he sat and watched you; then later, when I saw him walk, there was something cat-like in his gait as well. He was a young man, probably in his early thirties, though with those people it is hard to judge. He wore a cap lined with squirrel fur, and a voluminous scarlet robe, also fur-lined. He was a man of little ceremony but, although he received from his followers few outward signs of respect, his writ appeared to run effectively and all the time we travelled with him we were conscious that his will directed the caravan. Exactly what

118

he was prince of – how many people, how much land – we never rightly discovered. The Tsaidam has been studied less, has in fact been visited less, by foreigners than (I should think) any inhabited area of comparable size in Asia. All I know about the tribal organization of the Mongols who live there is that they are divided into four *hoshuns*: Dzun and Barun in the east, Teijinar in the south and west, and Korugu[1] (reputedly the largest) in the north.

Li, who had travelled the Tsaidam, on and off, for ten years, spoke Mongol well, and through him we conveyed fumbling courtesies. When the Prince asked where we were going I said 'To Teijinar' (which was the next place of importance after the Prince's own headquarters at Dzunchia); after that, I said, we didn't know. We had given him our cards, and presently we showed him our various Chinese passports, which neither he nor Li could read but which looked good and had our photographs on them. We were very much on our best behaviour.

At last the time came to produce our gift. It was a small second-hand telescope. I handed it across the fire with a low bow, holding it on the upturned palms of both hands in the approved style. With it went a *katag*, the flimsy light blue ceremonial scarf which must accompany all presents. The Prince had never seen a telescope before (which was just as well, for this one was a gimcrack affair). He and his staff spent some time peering through it, with faces contorted in the effort to keep one eye shut; and at first it appeared that visibility was poor. We were a prey to those misgivings which assail you when you give a child a toy and the toy, in spite of all they told you at the shop, declines to work. But at last somebody got the focus right, and there were grunts of amazement and delight as a distant camel was

[1] The spelling of this name, which I have never seen on a map, reproduces as exactly as possible the way the Mongols pronounce it. The name is also applied to the mountains north of the Tsaidam Marsh. There used to be, and perhaps there still are, five *hoshuns*; but I only heard of four.

brought magically nearer. We withdrew from the audience feeling that we had been accepted at court.

That first day, and for several days thereafter, life in camp was made irksome by sightseers. There was a crowd perpetually round the tent; all our actions, all our belongings, were closely scrutinized – by the Mongols with vacant gravity, by the Chinese with ill-concealed amusement and a magpie curiosity. 'How much did this cost, Mr. Fu? How much did this cost?' It was laughable to recall that we had brought with us a tiny portable gramophone (and three records) because it would be *so* useful to attract the natives; there were times, at this period, when we would gladly have exchanged the gramophone for its weight in tear-gas bombs.

After our call on the Prince I left Kini to play the two-headed calf alone and went out with the rook rifle. I had seen a couple of mandarin duck go down behind a little hill opposite the camp, and I followed them up and had a splendid afternoon, crawling about a soggy little valley through which a stream ran. There were a lot of bar-headed geese there; they had never been under fire before and they usually let me get within a hundred yards, crawling in full view. I shot very moderately, but came back to camp with three. I wanted to present one to the Prince, for this (I thought) would be taken as an appropriate and charming gesture; Li only stopped me in the nick of time. Buddhism, as interpreted in these parts, forbids the Mongols the meat of geese, ducks and hares, but allows them antelope and pheasants. To give the goose would have been a frightful solecism.

The Chinese were less scrupulous. As Moslems, they should have touched no meat which had not died by the knife; but there is a proverb about Chinese Moslems which gives a good idea of their attitude to Koranic law. 'Three Moslems are one Moslem; two Moslems are half a Moslem; one Moslem is no Moslem.' In other words, the eyes of man matter more than the eyes of God. So our fellow-travellers contented themselves with cutting the throats of the two dead birds we gave them and began plucking them without a qualm of conscience. We boiled ours – or as much of it as we could get into the pot – and ate it with rice. It was delicious. We felt very Swiss Family Robinson.

CHAPTER III

THE DEMON'S LAKE

AT dawn the next day the caravan moved and our journey began in earnest. It was the first of April, appropriately enough. Tents were struck and loads lashed on in the chill half-light, and presently a mile-long column of 250 camels, in strings of anything from four to ten, was winding westward through the silent wintry desolation.

In the middle of the morning we sighted the great lake which had been for so long a landmark in our plans. The Koko Nor covers an area of 1630 square miles and lies over 10,000 feet above sea-level. There are various legends about it, the commonest being that it was once a fertile valley which was flooded by a demon by means of an underground tunnel from Lhasa. Disaster threatened the surrounding countryside, for there was no telling to what lengths such malignance, backed by such plumbing, might not go; happily a god, disguising himself as a presumably very large bird, took a rock and dropped it on the mouth of the tunnel, thus saving the situation. The top of the rock still projects above the surface of the water, and a lamasery has been established on the island, which is said to be visible from the north shore of the lake. Nobody, for some reason, has any boats, and the monks can only receive their supplies in winter, when the pious bring them offerings across the ice. The lake is of course salt, but there are fish in it; I saw the bones of an unidentifiable five-pounder on the foreshore.

The lake when we saw it was frozen. The glittering ice stretched, unbroken and unsullied, as far as the eye could reach. It gave me a feeling of forgotten magnificence, of beauty wasted. Every year, unadmired, the waters hardened into crystal, carried snow, were swept by the winds; every year they became once more blue and dancing.

None regarded their majesty; none noted their moods, their rage or their tranquillity. The demon's malice and the god's resource had both been vain. The Koko Nor might just as well have not been there.

We had ridden ahead of the caravan with the more consequential Chinese, and in a hollow we all dismounted and fired the grass to warm our feet. When we were ready to go on Greys played me a dirty trick. I had one foot in the stirrup and was swinging myself into the saddle when he started bucking. He started bucking before I touched the saddle; the girth slipped and I came off on my head. The ground was as hard as iron, but no harm would have been done if Greys, still bucking like a thing possessed, had not come down with both his small hind feet on my right leg just above the ankle. Having done so, he bolted. My left foot was still in the stirrup and it looked as if I was in for a bad time; but by good luck I got it out before I had been dragged far, and Greys went off by himself.

My face, according to Kini, was the colour of a lettuce and I thought my leg was broken. But presently the pain went and I found that I could use the leg. That evening I took the rook rifle and went for a long walk, with some idea of preventing the leg from stiffening up; and although my shin was an odd shape for several weeks, and an odd colour for several months, I was never inconvenienced by it. Much more serious was the destruction by Greys of a tube of toothpaste in my saddle-bag; this reduced me to my last tube, which was of Chinese manufacture and tasted of nameless by-products.

Greys was odd. His trouble, I think, was an acute form of xenophobia, for he stood like a rock when a Chinese or a Mongol mounted him. But with me he almost always bucked like mad until I was in the saddle, after which his behaviour became exemplary. The habit was a nuisance, for one was always wanting to get off and have a shot at something and get on again quickly; and on one of his bad days it was impossible to get on again at all without the help of two able-bodied men. Otherwise he was a good horse, very much admired in the caravan.

Kini's horse was six years old, which was two years older than Greys; but he seemed much older than that. He wore an elderly, an almost *passé* air. He had a sad, bony face and an ungainly body. His paces looked awkward, but Kini was very comfortable on him, even when he broke, as he sometimes unemotionally did, into a strange, bounding, rocking-horse canter. He had no nerves and was very wise. At first he was a joke, but at the last we knew him for a loyal and gallant friend, whose loss for a time darkened our foolish enterprise with the shadow of tragedy. We called him Slalom.

We camped early beside a stream near the lake, having done only forty *li* (three li go to a mile). I made a barren expedition along the shore, where there was nothing to be seen but some big black-headed gulls; however, we had plenty of goose left over from the day before, and it was none the worse for being boiled again. Li, apologetically alarmist, insisted on our stowing all our gear inside the tent, as there were not-good men in the hills above the lake. The pressure on space was considerable; but everybody else seemed to be doing the same, and I even slept with the ·44 beside me, though not so much with the idea of using it myself in self-defence as in order to ensure that Li did not so use it. All night long a watchman paced the camp, from time to time rending the frozen darkness with a terrifying ululation. The Tangut bandit menace, it seemed, was being taken seriously.

Next morning it was snowing hard and bitterly cold. Our four camels were split up among four different strings, which meant that they came at different times to be loaded: a circumstance infinitely aggravating, for it interfered with our breakfast, which was the last food we should get for eight hours or more. As we scrambled cursing out of the tent, to find that a camel had kicked over the kettle, that it was even colder than we had feared, and that one of the boxes would not shut, how we envied the wise men and women at home the snug and dependable eight-fifteen which took them, replete with bacon and eggs, to warm and wind-proof offices!

Yesterday the caravan, moving slowly in pale sunlight through the dun wastes, had looked (according to my diary) 'like a couple of chapters out of Exodus'. To-day it recalled the Retreat from Moscow, with the Prince, wrapped in his scarlet robe and riding on a cream-coloured pony, as a far-fetched Napoleon. Snow clung to the camels' manes, plastered the loads. A violent and relentless head wind so peppered us with the flakes that we had to trudge (it was too cold to ride) with bowed heads and half-shut eyes. The pale immensity of the lake, the jagged wall of mountains on our left, were veiled by the driving storm. Our horses faced it as unwillingly as we did and kept their drooping heads close to the shelter of our backs. We reviled the experts, who had assured us that spring came to the Koko Nor in March and April.

At noon the wind dropped, the snow drew off, the lake and the mountains were reinstated. The sun was shining when we camped, two hours later, by a little stream; we pitched the tent and lunched cheerfully off tsamba with the first full stage behind us. I had heard, but forgotten, that distances were very difficult to judge on the Tibetan plateau, and when I set out for the lake shore I could have sworn that it was not much more than half a mile away; but it took me an hour to get there, walking fast. The geese that I had hoped for were absent, but as I wandered disconsolately back I saw a small herd of antelope about a mile away. They were down the wind and there was not enough cover to hide a stag-beetle; but I gambled on their curiosity overcoming their fears and walked slowly towards them. They let me get half-way, staring with heads up and dubious glances at each other. Then the warning to their nostrils grew too urgent; they wheeled and went racing off. But they were between me and the lake, and their course inland brought them a little nearer. They halted for a last look where a low ridge formed the sky-line. The ·22 was sighted up to a hundred yards and they were more than three times that range; but we were out of meat. I lay down, picked the biggest I could see, and sighted on the air two feet above his shoulder. Pht! At the diffident report

125

the herd jerked into flight as one animal, throwing up a cloud of dust which settled slowly in the sunlight. . . .

Settled very slowly. Did not, in fact, altogether settle, for it was being augmented. I realized incredulously that something was kicking on the ground where they had stood. It was the biggest fluke in history. I got up and paced the distance to where the buck lay struggling with a broken back; it was 403 paces. I finished him off with a shot in the neck.

Those antelope are small beasts, about the size of a roebuck, but it took me two hours to drag him back to camp. Altitude affected both Kini and me very little; but at 11,000 feet any unusual exertion must tell on you. The antelope made a profound impression on the caravan; the tiny ·22 bullets were passed from hand to hand amid exclamations of amazement, and I became the devil of a fellow. What else could my little gun kill? Yaks? Wild horses? 'Bandits,' I said, and got a cheap laugh.

We skinned the antelope, gave the forequarters away, and Kini made *shashlik* on the cleaning rod while the liver was boiling. That night we dined sumptuously. The wise men and women at home seemed much less enviable now.

CHAPTER IV

THE CARAVAN MARCHES

WE travelled for seventeen days with the Prince of Dzun. Life was peaceful, pleasant, and – by comparison with certain stages that were to follow – luxurious. There is something very reassuring about a big caravan. The liners, the luxury trains, at which we have been taught to gape complacently have no more than the ingenious vulgarity of gadgets when you compare them with a mile of camels; nor are they more efficient. To identify far-scattered animals in the darkness, to collect your own and bring them into camp before dawn, to do the complicated roping of the loads with frozen fingers, to move off without fuss in the first of the light – these things, which the Mongols did every day as routine, seem to me just as wonderful as the stenographers on the Business Man's Special or the Byzantine cocktail bar on the R.M.S. *Scorbutic*.

Li used to wake us in a grim half-light, thrusting under the flap of the tent what he called, aptly enough, 'eyewash water'. Cramped and cursing, we dragged ourselves out of our sleeping-bags, made some pretence of washing in the frying-pan, cleaned our teeth, and pulled on our boots. (It was far too cold to undress much at night.) 'God, I look awful.' 'Where the hell did you put my mug?' 'Get up, damn you, you're sitting on my sweater.' . . . We were usually bad-tempered in an amiable sort of way.

Then Li would bring the tea and we would swill it down (allowing ourselves one cup with sugar and three or four little cubes of biscuit each) and then mix our tsamba, all the time struggling to pack our things against the coming of the camels. The biggest box was the one in which we kept the plates and mugs and things we needed every day, and Kini, who from much living on small boats had a sailor's neatness in stowing things away, had charge of it;

so that hers was always the hardest lot at this unfriendly, inconvenient hour. Tsamba is not the easiest kind of food to eat with gusto in the early morning, and Kini was a slower eater than I was anyhow; I retain a vivid picture of her, protesting as vainly as Canute protested at the waves, combing her hair with a lump of tsamba held between her teeth and a mirror balanced on her knees, while I dismantled the tent about her and Mongols dragged away the box on which she was leaning.

Our camels were always among the last to be loaded. The snug community of tents that we remembered from the night before had vanished with the darkness, and over the ashes which alone would mark our passing we stamped our feet and grumbled while Li caught the horses. Then we mounted, to the forcibly expressed disgust of Greys, and galloped after the caravan.

There it wound, stately, methodical, through the bleak and empty land, 250 camels pacing in single file. At the head of it, leading the first string, usually rode an old woman on a white pony, a gnarled and withered crone whose conical fur-brimmed hat enhanced her resemblance to a witch. Scattered along the flanks, outriders to the main column, went forty or fifty horsemen. Both Chinese and Mongols wore Tibetan dress, which the Mongols, I suppose, originally adopted as a kind of protective disguise, for they are milder, less formidable people than the warlike Tibetans. The little ponies were dwarfed by the bulging sheepskins which encased their masters. Everyone carried, slung across his back, an ancient musket or a matchlock with a forked rest, and a few of the Chinese had repeating carbines, mostly from the arsenal at Taiyuanfu and all of an extremely unreliable appearance. Some people wore broadswords as well.

Thus we marched. For the first two or three hours it was always cold, and we would walk to restore the circulation in our feet. Sooner or later, every day, the wind got up. It came tearing out of the west and scourged us without mercy. It was enough to drive you mad. You could not smoke, you could not speak (for nobody heard you), and

128

after a time you could not think consecutively. The wind was the curse of our life; ubiquitous and inescapable, it played the same part on the Tibetan plateau as insects do in the tropical jungle. It did us no harm (except to chap our faces), but it plagued us and got on our nerves.

However, the wind never blew all day, and there were times when the sun shone and the march was a joy. Men climbed on lightly loaded camels and went to sleep in perilous positions. The Mongols and the Chinese ragged each other and played – with, I always thought, an underlying hint of fierce and ancient hatreds – a primitive game which consisted of lashing your opponent and his horse with your whip until you or he were put to flight; the whips were light and the sheepskins gave plenty of protection, but it was a tough game for all that. Sometimes a hare was sighted and pursued. Sometimes a few of us would ride on and sit down in the shelter of a hollow to smoke; the long-stemmed, small-bowled pipes would be passed from hand to hand, and mine with them if it was asked for, for I saw no reason to be haughty and exclusive in this matter. When people know no customs but their own, and when their own customs are few because of the extreme simplicity of their life, it is only courteous to respect those customs when you can. Besides, my pipe was a great marvel to them. They had little acquaintance with wood (many of them would not see a tree again until they went back to the markets on the edge of the plateau) and they were used to pipes with metal bowls; they could not conceive how I could smoke mine without setting fire to it. Mongols, though hopelessly uncommercial, know a good thing when they see it, and they appreciated the pipe in the same way that they appreciated my rook rifle or my field-glasses.

The hours passed at varying speeds. If it was warm and windless you fell sometimes into a meditation which blotted out a segment of the march, so that when you returned from the far-off things and places that had filled your mind you remembered the country you had passed through hazily, as you remember country in a dream. But if the wind blew no anaesthetic availed; for every yard of every

129

mile you had your wits too much about you, and progress was a slow and wearisome routine.

Towards the end of the seventh hour you began, like everybody else, to watch the Prince, riding his pale horse near the head of the column with three or four followers about him. The moment he wheeled off the trail and dismounted everyone who had a horse put it into a gallop. From all down the mile-long column ponies scurried out across the steppe, their manes and tails streaming, their riders whooping in the headlong (and quite pointless) race for tent-sites. We always chose one – at his invitation – near the Prince. While we waited for the camels to come up we unsaddled the horses (by no means everyone did this) and hobbled them. Even Greys submitted meekly to the hobble, which fastened both hind legs and one foreleg; I never saw a Tibetan pony object to having its legs handled.

Soon the camels arrived, string after string; were claimed and separated; knelt, roaring, to be unloaded. It was a scene of great confusion, yet it resolved itself astonishingly quickly into a neat, placid cluster of tents. All the tents except ours were circular; they were pitched with their backs to the wind, and the loads were stacked in a low rampart under their flaps. Men scattered to collect dung in the wide skirts of their sheepskins; others brought water in big kettles from the stream; and presently the smoke of cooking fires, flattened by the wind, was streaming from the door of every tent. But the Prince, who was a pious man, prayed before he cooked; a low, rhythmic mutter came from inside his tent, and one of his staff walked round and round it, his lips moving mechanically, sprinkling drops of water from a wooden bowl upon the ground.

It was always one of the best moments of the day when we had got our tent pitched and the things stowed inside it, and could plunge in and lie luxuriously on our sleeping bags, out of the wind. Out of the wind; it made such a difference. The air still roared outside and the thin walls bulged in upon us; but we could talk and smoke and rub butter on our chapped and burning faces and feel at peace.

Presently there would be tea with red pepper in it (no sugar ration was issued at lunch) and tsamba to abate the gnawing in our bellies. It is really impossible to describe how snug and comfortable we felt.

We marched usually from 6 a.m. to about 2 p.m., so we had several hours of daylight still before us. After lunch I always went out with the ·22, to wander happily along the lake or, when we left the lake, among the hills, recalling with an exile's pleasure many evenings similarly spent elsewhere, and coming back to camp with a goose or a duck or a hare or with nothing at all. But Kini never took the afternoon off, except to photograph, for there was nothing for her to do out of camp. She read or wrote or darned or slept; and whichever she did she was sooner or later interrupted by somebody who wanted medicine. The Mongols seldom bothered us, but any of the Chinese who were ill, or had once been ill, or thought they might be going to be ill, came regularly. They fell into three classes: those who had nothing the matter with them at all, those who had had something the matter with them for years and years, and those whom we were able to help. The third class was the smallest.

What with my wretched Chinese and their determination to pile on the agony, it took a long time to discover even approximately the nature of their various afflictions. We were at our best with cuts and sores, which Kini disinfected and bandaged with skill and care (she had once done some Red Cross training with a view to becoming a professional ski teacher). Internal complaints were not so easy, but when in doubt we gave castor oil, a policy which scored several medical triumphs and once won us the gratitude of the most important Chinese by curing him of a fearful belly-ache. One nice and unusually intelligent boy had an old abscess in his thigh and wanted us to cut it open; this we declined to do, but Kini worked on it so successfully with fomentations that in the end it was giving him hardly any trouble. At the close of a long day one of the last things you want to do is to attend to stinking sores on unwashed anatomies, but Kini did it cheerfully and took

131

immense trouble over it; all along the road it was she, not I, who did the dirty work.

It was she, for instance, who went out into the cold and saw to the cooking of the evening meal, while I squatted in the warm tent, cleaning the rifle or writing my diary or playing patience on a suitcase, and asking at frequent intervals how soon the food would be ready. When it was, we put the great black pot just inside the tent and Li brought his bowl and we got out our enamel plates and dinner was served: rice or mien or a kind of noodles which we called by its Russian name of *lapsha*, and whatever meat we had in hand. How we ate! We did not speak. We shovelled the food down until the pot was empty and we were distended. It was my misfortune that I had only a teaspoon to shovel with, for three or four larger spoons which we bought in Sining had broken almost on sight; but it is wonderful what you can do with a teaspoon when you are in the mood, and it equalled things up with Kini, who was a slower eater but had the only larger spoon. They were delicious meals.

As soon as we had finished eating we felt sleepy. Washing up was not a very arduous business, for we only had one plate and one mug each; all the same, it was usually omitted. We pulled off the soft sheepskin boots which I had had made at Tangar for use in camp, wriggled into our flea-bags, and covered ourselves with our overcoats. We made pillows of rolled up sweaters on a foundation of boots and field-glasses; Kini's was always very neat, mine was always a lumpy scrabble. Just outside, our horses munched their barley, making a sound as charming and as soporific as the sound of running water or of waves upon a beach. The tiny tent looked very warm and cheerful in the candle-light, and one of us would perhaps grow suddenly talkative, theorizing about the future or reminiscing about the past. But conversation became increasingly one-sided; monosyllables were succeeded by grunts, and grunts by a profound indifferent silence. Whichever of us was talking abandoned soliloquy and blew out the candle.

The wind dropped at night. Outside the iron land froze

in silence under the moon. The silver tents were quiet. The watchman moved among them squatly, like a goblin (thinking what thoughts, suppressing what fears?). A wolf barked. A star fell down the tremendous sky. The camp slept.

CHAPTER V

WINDS AND WILD ASSES

WE had sighted the Koko Nor on the day we started with the Prince of Dzun, April 1st; we did three marches along its southern shore.

The first two have been described. The third was a fine day, spoilt by a more than ordinarily fierce wind at noon. We were very close to the lake, and I lost face by shooting badly at a lot of geese in full view of the caravan. I got one, and a mandarin duck, but they both got up, hard hit, and fell a little way out on the ice; this was broken at the lake's edge and they could not be retrieved. My operations were hampered by an old Moslem who insisted on following me, brandishing a huge knife with which to cut the throat of anything I killed; his religious principles did him credit, but he got in the way. We called him the Bosun; there was something of the nautical about his gait and (less definably) about his white felt hat, and his genially villainous face recalled the Bosun in *The Tempest*, of whom somebody says 'His complexion is perfect gallows'.

The wind was terrible when we camped. A spark was whisked out of one of the Chinese tents and fired the sere grass. The flames licked through the camp as swiftly as a striking snake. They travelled so fast, were driven so hard by the wind, that they had no time to spread and the one tent that stood directly in their path was struck before they reached it. Everyone rushed up shouting and we beat on the flames with felts and sheepskins while kettles of water were emptied in their path. After five exciting minutes there was only a black scar on the yellow plain to commemorate a crisis. Afterwards, leaning sideways against the wind, I retrieved my reputation by bringing off a long shot at what seemed to be the only goose for miles around. That night, on the hills above the lake, angry golden whorls of fire crept eastward down the wind; we wondered if they had started from a Tangut encampment.

The next day, which was April 4th, we continued for four hours along the lake shore, then swung away left-handed towards the hills. We did a long stage, climbing gradually until we came to a narrow, rugged valley just short of the principal pass. Here we camped in half a gale, and this time it was our own fire (which, being outside the tent, was very difficult to control) that started the trouble. Once more flames ran along the ground, once more we beat them out; but our tent was pitched to leeward of the others and there was no threat to the camp. The wind, or the glare, or a combination of the two, had given me a kind of snow-blindness in my right eye; it was painful and made it impossible to shoot, but it only lasted two or three days. At this camp there was no water, but the men, knowing in advance, had loaded blocks of ice on the camels; so only the animals suffered.

We were off again at dawn. It was colder than ever. The pass was very steep, and owing to the altitude the animals had to be rested at short intervals while we climbed; it is called Tsakassu and according to our maps is about 12,000 feet above sea-level. From the top we got our last view of the Koko Nor, vast, glittering, and forlorn; to the south was a wilderness of hills. The wind was awful up here, and we tramped all day with hunched shoulders and stiff, stinging faces. 'I wish I was a nice warm debutante,' said Kini. After a long stage we camped in a naked and unfriendly plain. In the distance there was some kind of a low mud building. This was the only habitation (if it was a habitation) that we saw for several days; on the lake shore there had sometimes been a nomad's black tent crouched in a fold of the ground, but in the hills there was nothing.

My eye was better next day, and the march had hardly started when I was involved in a fruitless hunt after three wild asses. These animals, which we now beheld for the first time, were on this and many later stages of our route the only decoration of a naked landscape. They were a very good decoration too. The size of a mule, dark brown

135

in colour with pale bellies, they wheeled and galloped in the middle distance with heads up and short tails flying. They ranged in herds of anything up to fifteen, and in their manœuvres achieved that uncanny unanimity of movement which you see sometimes in a covey of partridges or a flock of teal; no troop of cavalry was ever more symmetrically ranked, more precisely simultaneous in its evolutions. They are known to Tibet and Ladakh as *kyang*, to the Turkis of Sinkiang as *kulan*, to China (always charmingly vague about natural history) as 'wild horses', and to science as *equus hemionus*. Their meat is edible, but they cannot as a rule be tamed, though I met somebody who had once seen one being ridden in Ladakh. They are very attractive animals to watch.

Towards noon we struck a marshy patch on the plain which we were crossing. The caravan made a detour to avoid a salt-caked bog and camped in a patch of withered grass beside a frozen salt lake about three miles long. I went out with the ·44 to look for wild asses, but though I covered a lot of ground there were none to be seen. The country was indescribably desolate. I shot a hare, which thought itself unseen, at a range of five yards, and the Bosun, who, in spite of threats had been following like a jackal at a distance, came up, skipping with delight, and cut its throat. That was the only thing killed by the ·44.

The next day we left the salt lake and climbed again, camping just short of another pass. Once more there was no water and the tents were pitched in two sections, each near a convenient snow-drift. In part of one of these we boiled the hare for dinner.

Soon after dawn on April 8th we crossed the second pass, which was an easy one, and dropped down on to a sloping table-land. It was cold, but the sun shone and the caravan looked very gallant as it drew away from the jagged mouth of the pass. In the middle of the day there was a deafening report ahead of us; an old Chinese with a wily face and a long pigtail had ridden on and broken the leg of a wild ass with his musket. Everyone galloped madly up and a revolting scene took place. They caught the beast

136

and put a halter on him and for ten minutes roared with laughter at his struggles before they finally cut his throat; they had no conception that it was cruel and I could do nothing about it.

Presently we came to a river called the Tsarsa. Kini stopped with some of the others to water her horse. Slalom put his forelegs in some kind of quicksand and started plunging. Kini came off into the ice-cold water and before they got Slalom out her flea-bag, which she kept folded on her saddle to sit on, was partly soaked; this was very bad luck, for the sheepskin took a long time to dry, and when it did dry it had shrunken and grown stiff. We camped under a cliff in a rocky little gorge, down which the wind came pelting, and dined off wild ass meat, a gift from one of our patients; it was tough and not as good as we expected. We had done a march of nine hours, our longest to date.

We were up at four next day. As the last camels were loading three Tibetans rode through the camp on ponies. They carried muskets and had no pack animals with them, and an uneasy silence fell on the little groups who watched them. 'Not-good men,' said Li. 'Bandits.'

I doubt if they were, but everyone seemed a little jumpy that day. A few of us, headed by the handsome and important Moslem whom we had christened Castor Oil, left the camels to follow the river gorge and took a short cut through the mountains. The Chinese unwrapped the cloth which protected the breeches of their rifles and from time to time uttered a kind of facetious war-cry. It was a brilliant day, and presently we came into a high valley where there were trees and turf on the ground. It was a lovely place. The trees looked like a cross between a cypress and a yew, and according to Li something about them (we couldn't make out what) was worth a lot of money. It was only when we saw the trees that we realized how much we had been missing them; in a thousand miles they were the only ones we came across. At the top of the valley we made a huge fire and rested round it, enjoying the sunshine and hating the wind. Then we rode on and dropped down on to another plateau, hedged on three sides by distant mountains but open at its western end. We lay up for an hour in a sheltered hollow, waiting for the main body to arrive. It was warm and pleasant and we talked nonsense, arguing about what would be the nicest possible thing that could happen at that moment. Kini said that we were well enough off as we were, but I contended that it would be even better if a large butler could be seen approaching, bearing a tray covered with scrambled eggs. We were always hungry all the time.

Presently the caravan arrived, long and deliberate, eating up distance as a caterpillar eats a leaf, and in the early afternoon we sighted dwellings; black tents and two or three low mud houses. Prayer flags fluttered over them and there were a few fields where barley was cultivated. We camped beyond them, close to a road built by the Chinese from Sining to a place called Shang and alleged to be practicable for lorries; we disliked the faint smell of civilization. Our supply of barley was running low, so in the evening Li and I rode two miles down the river to a flat farm-house belonging to a Tibetan. We drank tea and played with the children (whose mother had a startlingly beautiful Madonna face) and bargained with success. When we took our leave the people of the house kept their mastiffs at bay with great difficulty by pelting them with frozen dung.

The next day was April 10th and we did a double stage. We left the lorry road and climbed up a gentle slope towards a low pass beyond which no further mountains could be seen. Our sense of the picturesque was offended by the sight of what appeared to be telegraph poles astride the mouth of the pass; but when we got there they turned out to be tall posts between which were slung festoons of bones, mostly the jaw and shoulder bones of hares and sheep (at least that was what they looked like). There were also prayer flags and a good many *obos*, which are cairns of stones with a wide range of superstitious significance. Several small Tibetan caravans met us in the pass, coming up from the south by a road whose ultimate terminus was

Lhasa. Children in little gaudy bonnets were lashed on to some of the loads, their heads nodding drowsily to the stride of yak or camel. The men grinned darkly under their great fur hats. The women's plaits of hair were burdened with superfluous silverware like a Victorian sideboard. Few of them knew us for Europeans; nor was this surprising, seeing what sun and wind had done to us.

Beyond the pass we were in the Tsaidam basin. The mountains became, and for the next five weeks remained, a backcloth only. We left on our right the tents and mud walls of a small settlement called Kharakhoto and went forward into desolate dunes. Round Kharakhoto there was a crude irrigation system, and the crossing of one channel gave us trouble. The camels floundered gawkily, imperilling the loads; on the faces of the watching Chinese amusement alternated with acute anxiety, and it was easy to tell whose goods were carried by which beasts. At noon we halted in a tussocky plain but did not make camp.

Here we were not much more than 9000 feet up, and it was warm and almost windless. While we rested and the animals got what grazing they could, a kind of trial was held. That morning the Prince and one of his staff had ended an obscure dispute about a horse by beating up the plaintiff with their whips. The plaintiff was a disagreeable Chinese and the merchant in whose train he travelled protested. Feeling ran high in camp; there was a lot of shouting and flourishing of tent-poles. At last order was restored, and the parties concerned, with their followers, sat down on the ground in a circle. Castor Oil led for the defence. It was amusing to watch him – voluble, ingratiating, man-of-the-world – playing a stream of words over the dour façade of the Prince's representative. (The Prince did not attend the trial in person.) The Mongol sat with downcast eyes – eyes which, now childish and sullen, now uneasily evasive, seemed unsuccessfully bent on appearing inscrutable. His hands fiddled with his pipe. When he spat he spat self-consciously. Helpless, knowing from the experience of generations that he was no match for his adversary, that he was out of his depth in casuistry, the proud, pathetic Mongol, hunched in his sheepskin robe, epitomized the history of a once irresistible race; just as Castor Oil, triumphing with flashy subtlety over the slow wits of a barbarian, was in the true tradition of Chinese Imperialism, of conquest by cleverness. The Prince had to pay two bolts of cloth as compensation.

He was all-powerful in the caravan. His men were better than the Chinese, if it had come to force. But the Chinese controlled his only market, and next year, when he came back to Sining, Castor Oil and the others would have had their revenge. They might have had it through the officials, or they might have had it in a more Chinese way, by getting other merchants to refuse credits or to press for the settlement of debts. It was a risk, in any case, that the Prince did not care to take.

CHAPTER VI

NIGHT-MARCH TO THE END OF
THE WORLD

JUST before dusk we loaded up again and marched into the setting sun. Huge sand dunes closed in on us. The feet of camels and horses made no noise. The sunset gilded the haze of dust that we kicked up. There was no wind. As the light went men's voices died. Here and there, up and down the long slow chain of beasts, a rider would start a harsh, wistful, dragging song; but no one took it up.

Presently the moon shone. Scrawny feeble patches of tamarisk solidified, grew black, put on strange shapes and tired our eyes. The sand was silver, and the dust we breathed hung like an emanation, as of steam, around the caravan. Its flanks were pricked by little red eyes where men were smoking pipes. White horses gleamed like wraiths, the camels towered and were monstrous. Hour after hour the line of animals moved westwards with silent, shuffling strides. In all our world only the moon, the familiar moon, was real and linked us to a life we knew.

At eleven we halted in a waterless place, lit fires, lay down in the shelter of stacked loads, and slipped quickly out of those unearthly black and silver wastes. We were very tired.

Six hours later we were on the move again. It was freezing hard and our stomachs were empty, but Dzunchia was only two marches ahead and there was a sort of quiet gaiety in the caravan. Presently the sun rose and routed the frost. We thawed. The horses, thirsty and worn with marching, moved lifelessly, but we came into a country where the tamarisks grew taller and where here and there mosaicked beds of clay promised, at the right season, water. In one of these I saw the track of a bear, spatulate, sharp-toed, but somehow human. After four hours or so we stopped and had breakfast. This new world might be flat and featureless but at least it was warm; we ate and read and basked luxuriously.

At noon we went on. First flocks of sheep, then yurts, announced the end of desolation, the beginning of inhabited country. With a shock we realized that the Prince no longer led us. His own tents lay at some distance from Dzunchia and half the caravan was making for them. I felt suddenly sad as I looked back over my shoulder at our truncated column. Its full majesty was gone, its ragged unselfconscious pomp curtailed; because I had known it at full strength it seemed a poor thing now, and the pride which an ordered mile of beasts must give to one who rides with them was gone for ever. The liner or the luxury train you leave without a pang; the disintegrating caravan filled me with a queer nostalgia.

More dunes, more scattered yurts, then slippery flats, pitted with bog-holes, frosted with salt. The hard and knobbly ground had a shallow coating of grey mud; camels and horses skidded, crossed their legs, and stumbled. We forded a small river called the Bayan and zigzagged on through bad going, dodging the worst of it. Here at last was the reality behind those much-scanned symbols on our map, those little explosive trinities of exclamation marks with which cartographers convey a bog. Here was the Tsaidam Marsh. For the first (and I think the last) time, a landmark in the journey roughly coincided with our preconceptions.

We camped, late, on an island of dry ground. I brought off a long shot at a mandarin duck, but it was only wounded and we lost it in the grass. Wild fowl were on the move all round and, forgetting Tartary, I stalked geese without success in a grey, still, Hebridean evening in which only some gigantic herons seemed exotic and anomalous. Next day (it was April 12th) we reached Dzunchia after a long, dull, slithering ride.

You could not call it an impressive place; you could not, in your most romantic mood, endow it with a single attractive quality. Yet the first sight of Dzunchia thrilled

142

us as the Taj Mahal might thrill the simplest mind in all the Middle West. Far ahead, two hours' march ahead, an almost imperceptible square knob broke the unendingly flat and empty horizon. We drew nearer to it slowly, impatiently, expectantly, as castaways in a rowing boat draw nearer to an island. Squat, isolated, and somehow vigilant, the knob began to look more and more like a fort or a blockhouse. Full of excitement, we made ridiculous guesses about it; it was the local Opera House, it was a luxury hotel. There were times when the language difficulty, which prevented us from ever really knowing what was happening to us until it happened, lent a certain zest to life.

The fort was not a fort but a small, dilapidated lamasery. Round this had sprung up a little warren of mud huts, some of which were used by the Prince as store-rooms and some by the Chinese who came to trade here in the summer. That was all there was to Dzunchia: an unsightly, unexpected cluster of walls and roofs which grew like a wart in the middle of a vast bare plain. The poor gesture which man had made towards establishing himself there, the dingy skeleton of domesticity, enhanced to an overpowering degree the desolation of the place. Dzunchia looked, felt, and smelt like the end of the world.

We spent three days there. The elation of having arrived, of having finished another chapter in the expedition's history, quickly wore off. Nor did we take kindly to sleeping under a roof again. Our squalid, cave-like room, even after it had been swept of litter, had two great disadvantages as compared with the little tent. For one thing it was not wind-proof, and when we lit a fire to warm it the smoke drove us, choking and weeping, out of doors. For another, it was spacious, so that we were never without company, never without the obligation to be polite, to show off our belongings, to tell how much they cost. Every day for an hour or two the sky, without darkening, became less blue and a dust storm bore down on us from the west, coating everything with a fine grey powder. We may not have been much dirtier, but we felt much dirtier than on the march.

It is always the way. The desert is clean and comfortable, and the Ritz is clean and comfortable; it is on the first of the stages from the desert to the Ritz that you find the real dirt, the real discomfort.

The remnants of the caravan disbanded at Dzunchia and from now on we had to proceed under our own steam. On the day we arrived Li got in touch with a Mongol who was prepared to hire us camels, but the camels were far away at pasture and delay was inevitable. While we waited there was nothing to do. It was fun to lie in our sleeping bags in the early morning, instead of having to scramble out into an urgent unkind world; but as the day wore on we grew discontented and restless. The future was still a riddle. We had been gone two months from Peking, but on the map of Asia the thin, red, reassuring line which wriggled along the Himalayas looked inconceivably far away and it was impossible to say how much nearer to India we should get, where and when and how we should be eventually defeated. We mentioned Sinkiang to no one, not even to Li. We pinned our hopes on Teijinar where, two years before, a Cossack friend of the Smigunovs had been living; it was extremely doubtful if he was still there, but if he was we had an opportunity of at any rate assessing our chances of crossing the frontier into Sinkiang. Teijinar was said to be some fifteen marches further west.

Apart from two or three lamas and one Chinese, there appeared to be no one so unfortunate as to be a permanent resident of Dzunchia. One of the lamas, a gigantic, grizzled man with a Johnsonian manner and an intolerably loud voice, sat in our quarters for hours on end, twirling his prayer-wheel and marvelling at us. The Prince called one day to say good-bye, and gave us his visiting card and a present of milk. To the end we remained, I think, a mystery to him and indeed to all the people of the caravan. Very few of them had seen a foreigner before. They addressed me always by a respectful Chinese term which means 'Pastor' and is applied to missionaries; Kini, whose native country was not on their map, they spoke of as 'that French person'. In general they treated us as an obscure kind of joke, of which they could not be certain that they really saw the point; this suited our purposes well enough.

In the cultural history of the expedition Dzunchia marks the closing phases of what may be termed the Leblanc-Simenon period. The blessed Urechs had given us, on parting, a substantial paper-backed supply of the works of MM. Maurice Leblanc and Georges Simenon. In the tent and on the march both the former's hero (Arsène Lupin – *gentleman-cambrioleur*) and the latter's (Inspector Maigret) were our inseparable companions; the one romantic and superhuman, the other plausible and earthy. We fought each other for these books and dreaded the day when they would be finished. As each was jettisoned the influence of French detective fiction spread gradually throughout the caravan, and it was no uncommon thing to see a Mongol stalking along with the lively cover of *La Demoiselle Aux Yeux Verts* stuck in between his forehead and his fur hat to form an eye-shade, while the dramatic pages of *Le Fou de Bergerac* stuffed up the holes in several pairs of boots. The only other form of literature the Mongols can ever have seen was prayer-books in their own lamaseries; if they thought that our books were prayer-books too we must have struck them as very sacrilegious people. They had an odd habit of looking at all photographs through an imaginary pair of field-glasses; but still odder (to us) was their astonishment at our gloves, which they were always asking to see and which they clearly regarded as a most ingenious but rather effete invention. Their hands were protected only by their long sleeves; there is a big future for the glove trade in Central Asia.

We stagnated impatiently at Dzunchia. We wrote a further batch of farewell letters and left them with the Chinese whose abscess Kini had treated, to be sent back to Tangar with the first east-bound caravan. (These letters, which eventually reached Europe, were the last anyone heard of us until we got to Kashgar.) We were feasted on mutton by Castor Oil. Kini was bitten in the behind by a dog. I got a right and left at mandarin duck, and also shaved, a thing which I did about once a fortnight throughout the journey; for some reason I only had six razor-blades with me. In the evening we watched rare caravans crawling up out of the horizon. 'A limitless expanse,' says my diary; and though it has the decency to drape the *cliché* in inverted commas they were not really needed, for the *cliché* was an accurate description.

On the second evening we had a slice of bad luck. A big west-bound caravan passed without calling at Dzunchia, and as I watched the long file of beasts I had a kind of intuition that they meant something to us. It was late and I knew that they would camp near. When I was out after geese that evening I found their tents, walked into the chief one, and drank tea with half a dozen Chinese. They were tough, unceremonious people and I was not sure what to make of them. Their leader said that they were headed for Teijinar and claimed that they were travelling fast. Had they any unloaded beasts for hire? Yes, they had several; plenty for us, if we only needed four. I said that I would send Li to fix things up and walked back to Dzunchia, feeling resourceful and conceited.

I sent Li, but he returned saying that I must have made a mistake, that the people in the tents had no spare animals, that I couldn't have understood them properly. I said that I was sorry and forgot about it. But later, at Teijinar, we discovered that Li had gone to the wrong camp; the men I had seen had waited for us till late the next morning before moving on. If we had joined them we should have saved ten days, a certain amount of money, and much agony of mind.

At last, before dawn on April 16th, our four camels arrived and with them a wretched horse for Li to ride. The only other members of the Prince's caravan who were going further west were a party of a dozen Moslems; they were bound for the mountains south of the Tsaidam, where they were going to wash gold in the rivers. They were inexperienced people, none of them knowing the country, and we had no desire for their company on the road; but we had perforce to accept them as travelling companions, since they were going the same way at the same time. Most of them had left the day before, but the remainder started off with us, in charge of eight half-bred yaks carrying loads for which they had been unable to procure camels.

We said good-bye to Castor Oil, the lamas, and the abscess man. It was a warm, sunny day, and with light hearts we rode westwards once more, leaving behind the smoky rooms, the litter of bones and excrement, the listless mongrel dogs, the verminous monks, the torn prayer-flags, the ignoble desolation of Dzunchia. We would have given a lot to be sure that we should never see the place again.

PART FOUR

NO MAN'S LAND

CHAPTER I

THE LOST CITY

Now began a period in which incidents were fewer, delays more numerous, and the country more monotonous than in any other part of our journey.

The squat silhouette of Dzunchia, whose slow growth upon the horizon had riveted our eyes four days ago, now dwindled and vanished without a backward glance from us. The horses moved easily after their rest. The sun shone on Li's wine-red *polu*, on the russet and gold of mandarin ducks which circled in pairs about the bog-holes, croaking. A heat-haze danced over the marshy land and one or two of the huge mosquitoes which are said to make life in the Tsaidam unbearable in summer buzzed and bit us ineffectually; they assorted oddly with the drifts of snow which still lay here and there in hollows. To the south an unbroken chain of peaks stood up against the blue sky, marking the northern bulwark of the main Tibetan plateau. It felt good to be on the march again.

But we had not gone far before the bright day was clouded by misgivings. Li revealed for the first time that our new camels and the Mongol in charge of them, so far from taking us to Teijinar, would go no further than Nomo Khantara, a mere three stages further west. Nomo Khantara marked the tribal boundary between the Mongols of Dzun and the Mongols of Teijinar, and there we should have to change our animals again. I hated the sound of this. It meant at least two days' unforeseen delay and might mean much more; this was a bad season to travel in, for the camels were in poor condition and the Mongols were reluctant to bring them in from the pastures to be used on the road where there was little grazing. Our escape from Dzunchia began to smell of anti-climax.

In the middle of the march the track led us out of the

salt-flats into a strange country of small dunes and twisted tamarisk. There was something forced and unnatural about the landscape. The little hummocks, the naked branches, looked – against the too bright, too picturesque background of sky and mountains – like the synthetic scenery which surrounds stuffed wild animals in a glass case. The snow and the mosquitoes, the dry hollow contrasting with the bog on top of the ridge beyond it – everything seemed freakish and abnormal.

Li, who had ridden ahead, stopped without our knowing it at the only yurt we saw. Kini and I went on until the length of the march made us suspicious; then we turned and rode back and found the camels unloaded and grazing. We made a pleasant camp under a tamarisk and decided to do the two remaining stages to Nomo Khantara in one day.

We woke to a changed world. The sun had gone and an icy wind bore down on us from the west. We moved off in some disgust, for we had fondly imagined that we had finished with the cold; did a dull, chill march; halted at midday for tsamba; then forced the pace and arrived at Nomo Khantara in the afternoon, an hour ahead of our camels.

At first sight Nomō Khantara was rather an attractive place, as attractive places go in the Tsaidam. A few yurts were dotted about the centre of an enormous grove of tamarisk, or some scrub like tamarisk, which grew to a height of about twelve feet and gave you the illusion of a forest. A little stream, opaque with yellow mud, followed one of the many channels of a dried-up river-bed which would not fill till summer melted the Tibetan snows. It felt (at first) very snug after the bareness of the salt-flats.

We pitched the tent next to what Li referred to as 'my house'. He had been talking about his house for several days, to our mystification. It turned out to be two yurts, one used as a store-room and the other inhabited by one of Li's brothers, who was also acting as an agent for Ma Shin-teh. The other members of the household were a Mongol woman with a wrinkled, humorous, and charming face and an unusual dignity of carriage; a small, irritating child called, as nearly as we could make out, Gumboil; and a varying but substantial number of goats. The premises included stables, which were brilliantly contrived by digging a kind of grave large enough to contain, and deep enough to imprison, two horses. Nearby was a handsome tent with a bold pattern worked on it; it belonged, we learnt, to two itinerant lamas from Tibet. In the same clearing was also pitched the blue tent of the gold-seekers, who had arrived the day before.

It was a different sort of place from what we were used to, and we made camp cheerfully enough. But over bowls of tea in Li's yurt we heard the local gossip, and the local gossip was far from reassuring. The stout, somehow despicable Moslem who led the gold-seekers looked dejected. The Mongols here, he said, were not-good men. They had refused to hire him camels. They had even refused to hire the lamas' camels, although the lamas were very holy men and very anxious to get to Teijinar; the Mongols had gone on refusing for a fortnight, and now the lamas were going back eastwards to Shang by the way they had come. It all sounded most depressing.

We spent what afterwards turned out to have been the Easter holidays at Nomo Khantara – six interminable days. It is not really a good place to go for Easter; secluded and salubrious it may be, but the visitor will not find it gay.

On the first day Li rode over to the Mongol encampment, a couple of miles further west, and was refused camels. On the second day I went with him and the Mongol front seemed to weaken slightly. On the third day we both went and flourished our Chinese passports (which of course they could not read) and made menacing talk; the head men gave in. But before we could get the camels the clan had to be gathered and men detailed to go out to the pastures and fetch them in, and so incalculable was the temper of these Mongols that until the very last moment we could not be sure that they were really going to produce the animals, could not be sure that we were not condemned indefinitely to the tamarisk until a caravan should pick us up in the summer.

The place, we very soon discovered, was more of a prison than it looked. The little trees (if you could call them trees) did not grow thickly; there were ten to twenty yards between each, and at every step fresh devious glades presented themselves, tempting you to explore further. This it was unwise to do. There were no landmarks, no tracks, and every tree looked exactly like the next. The ground was bare, the cover seemed thin; but once you were out of earshot of camp you had nothing to guide you but the sun, and you quickly noted how deceptive was the sparseness of the trees, how difficult it was to steer a course.

The first day we were there a boy attached to the gold-seekers went off into the tamarisk and never came back. Search parties ranged by day, huge bonfires blazed by night, and the lamas put in some fairly intensive clairvoyance, chanting and throwing dice to establish his geographical position. I interrupted, by special request, a game of patience and put the problem to the cards, one suit standing for each quarter of the compass. But the boy was never found; he must have died of hunger and thirst, perhaps only a little way away.

Kini, as usual, endured delay with a better grace than I did; but there was little to fill our life except anxiety and misgivings, and neither of us enjoyed Nomo Khantara much. Apart from food, the tattered patience cards, and our dwindling supply of books, we had three potential sources of interest and amusement: the Mongols, the hares, and the Lost City.

The Teijinar Mongols were surly, bearish people. They looked wilder and woollier than their neighbours of Dzun, and none of them spoke a word of Chinese, in which some of the Prince's followers had been quite proficient. At Nomo Khantara they were living away from their tents, in curious open bowers scooped out of the lee side of unusually thick growths of tamarisk. Like the scenery in a Chinese play, the walls, the door and the roof were left to the imagination; the skeleton of a dwelling was suggested

154

by the central fireplace, by sheepskins and matchlocks hanging from the branches, by an old painted chest wedged in the crotch of a tree. Most of the men went about naked to the waist, their shaggy robes gathered in great unwieldy bunches round their middles, the wrinkled tubular sleeves dangling flaccidly like the trunks of dead elephants. Dust and wind and sun had given them a crusted look; their small bloodshot eyes glittered redly in their broad dark faces. A Mongol on foot lacks his native centaur dignity, and these people, shambling half furtive and half truculent through the thickets, suggested, more strongly than any human beings I have seen, the poor monster Caliban. For all that, they represented a type of civilization which the world for some unknown reason considers higher, or at any rate more respectable, than the nomad's. They were agriculturalists. The ground, watered by the shifting river-bed, sheltered by the tamarisk from the eroding wind, was split up into fields over a wide area; those near our camp were clearly old and had long been fallow, but round their settlement the Mongols were already breaking the ground and repairing little irrigation channels. They grew barley and stored it underground. They were the only agricultural community I heard of in the Tsaidam, and I like to think that their bad manners were the consequence of their deserting Mongol tradition and settling down.

As for the hares, there were plenty of them. With much caution and a compass I used to range the environs every day, and in a couple of hours always got as many as I could carry; they were amusing to stalk, for the Mongol dogs had made them wary. One evening I was startled by a sound at once familiar and anomalous; if a telephone had started ringing, or a boy had shouted 'Football Results!', I could hardly have been more taken aback. I listened . . . There it was again. This time there could be no doubt. It was a cock pheasant crowing. I followed him up and got him as he strutted in an open place. He was a very handsome bird, differing slightly as to plumage from *P. colchicus*. Later I got two more; they were welcome, for a diet of boiled hare palls after a time.

155

Then there was the Lost City. We christened it in the Fawcett tradition; but I know that it is not a city and I cannot be sure that it is really lost, though I can find no reference to it by the few travellers who have penetrated the Tsaidam. It consisted of two old mud forts, situated about a mile to the north of our camp. The bigger was some 300 yards square, with crenellated walls about thirty feet high by ten feet thick; you could walk along them behind the ramparts and there were gates in the middle of the eastern and the western walls. The smaller fort was about half that size and quite empty, whereas the bigger had the ruins of some unidentifiable building in the middle of it. They were both in a good state of preservation, thanks presumably to the dryness of the air and the protection against wind-driven sand afforded by the tamarisk. Anything which breaks the monotony of a featureless country is appreciated, and it was pleasant to wander round the deserted walls, sniping at hares in the dead grass below you and wondering who last fired across these battlements, and with what weapons.

The Chinese could not, and the Mongols either could not or would not, tell us anything about the history of these forts. They looked Chinese to me, if they looked anything at all; but five or six miles to the west we found a domed mausoleum of an unmistakably Turkic design and apparently belonging to much the same period as the forts. The matter is one for the learned men; I can only make a few obvious deductions. At a period unknown and for purposes unknown somebody maintained a garrison at Nomo Khantara, and from their conquerors (or protectors) the Mongols learned to practise the arts of husbandry. One might surmise that the garrison did not stay there long, otherwise the ruins of buildings would have been visible inside the walls; one might even guess, rather wildly, that they stayed only for the inside of a summer, otherwise they would have taken the trouble to build themselves some better protection against the great cold than was offered by their tents.

Having gone thus far and being a little dizzy with conjecture, I ask myself whether the forts could have had anything to do with General Tso Tsung-tang. In the latter half of the last century General Tso set out from the coast at the head of 2000 ill-conditioned soldiers and marched some 2500 miles westward to Kashgar. In Kashgar the adventurer Yakub Beg, an ex-dancing-boy from Khokand, had raised the standard of revolt and established himself so firmly in power that in 1875 Queen Victoria went so far as to send a mission to him under Sir Douglas Forsyth. When General Tso got to Kashgar he turned out Yakub Beg and restored the authority of the Emperor; but it took him two years to get there, and on the way his small army (which must have become considerably smaller as the road grew long and the pay-chest light) used at intervals to halt, fall out, and cultivate the land until they had enough provisions for the next stage.

There are several good reasons why I cannot say whether the forts at Nomo Khantara could have been built by General Tso's army, or by a detachment of it. I do not know either which way General Tso went, or how the old forts are, or how long they would have taken to build; I have not, in fact, any of the necessary evidence to make the guess plausible. But General Tso, whose campaign, reflecting something of China's former military greatness, contrasts so strikingly with her recent conduct in the field, at least might have had a motive for erecting fortifications at a point of no strategic value on the edge of a useless swamp; and I can think of nobody else who could have had even a motive.

CHAPTER II

PATIENCE

LIFE in camp was irksome and monotonous. A proper expedition, when it gets held up, can pass the time with contentment and profit, sorting out its specimens, taking meteorological observations, checking its stores; but we, alas, had no specimens to sort, nothing to take meteorological observations with, and no stores worth checking. Kini washed some clothes. But a dying sepoy, or an old fishwife, or some such person had once told her that clothes were best washed in water which had ashes in it, and the only result of her public-spirited laundering was to turn everything she washed dark grey. Then she boiled some hares against a potentially meatless future, but a cat stole most of them in the night. We were down to the last Arsène Lupin. It was all rather dreary.

I played patience endlessly. I had caught the habit in Sining, and it was terrifying to think how many games I had played since then. I knew an increasingly large number of the cards by their backs: the ace of diamonds had a corner off, the three of spades was almost torn in two, the queen of clubs had gun-oil all over her. I only know one kind of patience and I don't really like playing that, but by now I had perfected a method of foretelling the expedition's future by the results I got. If it came out (which hardly ever happens with me) we were going to get to India. A score of twelve represented the Sinkiang frontier, and anything over twelve the amount of progress we should make inside the Province; you could tell whether our downfall was going to be through Soviet influence or through the Tungans by seeing whether you had got more red cards or more black cards out. Patience was quite a good drug, and anyhow it kept me from wolfing our iron rations of literature.

One day Li came to us and begged to be excused from going any further. Nomo Khantara was really his headquarters and he had business to do there; neither he nor Ma Shin-teh had originally realized that, when we said we wanted to go to Teijinar, we meant the place called Teijinar and not merely the territory of the Teijinar Mongols. He was very nice and apologetic about it and promised that his brother, whom we had greatly taken to, would go with us instead. But next day his brother backed out too, and between them they produced from heaven knows where a gnome-like boy called Tso. Tso didn't want to go at all and asked for fifteen dollars a month, which was half as much again as we were paying Li; we compromised at thirteen, but Tso looked very unhappy about it and eventually called the deal off altogether. Li, whose association with us had given him a cosmopolitan, man-of-the-world manner, said loftily 'That boy is frightened of foreign persons', and forthwith changed his mind and agreed to come with us after all.

We always called him Brother Li, which is the custom of the country. He was not really our servant; we ate together and shared whatever work there was to do, though Li did most of it. He was extraordinarily loyal to us. Not only his own face, but that of his master Ma Shin-teh, was involved in our safety and well-being, so that we were a much more sacred charge than we would have been if we had merely hired his services in the ordinary way. He had never had anything to do with foreigners before, but he had evidently heard something of their ways; at the Mission in Tangar he asked Mr. Urech to ask me 'not to become passionate if affairs went badly'. Luckily I am fairly good at this, and we always got on well.

The days dragged by. The gold-seekers sat round their fire, whittling moodily away at handles for their spades and mattocks. From the lamas' tent came the sing-song mumble of devotions, interrupted at all too frequent intervals by the ringing of a silver bell with an unmistakably boarding-house note. In the evenings the lamas used to call on us. They took us at first for Japanese. This mistake has been

159

made with me three times in remote parts of Chinese territory: once at Nomo Khantara, once in a village in the extreme south of China, and once at Dolon Nor in Chahar, where the Chinese garrison, who were paid by Manchukuo, saluted me whenever they saw me. The chief lama was a fat, merry man; he had rolling eyes and a little moustache and looked exactly like a Frenchman in a farce. The other was much thinner – a jerky cadaverous creature who hooded himself with his robe against the sun and corresponded very closely to my idea of a Martian. The fat lama was intelligent and much travelled; he came from Lhasa and had been to Calcutta, which he called Galligut. He was the only person we met in these parts who had a rudimentary idea of what a map was for. We liked him for his infectious high spirits and gave him a photograph of the Dalai Lama when we went away.

The last day was the worst. A great wind shrieked through the tamarisk and dust crept in to plague us by unsuspected chinks in the tent. Dust-devils – slim, unwavering pillars 300 or 400 feet high – waltzed slowly through the brittle groves; the twigs and dead leaves that were caught in the fierce eddy at their base made an eerie, crackling rustle as they raced round and round on the bare earth. The camels should have come at dawn but hadn't. There was nothing to do. We had fried a lot of cubes of dough to replace our biscuits, which were finished; we had boiled the hares, written up the diaries, packed the gear. We gave up making shifts to pass the time. We lay all day in the tiny tent, numb with boredom.

Next day, in the morning, the camels came. No castaways ever hailed a ship with more delight than we hailed those shaggy and incurious monsters. Li paid out a stiff price in cloth and bricks of tea and we loaded up. The tent was struck, and the little rectangle of hard earth on which we had lived for nearly a week lost its status as a floor, reverted in the twinkling of an eye from cramped, important domesticity to being an infinitesimal part of a desert. At the last moment, over the fire in Li's yurt, it seemed that there was going to be a hitch. The Mongols, as far as we could make out, had become suspicious, not of our intentions, but of Li's; they thought he was leading us into the wilds for some fell purpose of his own. But in the end he calmed them, and we were riding west once more, through tamarisk and more tamarisk, out into a naked desert of hard grey gravel. It was April 23rd.

Again we were cheated of a due elation. As before, Li casually revealed that these fresh camels would not take us through to Teijinar, that we should have to change animals half-way, at a place called Gorumu on the Naichi River, five or six stages ahead. This was bad, and it was also bad that the gold-seekers had got their beasts at the same time as we, for their loads were heavy and they were one camel short, so that the pace of the caravan was reduced. There were two Mongols in charge of the camels; one was young, lively, and handsome, the other was a phlegmatic man who rode a white horse and bore a startling facial resemblance to Mr. A. P. Herbert. We urged that the caravan should split up and that the young man should take our four camels along at their own pace; but this the Mongols would not do, since they had been put jointly in charge of the whole lot. A faint ray of hope appeared when the young man told us, through Li, that his wife had been stricken dumb in her sleep seven months before; he would do anything for us, he said, if we could cure her. We told him to fetch her when we camped.

He did fetch her. We halted after a long, slow stage in a shallow basin where there was water, and when we woke next morning found that the horses had vanished, departing in a body back towards Nomo Khantara. This held us up till they were recaptured and brought in at noon; I had a dreary feeling that the expedition was petering out uncomfortably, jarringly, like a record on a gramophone that is running down. Meanwhile the Mongol produced his wife, who turned out not only to have lost her voice but to have one arm paralysed as well. Kini tried to jolt her nerves with smelling salts and a dose of strychnine pills, and we both stared at her with solemn, tense expressions, as though we

161

were going to burst, in case we should happen to bring off a faith cure. But the poor girl only gazed back with shy, wondering eyes, like an animal; her family, who had pressed on us a gift of butter which we did our best to refuse, waited for a miracle with an embarrassing air of expectancy, but after half an hour she was, not very surprisingly, just as dumb and paralytic as before. We apologized to the Mongol, whose hopes we had from the first been careful not to raise, and I told him that when he came back he had better try firing a gun off in her ear when she was asleep. I often wonder if he did this, and what were her first words to him if it restored her speech.

CHAPTER III

EMPTY DAYS

WE made Gorumu in six stages, arriving on April 28th; there is not much to tell about them.

Though water still froze in the tent at night, the days were hot; we both had faces the colour of Red Indians, except for my nose, which periodically lost its skin and became a striking shade of pink. We were doing long nine-hour stages, winding slowly through an empty world. Low belts of tamarisk: mazes of castellated dunes: huge tracts of dried-up marsh, caked with salt which gave them the colour and texture of a ploughed field by moonlight: soggy going where the camels waltzed and floundered: stretches of hard desert on which the heat-haze danced and mirage hovered in the middle distance: more tamarisk, more dunes, more bog . . . And always, marching proudly on our left, the mountains, tipped here and there with enviable snow.

There were few incidents. Game was scarce and I only just managed to keep the larder filled. When we broke camp I used to go on ahead of the animals for two or three hours, on the chance of a duck or a hare. One day, following the main track, I came to a big salt-lick with a solitary antelope out in the middle of it. There was no cover, so I tried to fluke him and broke his back at 300 yards with my habitual luck. I sat down, feeling very pleased with myself, and waited for the caravan to come up. The minutes passed. No caravan appeared. I knew I gained about twenty minutes on them in the hour, but it was only two hours since we had moved off and it soon became obvious that something was wrong. I fired a little patch of scrub, but it only sent up thin and wispy smoke. Thanks to the bareness of the salt-lick I had a big field of vision, but there was nothing in it and I faced the sorry prospect of abandoning the antelope and going back to pick up their tracks.

Then at last I saw them, a little louse-like string crawling along the dunes which bounded the salt-lick to the south; they must have made one of our usual detours away from the marsh to avoid bad going. I shouted, but the breeze carried the sound away, and even if they could have seen me, which I doubted, I knew how seldom they looked about them on the march. Sadly, and with a very blunt knife, I hacked off a haunch and made after them across the blinding, sharp-edged furrows. Kini, who was riding in rear, spotted me as she passed, and waited with Li and Greys; but the salt was cruel going for the horses, so we could not fetch the rest of the venison.

Kini had found the hindmost camel adrift, its head-rope having broken unnoticed; and when she dismounted to retrieve it Slalom, who hated camels, had kicked her in the back. So that day was packed with incident, as those days went.

On April 27th, in a pleasant camp by a little stream called the Tukhte, we were woken by the sound of groans; one of the Mongols – it was A.P.H. – was down with what seemed to be rheumatic fever. We gave him quinine, got another Mongol from a nearby yurt, and went on. Early the next day we came to a wide stretch of pasture-land, dotted with cattle, sheep, and camels, and at noon camped in a sheltered gully which was one of the three beds of the Naichi River. Gorumu was a likable place. The little river ran musically past our tent and the sparse scrub which lined its banks was full of unsuspicious hares; I addressed myself without enthusiasm to the now rather melancholy task of decimating them.

We were prepared for the worst: for a week's, for a month's delay. Actually we were there only three days. We got hold of a Mongol who had two camels of his own and scrounged another; and Li bought a she-camel in calf which he hoped to sell at a profit. Camels carry their calves for thirteen months; Li's was four months gone, of dwarfish stature, and altogether ludicrous to look at. We always laughed at her, and Li, though at first perplexed, got into the habit of laughing too, without quite knowing why.

At Gorumu we went about in shorts and Kini even bathed, or claimed that she had bathed, in the river. There were said to be a lot of Mongols there, but the yurts were widely scattered and most of the men were up in the mountains hunting yak. We struck up a friendship with one of their grass-widows, a handsome girl whom we christened the Sleeping Beauty because when I first met her she was asleep in the sun, clutching her horse's reins and tending a flock of sheep who had long ago moved out of sight. She feasted us, too heavily for Kini's digestion, on tsamba and very rancid butter. I also called on the vicar, who was an itinerant lama from Tibet; he lived in a small blue tent with an alarm clock which was either five hours fast or seven hours slow.

The gold-seekers camped next door to us. Li, who had a low opinion of them, said that they thought there was gold in the Naichi and that two of them were going upstream to see if there was enough to make it worth while washing. 'Is there really any gold in this river, Pastor?' he added sceptically; foreigners are expected to know everything.

Early on May 1st the camels arrived. The Moslems gave us a parting present of yak's meat and red pepper, but we said good-bye to them without regret. We knew, and they knew, that they were travelling on my face, that they would never have got their camels at Nomo Khantara if Li and I had not broken down the Mongols' resistance; they had been a drag on us and we were tired of their society, tired of their harsh unending songs, tired of their habit of borrowing things, tired of their sores, tired of their faces, puffy and blackened with exposure. Nevertheless, because we had travelled together for so long, I had a little involuntary pang as we rode off, a tiny illogical feeling of desolation at the thought that if we were lucky we should never again see the plump, sly chief, or the Bosun, or the cheerful little boy who said he was a Tibetan and couldn't eat hares, or the lout with a poisoned hand, or the old man with a pigtail who had shot the wild ass and who was the most effective of them all. A hard journey makes you curiously tender to even your most maddening companions.

This time we did feel elated at departure. We had got away quicker than we expected; we were on our own at last; and Teijinar was only five or six stages farther on. The sunlit world seemed a very satisfactory place.

But after two hours we stopped at a yurt belonging to a Chinese with a Mongol wife, and Li said that we must stay the night there because our Mongol, who lived close by, had yet to grind his tsamba and make his preparations for the journey. Li had told me this the day before but I had not understood him. I was angry with myself. The incident reminded us what innocents we were, how effectually the language difficulty prevented us, not only from learning anything worth learning about the people and the country, but from ever really knowing for certain what was happening to us.

I am fairly quick at languages and in normal circumstances so long a journey without interpreters would have given me a decent smattering of the language I had to use. I had left Peking with a minute and rudimentary Chinese vocabulary, based on the first half-dozen records of a linguaphone course supplemented very slightly by travelling in Manchuria. After we lost the Smigunovs this vocabulary increased quite fast up to a certain point, then stopped increasing. I had mastered the paraphernalia of travel in Chinese, but I never mastered any more (a) because there was no common language in which our fellow-travellers could explain the meaning of words, (b) because they were uneducated, unimaginative and slow-witted, and (c) because the paraphernalia of travel was the principal topic of conversation on the road. The Russian that I had picked up the year before, with half the opportunities and starting completely from scratch, was much better than my Chinese ever became.

It was, furthermore, a shaggy and outlandish kind of Chinese. In the extreme north-west of China they speak what I take to be a variant of the Shansi dialect. It is not as incomprehensible as the southern dialects, being based closely on mandarin; but it was disconcerting to find (for instance) that 'water' was *fi* instead of *shui*, that *she-me* (meaning 'what') had contracted to *sa*, and that *normen*, not *wormen*, meant 'we'. I found myself, *mutatis mutandis*, in roughly the position of a Chinese who, after cursorily studying the first chapters of a modern English primer, is turned loose in the remoter parts of eighteenth-century Yorkshire.

I filled in the wasted day with a long, fruitless walk after antelope. The Mongol, who had a fierce, wild face and was christened Attila, ominously failed to show up that evening, but sent an old woman over to say that his clothes were being mended and he would come at dawn. But at dawn, or soon after it, the old woman was back with the irritating news that one of the camels had dragged its moorings in the night and returned to the pastures. So in the end it was noon before we started.

But Attila, it soon appeared, was quite prepared to force the pace, and we settled down to a series of the longest stages yet, usually halting in the middle of the day for tsamba and then pressing on. I will not describe them in detail, for there is very little detail to describe. I remember that on May 3rd, after our first camp, we had breakfast outside the tent, with the mountains very clear and lovely to the south. That day we marched till after dark, finishing up at a water-hole which, to the Mongol's surprise and our disgust, contained no water. We were not very thirsty, but we had nothing we could eat uncooked; in the end we soaked some tsamba in the dregs of the Chinese spirit, producing a dish which suggested *baba au rhum* to Kini. The next day there was a head wind and it was bitterly cold, reminding us that, whatever the calendar might say, we were 9000 feet above sea-level. It looked as if we were going to go without meat for the first time until I happened on a mandarin duck and had the joy of killing something which we badly needed and which we didn't expect to get. Another duck I shot was in the family way, and we ate

167

what it is reasonable to suppose are the freshest eggs we shall ever eat; they tasted pungent and delicious.

Thus we drew slowly near to Teijinar, the place where our fortunes would be made or marred.

CHAPTER IV

THE GOOD COMPANIONS

It occurs to me that there is too much grumbling in this book. I am trying to give an honest account of this journey, but perhaps fidelity to the facts unwittingly distorts the picture, misapplies the emphasis, fails to reflect past reality by just as wide a margin as the unscrupulously imaginative treatment which until quite recently was alone considered capable of securing a public for books of travel.

I cannot tell if this is so or not. But, when I try to recall what I have written, the pages seem loud with complaint; the wind, the delays, the monotony, the long stages, the tedious fare – these and many other factors, even if not explicitly inveighed against, must be building up for you a picture of a hard life in an unkind world. This picture is a false one.

There are, I know, many people to whom our existence would not have appealed; but actually it was a very good existence. We were down to brass tacks. We were engaged on an enterprise in which we were both passionately anxious to achieve success and in which we were both convinced that success was, by any standards, worth achieving. This sense of what the politicians call, usually with more unction than accuracy, a 'high purpose' provided a translunary background against which we were content to lead sublunary, not to say bestial lives. We were not so very far above the animals. Our days, like theirs, were ruled by the elemental things – the sun, the wind, the frost. Like them, we lay on the earth to sleep. Like them, we were interested above all else in food.

We were never short of food; but, with the exception of perhaps an hour after the evening meal, there was no single moment in the day when we would not have eaten, and eaten with the greatest relish, anything that appeared remotely edible. Dog biscuits would have been welcome. A plate of cold tapioca pudding would have vanished in a flash. Your dust-bins, had we come across them, would not have been inviolate. We were leading a very healthy if not a particularly strenuous life, and the keen upland air was a great appetizer. Moreover, though I will not hear a word said against tsamba, we were not getting a great deal of what one's mother tends to class as 'Proper Food'. As the stages got longer we used to carry something in our pockets – a doughy lump of tsamba wrapped in newspaper, or a bone with meat on it – to stave off the pangs that assailed us after four or five hours' marching. But our hunger was not of dimensions to be reduced by snacks, and sooner or later we began involuntarily to talk about food. It was our favourite topic; all others were remote and academic by comparison. The present was empty of incident; the immediate future was maddeningly uncertain; and the rest – our respective pasts and our respective futures – seemed so infinitely far away that as subjects for discussion they only had the irrelevant quaintness of a dream related at the breakfast table. Food was the one thing that we could always talk about with feeling and animation. Of certain stages of a journey in Brazil I once wrote, 'Continuous hunger is in many ways a very satisfactory basis for existence'; and in Tartary it proved its worth again.

But there were days, or parts of days, when no such material stimulus to thought and conversation, no such gross foundation for peace of mind, were needed: days when we rode or walked for hours, singly or together, filled with contentment at our lot. The sun shone, the mountains were alluring on our left, and we remembered the virtues of desolation and felt keenly the compensations of a nomad's life. Each march, each camp, differed very slightly from the one before; but they did differ, and we appreciated the slight but ever present freshness of our experience as much as we appreciated the tiny changes in the flavour of our food.

We took, besides, a certain pride in the very slowness and the primitive manner of our progress. We were travelling Asia at Asia's pace. In Macaulay's *History of England* (which had now succeeded Arsène Lupin in our intellectual regime) he speaks with smug Victorian condescension of 'the extreme difficulty which our ancestors found in passing from place to place'; and there was a certain fascination in rediscovering a layer of experience whose very existence the contemporary world has forgotten. We had left the twentieth century behind with the lorries at Lanchow, and now we were up against the immemorial obstacles, the things which had bothered Alexander and worried the men who rode with Chinghis Khan – lack of beasts, lack of water, lack of grazing. We were doing the same stages every day that Marco Polo would have done if he had branched south from the Silk Road into the mountains.

In all this I felt an obscure pleasure; it may, of course, have been partly a kind of snobbishness, but I don't think it was. In these days it is difficult to do anything in the old and natural way. Nobody in England now walks without putting on fancy dress to do it in, and the word 'caravan' has come to be applied only to a stream-lined state-room on wheels which you tow behind a fast car. If you go by train when you might have gone by air you are certainly either old-fashioned, hard up, or a fool; and anyone who travels anywhere without a machine of some sort can only be advertising something. Those scientific expeditions which scour the desert in caterpillar tractors, with film cameras whirring by day and broadcast music in the tents at night, bring back a mass of valuable data; but I doubt if they know what the desert feels like. In all else ignorant, we at least knew this.

In the routine of life there was only one extraordinary feature, and that was how well Kini and I got on. We had been travelling together for three months already, and the journey lasted another four; all this time we were living together at the closest of quarters in conditions which were often uncomfortable and sometimes rigorous. By all the conventions of desert island fiction we should have fallen madly in love with each other; by all the laws of human

171

nature we should have driven each other crazy with irritation. As it was, we missed these almost equally embarrassing alternatives by a wide margin.

I suppose this happy state of affairs was due partly to a certain balance maintained between the differences and the similarities in our characters. If we had been too much alike it would have been bad; and if we had been completely opposite sorts of people it would have been bad too. While we were outwardly very different we had certain fundamental things in common. The most important of these was a liking for the kind of life we were leading. We neither of us particularly minded discomfort and uncertainty and doing without most of the things which civilized people consider, or imagine that they consider, essential to the conduct of a rational life; and we both liked fresh air and exercise, of which we got plenty. We were both adaptable and fairly phlegmatic; and we were both fatalists, as all travellers, and especially travellers in Asia, ought to be.

Perhaps one of the main reasons for our getting on so well was that Kini always had a certain friendly contempt for me and I always had a sneaking respect for her; both sentiments arose from the fact that she was a professional and I was eternally the amateur. The contrast showed all the time. Kini believed that the best way to get a thing done was to do it yourself; I believed that the best way to get a thing done was to induce somebody else to do it. It was I who shot the hares; but it was Kini who, noticing that if Li or a Mongol skinned them the liver and kidneys were always thrown away, taught herself to do the job. If anything wanted mending or making fast, if a box needed repacking, if one of the saddles was coming to bits, it was always I who said, 'Oh, that'll be all right', always Kini who expertly ensured that it would. On my side it was partly laziness and partly incompetence; on Kini's it was the knowledge, acquired from experience, of how important the little things can be. In so far as you can audit a division of labour, ours would have worked out something like this:

172

I did	*Kini did*
all the shooting	all the cooking
most of the heavy	all the laundering
manual labour	all the medical and
all the negotiating	veterinary work
all the unnecessary	most of the fraternizing
acceleration of	most of the talking in
progress	Russian
all the talking in Chinese	
and (later) Turki	

I suppose I was the leader, because I made decisions more quickly, guessed more quickly, knew more quickly what I wanted than Kini did. But she did all the work that required skill or application, and almost all the work that was distasteful or annoying rather than merely arduous, the work that gets left undone if there are only second-rate people to do it; we both knew that she was, so to speak, the better man, and this knowledge evened things out between us, robbed my automatically dominating position of its power to strain our relations. We had complete confidence in each other.

We were both reserved by nature, but Kini was the less taciturn. I can only talk nonsense with fluency and conviction, for all serious subjects, and particularly anything to do with myself, seem to me, almost as soon as they have been broached, to be not worth discussing after all; in any case I talk badly. But Kini, in the mood, could talk extremely well and was not restrained from airing her opinions or recalling her past by any inhuman intimation that the former were worthless and the latter was a bore. This was a boon to me, for she had an interesting, rather barbarian mind, and her life had been lived in many places and all sorts of conditions. Against the monotony of scrub and desert, or in the tented candle-light, the places and the people she knew crowded an all too empty stage: Pudovkin's house in Moscow, the snows of Italy or Austria, a kindly monk in Corsica, the fears of an *émigré* in Samarkand, Alain Gerbault, the school in Wales where she got

her first job, a British flagship's hospitality, the customs of
the tunny fleet, White Russian taxi-drivers in Berlin, a trail
of *gaffes* from Paris to Peking, stagefright, the Olympic
games – her talk made so vivid and so valuable a decoration
to the long slow hours that sometimes even I was shamed
out of silence into some pawky anecdote about an alligator.

Occasionally we discussed without relish the books we
should one day have to write about this journey. The
prospect of sitting down and committing our memories to
paper was welcome to neither of us; but at least I knew
that I could get the horrid job done quickly, whereas Kini
was sure that she could not. Travel books in French (at
least the ones I have read) are commonly more vivid and
exclamatory than travel books in English; and I used to
tease Kini by concocting apocryphal quotations from her
forthcoming work: '*Great Scott!*' s'écria Pierre, dont le
sangfroid d'ancien élève d'Eton ne se froissait guère que
quand ses projets sportifs s'écroulaient, 'Voilà mon vinch-
ester qui ne marche plus!'

Kini was often irritated by me; and sometimes when I
called her a bloody fool I thought I meant it. But we were
both essentially what the Fox-Hunting Man calls 'solitary-
minded' and the detachment in our natures prevented us
from interfering with each other's lives; we had come to
take each other as much for granted as we took our horses.
It was only at times that one would remember, fleetingly,
how valuable the other's presence was, how trying the
journey would have been alone. Perhaps we were less
independent of each other than we felt.

CHAPTER V

TRAVELLING BLIND

As we approached Teijinar it became increasingly obvious that we should not get much further west without reinforcements of some sort. Li was leaving us. What we needed was a fairy godmother, somebody like Lu Hwa-pu, somebody who would help us and whom we could trust. Above all we needed information – information about the road and information about the situation in Southern Sinkiang.

I had better perhaps recapitulate the relevant parts of our plan of campaign. The Tsaidam route would bring us into Sinkiang through the 15,000 foot passes of the Altyn Tagh, whence we should drop down into one or other of the oases lying south of the Takla Makan. Rumours – stale already when we left Peking – had alleged that the rebel Tungan armies, which, under Ma Chung-ying, had been repulsed before Urumchi by Soviet Russian troops and aeroplanes, were in control of these oases; and we had calculated, airily enough, that the Tungans, being hostile to the U.S.S.R., hostile to the Provincial Government at Urumchi which was dominated by the U.S.S.R. and hostile or indifferent to Nanking, would neither turn us back because we had not got passports for the Province nor imprison us (as several foreign residents of Urumchi had been imprisoned) lest we should bring to the outside world news of what was going on in Sinkiang. We even went further, chimerically contending that the Tungans, whom gossip and probability alike portrayed as angling for arms from India and among whom (according to Moscow) T. E. Lawrence had for some time past been at work, would welcome two special correspondents – one of them British – whose revelations might react in their favour by discrediting Urumchi and the Russians behind Urumchi. The attitude of the Tungans was, it will be seen, a crucial factor in our plan.

Our plan was a very good plan to talk about, and not a bad plot for a thriller. But now that the time was coming to put it to the test of execution we could not help wishing that we knew a little more about its chances of success. The Tungans[1] are the fiercest fighters, the cruellest pillagers, and altogether the stormiest petrels in Central Asia. All we knew about their recent treatment of foreigners was that they had wounded the wife of the British Consul-General in Kashgar, captured several missionaries, and temporarily paralyzed Sven Hedin's expedition by commandeering his lorries; they didn't sound very hail-fellow-well-met.

Were they still in the southern oases? Were they again at war with Urumchi? What about that impending revolt at Khotan of which we had heard at Sian? To these and other questions we badly needed answers, for although a little danger would have relieved the monotony of life we were neither of us feeling suicidal.

The answers we hoped to get at Teijinar, possibly from two sources, certainly from one. Every year, according to the Smigunovs, a few Turki merchants came from the southern oases to trade at Teijinar, and from them we could learn roughly how things stood. But there was a chance of something much better at Teijinar, a chance of a source and a fairy godmother rolled into one in the shape of Borodishin, the Smigunovs' Cossack friend who has already been mentioned. We carried letters to Borodishin, and we knew that if he was there one at least of our greatest difficulties – the language difficulty – would be temporarily over. But was he there? The odds were against it, for he had last been heard of two years ago, at a time when the

[1] The Tungans are Chinese Moslems from the North-western Provinces. 'Tungan' is merely the name given by the Turki inhabitants of Sinkiang to Chinese Moslems who have settled in or invaded their Province. A typical Tungan has a swarthier face, a more aquiline nose, and generally a more Latin look about him than an ordinary North Chinese; but the racial difference, which I believe is due to an infusion of Turki blood, is not clearly marked in all cases.

Smigunovs themselves were evacuating on account of the
civil war. We questioned everyone we met. Some said there
was a foreigner at Teijinar, some said there wasn't; most
said they didn't know. The question was of supreme
importance to us; it looked as if the answer to it might
make all the difference between success and failure,
between reaching India and returning (we dreaded this
above all) by the slow and dreary way that we had come.

On May 6th, in the middle of the last march but one to
Teijinar, I realized that something was happening that had
not happened for nearly a month. We were going uphill.
The ground sloped slightly but indubitably, and life became
illogically more exciting. Presently we halted at water for
a meal. Four or five Mongols rode up out of nowhere, and
one of them, greeting us, said 'Kharasho!' which is Russian
for 'good'. We questioned them eagerly. Yes, there was a
foreigner, an *oross*, at Teijinar; they had seen him the day
before. The odds against us shortened with a rush.

In the evening we rode on, crossing a naked billiard-
table of sheer desert towards a hazy sunset. Never had the
world seemed more silent and more empty. I was ahead,
and not even the rhythmic shuffle of the camels' feet came
to my ears. Tomorrow, I thought, we shall at least know
something; we shall have some light by which to read our
destinies. And whether they are dark or fair, whether it is
retreat or advance, this is at least the end of Part One. I
was not sorry.

We camped that night in an island of dry grass without
water or fuel. Next morning we came to dunes again, and
beyond them to soggy pastures, alive with flocks and
antelope and wild fowl. This was Teijinar, but the Russian's
tent was said to be two hours further west, at a place called
Arakshatu; we halted for tsamba and went on.

In the evening, guided by an old man on a red horse, we
reached an inlet of the marsh which ran up to a cluster of
bluffs. Beyond it stood two yurts, side by side. '*Oross*,' said
the old man, and left us. Kini and I put our tired ponies
into a canter. At the drumming of their hoofs the felt

177

hanging over the door of one of the yurts was pushed aside and a white man came out.

'*Zdravstvuite!*' we cried.

He looked at us with incredulity — a squat, stooping figure in a skull-cap and an old Russian blouse. Slowly his sad eyes brightened, his bearded face broke into a grin.

'Welcome,' he said in Russian. 'Where the devil have you come from?'

CHAPTER VI

BORODISHIN TAKES CHARGE

WE had a splendid evening. It was a great relief – especially for Kini – to be talking Russian again, to be no longer dependent on my sparse and uncertain Chinese; and it was a great relief to be able, for almost the first time since we had left Peking, to speak openly of our plans. We were installed luxuriously in the second yurt, which was normally used as a store-room. We cooked a duck that we had with us and got out one of our precious bottles of brandy and had a gargantuan meal with Borodishin and Wang Sun-lin, his Chinese partner in trade. Wang both spoke and wrote Russian, and in the rumours of his existence which we had picked up on the road he had always been referred to in words connoting great scholarship and learning; it was strange to meet the tubby, insignificant reality behind our subconscious image of a tall, frail sage.

The atmosphere was a good deal mellower than it had any right to be. The news we had counted on obtaining at Teijinar was not obtainable. Ever since the outbreak of the civil war in 1933 communications between Sinkiang and the Tsaidam had been cut; no merchants had come through. After the first bloody rumours silence had fallen, and none could tell what was happening beyond the mountains. We were as far from being able to assess our chances of getting further west as we had been in Peking, nearly three months ago. It was maddening.

No news was unlikely to be good news, but neither of us was minded to turn back. We discussed the situation over maps with Borodishin, who had volunteered, as soon as he knew our plans, to do all in his power to help us. Borodishin said that the direct, the obvious route to Sinkiang lay through Ghass Kul, whence a comparatively easy road led you up over the Chimen Tagh and down to the oasis of

Charklik. But the Tungans, or whoever else was in control of the southern oases, almost certainly maintained a frontier-post on this route, and frontier-posts were institutions which we, being heavily under-passported, were anxious to avoid. There was, however, said Borodishin, another road, much more difficult – indeed at this barren season barely negotiable – but preferable to the first because it was hardly ever used and therefore probably not watched. To follow it, we must leave the Tsaidam forthwith (an idea which greatly appealed to us) and strike south-west into the mountains, then bear west up the gorges of the Boron Kol, on whose lower waters Teijinar was situated; twelve marches, or thereabouts, would bring us to Issik Pakte, where there was a Turki encampment. Here news of the southern oases would surely be available, and if it was of a reassuring kind we could carry on for some twenty stages through the mountains and drop down on the oasis of Cherchen, well to the west of Charklik. Borodishin said that he would willingly act as our guide as far as Issik Pakte, but he could hardly come further, for he had no papers of any sort and White Russians in Sinkiang had a low survival-value. It was good to know, when we went to sleep that night, that though we should still be taking our fences blind we were at least going to get a run for our money. It was all we asked.

It took us eight days to make our preparations. The sun shone, and we led a placid, uneventful life in shorts. The more we saw of Borodishin, the more we liked him. '*Un brave homme*,' Kini had guessed at our first encounter, and that was exactly what he turned out to be. He was about fifty, and came of a respectable family in Akmolinsk. In the Great War he had seen service on the European front, but the outbreak of the Revolution found him in Siberia and he became an N.C.O. in the White Army commanded by Annenkov, who for all this bravura seems to have been easily the least hopeless – except for Kolchak – of the White leaders in eastern Russia and who had certainly inspired in Borodishin a touching devotion. At last his forces – ragged, typhus-ridden, and disillusioned – accepted

180

their fate, abandoned their wild plans for further resistance to the Reds, and were permitted to enter Chinese territory by way of the Tien Shan on condition that they laid down their arms.

Most of the men drifted down through Kansu towards the coast, but Annenkov stayed for a time in Sinkiang and Borodishin stayed with him. Then Annenkov moved further afield, was betrayed by Feng Yu-hsiang to Soviet agents in Outer Mongolia, and shot. Borodishin, after trading in Ili and Dzungaria, eventually wandered down to join Smigunov in the Tsaidam. He had been in the hills buying up yaks' tails when the Smigunovs went east with Norin, and the accounts and papers relating to the trading concern had been left with Wang Sun-lin, who was therefore technically Borodishin's superior. They seemed to get on well enough together, but from things that Borodishin said I knew that Wang's domination rankled. We were the first Europeans he had seen for two years; his was a terribly desolate life. With us he was always cheerful, or at any rate tranquil; but you had an awful feeling that perhaps his heart was breaking slowly. When he first came into Sinkiang he wrote to his wife and children in Siberia, telling them to join him on Chinese territory. Preparations were started at both ends, and they were actually on their way to the frontier when his letters suddenly ceased to be answered; a little later he was advised in a roundabout way that for their sakes it would be better if he gave up trying to get in touch with them. That was in 1927. He still yearned for them, still (sometimes) had hopes that he would see them again; he spoke of them impassively, but it was easy to guess how large they loomed in his life. He smoked a Mongol pipe incessantly. 'I never used to smoke at all,' he told us. 'But when I got that last news about my wife I started, because it seemed to make things easier. I shall stop when we are together again.'

It took us very little time to discover that none of the Mongols would hire us camels for a journey from which camels were by no means certain to return; if we were to get animals at all, we should have to buy them. The Prince

181

of Teijinar was away, but the day after we arrived an emissary came from his twenty-year-old son, requesting us to visit him; he asked for a day's notice, and we had heartening visions of a mutton feast, a little post-prandial haggling, and the speedy purchase of four fine camels. We said that we would come the next day.

Washed and brushed and dressed in clothes which might by a long stretch of a tramp's imagination have been called presentable, we set out in the morning, accompanied by Wang Sun-lin on a camel. It was a hot day and we had a two hours' ride back to the yurts of Teijinar; we had purposely made a light breakfast lest, when the time came for feasting, we should be unable to distend ourselves with the zest which civility demanded. By the time we reached the Prince's tents our hunger was in its prime, had not begun to stale and numb itself and lose its edge as we found it used to at the end of a long march. We looked forward keenly to the audience.

It took place in a yurt which was bigger and more magnificent than most, and outside which we discarded our whips, as custom decrees you must.[1] Along the walls were stacked painted chests which clearly belonged to some part of Turkistan, and there were carpets both from China and Khotan. The old Prince's son sat opposite the door, with elders and notables squatting in two convergent ranks on either hand. He was a handsome, surly young man with a pout, who sat lollingly and made no outward show of courtesy. We took humble places near the door and paid our compliments through Wang. Then I went up, feeling like a child with a mayoral bouquet, and presented our cards, laid reverently athwart a ceremonial scarf, and after them our presents, with another scarf. They were not, I freely admit, very good presents; they consisted of a knife, a pack of cards, and a box of cigarettes. The young prince's face showed that he had hoped for something better from such fabulous beings.

Tea was served, with rancid butter in it; but not very much tea, and the neat, alluring, golden piles of tsamba

[1] You may not whistle in a yurt, either.

which stood about the felts in wooden bowls were left inviolate. We eyed them wistfully, and the long silences were more than once broken by poignant internal whinnyings from the distinguished strangers. Laboriously, through Wang, we answered the usual questions, made the usual polite remarks; but the atmosphere was cold and unpropitious, and when we had finished identifying ourselves conversation languished. I brought out a tube of quicksilver from a broken thermometer and played with the stuff idly, hoping to capture at least their curiosity; but the foolish gambit failed, and we told Wang to open negotiations for the camels.

He did; a flicker of intelligence and interest passed through the dour assembly. But we soon saw that things were not going well; the young prince's face was surlier than ever, and Wang looked rueful. The talk dragged on. The prince asked an impossible price and wanted payment in solid silver which (as no doubt he knew) we had not got. At last, in disgust, we closed the interview, exchanged frigid farewells, and rode hungrily home. Next day we learnt that the young prince had sent out messengers forbidding all his subjects to sell us camels.

The question of camels apart, neither Kini, who had lived among the Kirghiz in the Tien Shan, nor I, who had travelled more cursorily in Mongolia, could find in our experience a parallel for such treatment of guests by a nomad. Perhaps our presents were too small. Perhaps we were too meanly dressed, too poorly attended. Perhaps he took a dislike to our faces. Whatever the cause of his resentment, the young prince did himself no good, and us no harm. He badly needed dollars, as Borodishin knew; his father had to pay annual tribute to Sining, and the Chinese did a good deal more than protect their own interests in assessing the cash value of a payment made in kind. Moreover, we got our camels. The news of the embargo had hardly reached us when we received a call from the most venerable of the young prince's entourage, whom we had conjecturally identified as the Prime Minister. The Prime Minister was a shrivelled but vigorous old man with a long, tapering silver beard and a humorous eye; he was also a camel-fancier in a big way, and after much circuitous talk over the fire in Borodishin's yurt we knew that the Prime Minister's loyalty to his master's son was no match for his commercial sense.

In the end, for an average price of about £4, we bought one good camel from him and three more from a Mongol-Chinese half-caste called Yanduk. Yanduk, who seemed to be a prominent figure in these parts, was the man who had offered me camels at Dzunchia, and from him we learnt of Li's mistake, and how it had lost us ten days: when we remembered that awful week at Nomo Khantara and the wasted time at Gorumu we cursed our luck.

All this, of course, took time; and it took time – because all the yurts lay so far apart – to buy the primitive packsaddles and the ropes, and a fresh supply of barley for the horses and of tsamba for ourselves. Meanwhile we lazed about, reading Macaulay and writing a further salvo of farewell letters which were to be sent out to Tunghwang when next a caravan should go that way; these reassuring effusions are still, unfortunately, in the post. I made a few successful raids on a patch of marsh, two or three miles away, which housed duck and snipe and a number of amphibious pheasants. In the evening the two horses, led by the punctual Slalom, came up to the yurts from the bog in which they had been cropping the rare blades of fresh grass and drew a half-ration of barley. Redshanks called in the dusk, and dogs, far away, barked at the herdsmen coming home. The sun dropped below the horizon without flamboyance. We went into the yurts to dine and talk and play our three records on a collapsible gramophone some six inches in diameter. We were getting to know them pretty well.

Li left for Nomo Khantara on the third day. We paid him off – he had been serving us for a wage of ten dollars (about 15s.) a month – and made him a present of money and gave him various trivial things (among them a photograph of the Dalai Lama) which he had long coveted. At Teijinar he had traded some tobacco that he had with him for two fox-skins, and he seemed well pleased with his journey. For the last time we laughed as he mounted his pregnant camel; for the last time – perplexed to the end at this obscure joke – he laughed politely back. Then he rode away. He had been very loyal; we were so green, such innocents, that he could have taken advantage of us in any number of ways, but he never did. He was rough and ignorant, but he had a kind of clumsy courtesy towards us, and though I think he thought us mad he seemed to have our interests genuinely at heart. It was sad to realize that we should never see his unattractive face again, with the eye-slits so narrowed by the sun and wind that you had the feeling he was blind: sad, even, to be immune for ever from the sudden bursts of harsh song with which he emphasized rather than relieved the monotony of the march. He had been a good friend to us.

At last everything was nearly ready. We collected great armfuls of scrub for fuel and devoted a day to frying little cubes of dough, the successors to our original supply of biscuit. On the edge of the desert behind the bluffs I shot an antelope. That was the biggest, the most scandalous, of all my flukes with the rook rifle; she was just under 400 paces away and I got her in the head. It was a good omen and, better still, assured us ten days' supply of meat. Kini made shashlik on the cleaning-rod and we spent our last evening at Teijinar in feasting.

The next day, just before noon, we started. No Mongol would come with us. We loaded up, said good-bye to Wang Sun-lin, and rode away from the yurts, past the bluffs, and out into a shimmering desert of piedmont gravel beyond which, formidable and mysterious, a great wall of mountains challenged the sky.

It was May 15th. We had been exactly three months on the road to India.

PART V

NO PICNIC

CHAPTER I

THE GORGES OF THE BORON KOL

IT was a hot, still day. The sun beat down and mirage
waterishly streaked the periphery of our field of vision.
The little caravan of four camels, two ponies, and three
humans crawled punily across that empty place towards
the mountains. Not a rock, not a tuft of scrub, was seen in
the naked desert; here was the starkest desolation.

We were not oppressed by it. The horses, underfed still,
but fresh after their eight days' rest, moved easily, and it
was pleasant to be able to steer a straight course instead of
being forced into a series of southerly detours by the
sprawling marsh. We scanned curiously the gashed and
non-committal faces of the mountains ahead; we were
immensely glad to have done with the Tsaidam. The four
camels began to assert their personalities, and we noted
that the last – the one we had bought from the Prime
Minister – lived up to Yanduk's disparaging description of
him. 'He has a bad heart,' Yanduk had said, and sure
enough the camel kicked at the horses when they followed
him too close; there was an intractable and mutinous air
about him.

After five hours we struck the Boron Kol, here flowing
dispersedly, its waters opaque and yellow with silt, and
presently climbed a wind-hardened ridge of dunes on to
another shelf of desert. We had been riding in our shirt-
sleeves, but now a haze obscured the sun and a wind began,
gently at first, to plague us. I put on a leather jacket with
a zip fastener, but Greys, who was touchy and nervous if
I did anything unusual in the saddle, incontinently bolted.
I let him gallop until (I hoped) he felt a fool, then finished
putting on the jacket; but in the process the fastener had
dislocated itself and the wind, which was fast increasing in
strength, found a vital chink in my defences.

It was a bitter wind. The hot hours behind us were forgotten; in twenty minutes we had ridden out of one season into another. A dun, vaporous, impalpable wall marched up across the sky and bore slowly down on us from the west. From the dunes pale writhing snakes of sand licked out across the dark grey desert, and almost before we realized what was happening the sand storm was upon us. The mountains vanished. We could see no more than thirty or forty yards, and our faces were stung as though by innumerable, unceasing blows from an invisible hair-brush. It was far too cold to ride. We dismounted and trudged with half shut eyes under the lee of the camels. Borodishin, hunched on the leader, followed with difficulty an old faint track made by animals in single file. The wind screamed vindictively.

Dusk fell unnoticed; only my watch registered the approach of night in that unnatural twilight. But presently the wind lost something of its turbulence, the air was no longer full of sand, and we found that we were coming in under a strange conical hill, oddly patterned with sheets of black rock. Night was nearly on us. At the foot of the hill a broad ravine yawned obscurely on our left, and a steep slanting track led us down into a patch of sparse scrub beside the swift but soupy current of the Boron Kol. We made camp gropingly in the darkness, cooked ourselves a meal, and went to sleep full of curiosity to see, next morning, what sort of a place this was.

That pleasure was, however, denied us. We rose at four to find that snow was falling heavily; the world was veiled again. While the kettle boiled I caught and saddled the horses, and after tsamba Borodishin and I loaded the camels. This was a task requiring strength and skill; in the former Borodishin and in the latter I was deficient. Borodishin had a weak heart, which is no asset on a journey made at altitudes ranging from 9000 to 15,000 feet, and we did all we could to spare him violent exertion. I am unhandy with ropes and had studied too superficially the Mongol trick of lashing boxes and sacks on to the straw-stuffed packsaddles which squeeze the humps on either side. Still, we managed well enough in spite of numb fingers and slippery cords, and I was pleased to be doing a little honest work; it made me feel less of a tourist, less of an amateur.

We led the animals up out of the ravine, on the lip of which a minor blizzard met us. Again it was too cold to ride, and we stamped mechanically along with our chins on our chests, reflecting that we were not going to see much of the Altyn Tagh as long as climatic conditions made it impossible to keep our eyes open. But after a couple of hours the wind dropped and the sun came out. We found ourselves crossing a bleak tableland towards a sudden jagged cluster of little peaks which the Mongols called – aptly enough, we thought – the Black Cold Mountains. With astonishing rapidity the snow vanished. The world turned from white to streaky, then from streaky to drab; the ground steamed a little, and the storm was forgotten.

Borodishin took the camels along at a good pace; we were marching faster than we had ever marched before. We dropped down under the steep cliffs which here enclosed the river. The track was narrow and at times mildly dangerous; its giddier passages were marked by little *obos* erected by the superstitious. Rounding a corner one of the camels bumped his load against the overhanging wall of rock and for one sickening moment lurched out over a nasty drop before he recovered himself. We were glad when the valley widened slightly and we could march above the gorge.

After a stage of nine hours we halted in another patch of scrub which provided fuel and a minimum of grazing. Here there were a few antelope, the first living creatures, with the exception of two extremely small lizards, that we had seen since leaving Teijinar. While we made camp it began to snow again, and the tent was colder than it had been for weeks.

At dawn next day we loaded the camels under a windless sky in which the stars were dying; the first two hours of the march were brilliant and idyllic. Then, without warning, another snowstorm hit us, and once more we tramped with numb feet and stiff faces, silent automata plastered in front with white. When the snow stopped the wind continued, blustering down on us, stinging us with sand, making a drudgery of the march. We passed, on the southern bank, a little tributary called Ulan Ussu or Kizil Su, the former a Mongol and the latter a Turki name meaning the Red River; it was this stream that dyed the Boron Kol ochre with silt and above its point of confluence the main river was relatively pure. We made camp at Tashpi, a place where a fort-like mound stuck up out of the scrub in the river bed. Borodishin was troubled by his heart and we gave him some valerian. That was another cold camp, but we were making good going and morale was high.

The next day was frosty, brilliant, and mercifully windless. At noon we met two Mongols on camels, the first human beings we had seen for four days and one of them, according to Borodishin, the son of the Prime Minister. He was a pleasant boy, with a lamb peeping biblically out of his sheepskin robe. Guided by him, we crossed the river, which here ran diffusely in a wide, shallow bed; the camels floundered alarmingly in one or two bad patches of quicksand. Ahead of us we could see three yurts. As we made for them a queer thing happened; Greys gave out. It was as though he had suddenly lost all his strength. I got off and dragged him along, slowly and with difficulty, wondering what could be the matter. It was true that we had been doing long stages, but not long enough to worry a horse acclimatized by six weeks' marching; besides, I had done a good part of them on foot. He was underfed, but no more underfed than Slalom. His collapse was mysterious as well as disheartening. When I got into camp we decided to lie up the next day, partly to rest Greys and partly because we hoped to induce one of the local Mongols to come with us to help with the loading and the work in camp.

The idle day was welcome. The sun shone, *The History of England* was extremely exciting, and there was nothing to do except from time to time catch the camels before they strayed too far. Borodishin opened negotiations with the Mongols. None of them wanted to come with us, for it was a bad season to take a camel on this barren road and in any case they had their hands full with their flocks. But in the end one of them, a middle-aged man with a sour, puckered face, signed on as far as Issik Pakte in return for a high wage, paid in advance. The Chinese Republic can have few remoter subjects than the inhabitants of these yurts, and only one thing there reflected Chinese influence, this was a large stone which the Mongols brought with them and on which they proceeded to ring our dollars. Luckily these were all good, an unusual circumstance in China.

We had meant to start at dawn the next day, which was May 20th, but our Mongol was at his devotions, praying for an auspicious journey, and his devotions were protracted. It was 6.30 before we moved off. Greys seemed better, and Slalom was on top of his form; Kini, in fact, cut a voluntary while galloping after the camels. The Mongol joined us with two riding camels – one for himself and one for Borodishin's return journey – and a yearling camel calf which, from its thin, flat head and serpentine neck, was always known as the Lizard. The Lizard was a creature of indescribably desolate appearance; it trailed along behind the caravan, dropping even further and further astern, until suddenly it would become alive to its forlorn situation, pull itself together, and come lolloping after its mother with ludicrous anxiety. Like all the other animals it got very little to eat, and one day it picked up a huge white bone and carried it pathetically in its mouth for several hours. It was the silliest animal to watch that you can imagine.

In the middle of the morning we sighted geese in a patch of marsh by the river. They were reasonably tame, and my first shot wounded one which flew staggeringly away and settled on the opposite bank; in the end, after a long-range bombardment, I waded across and retrieved him. Kini had waited for me and, since Greys hated anything dead, I gave the goose to her. But necrophobia was rife that morning; Slalom went off in a panic, bucking madly, and Kini took her second toss that day. Finally I slung the corpse on my

193

saddle, and Greys' dislike of it increased his pace, which was already beginning to flag ominously.

In contrast to the former marches, the morning was very hot, and we broke the stage, which was an extra long one, by halting for three hours under some jagged bluffs which looked white and somehow African in the strong sunlight. We plucked the goose, working in relays, ate some tsamba, and went on. Soon afterwards we sighted for the first time a new and much larger kind of antelope; their scientific name I do not know, but Hedin calls them *orongo*. I sniped them fruitlessly at long range, skirmishing on the flank of the caravan while Kini led Greys. But Greys was not easy to lead to-day; the old lassitude was creeping over him, and we only managed to finish the stage by dragging him along behind Slalom while I threatened his quarters with a whip. I felt sad and exhausted. Poor little horse! I remembered the fiendish vigour with which he had so often bucked me off and wished that he might recover some part of it now.

The wind was up again and little local storms of rain and dust were scouring the valley when we trailed slowly down a long grey slope of desert into a patch of sere grass. It was an hour's march short of the place we were making for, but Greys was all in and two of the camels were showing signs of weakness. For the first time we had an intimation that perhaps, after all, this journey was to be no picnic.

CHAPTER II

LOST

BORODISHIN diagnosed Greys' collapse as being due to the fresh grass he had eaten at Teijinar. There had been little enough of it in all conscience, but according to the Mongols the first fresh grass of the year always weakens horses. There was nothing we could do about it.

Next day we gave both horses a little barley before we moved off, and I tied Greys on behind the last camel. There were a lot of the new antelope about – the bucks very handsome, with long black horns, black faces, dun flanks, and whitish forequarters. The rook rifle had achieved some fantastic results, but it was too much to expect it to knock over animals of this size, so I slung it on my back in reserve and took the ·44 along as well. Alas! the fifteen-year-old ammunition was well past its prime; I could have made better practice with a bow and arrow. The little herds streamed gallantly past, astonished but unharmed; there were no casualties, and I never used the ·44 again.

Near the place where we had camped there was a Turki burial ground – a big, flat-topped mound with eight or nine small tombs on it; above each a black yak's tail hung from the top of a pole. These tombs, and the fact that all place-names in the Boron Kol valley had a Turki as well as a Mongol version, seem to indicate that what is now Teijinar Mongol territory was once inhabited by Turki hunters from Sinkiang.

Presently the bright morning clouded and a strong head wind sprang up. The going was sandy; walking ceased to be a pleasure and became hard work. We had to ford the river where it made a sharp bend between two cliffs, and I begged a lift on Slalom's crupper. At length, after about five hours, I swallowed my pride, gave up battling with the wind, and mounted the Mongol's spare camel after he had removed a saddlebag which contained his prayer-book; he could not read the prayer-book, but knew it was too sacred to be sat on. I discovered that to ride a thin camel bareback is one of the least agreeable methods of locomotion.

On the next day the wind had gone and sunshine tempered the desolation. Snow peaks stood up bravely on our left. The river up here was frozen, and from time to time the ice cracked loudly, making a report which would have justified more romantically-minded travellers in believing, or at any rate in saying, that they had been sniped by bandits. Antelope and wild asses roamed the terraces of iron-hard desert, subsisting on heaven knows what. In the middle of a hot morning I found a buck dying by a little stream and finished him off with a ·22 bullet in the neck; but we did not like to touch meat which was presumably diseased. Further on, after shooting a good deal worse than usual, I knocked over a yearling buck at 150 yards (it was easily the closest shot I ever had at an antelope); he was hit far back, but after an ignominious chase I killed him and we halted to skin him and to rest the animals. Alas, we found on his hind quarters, under the skin, a colony of a dozen great bugs, the size of slugs and so unattractive in appearance that in a fit of unwonted squeamishness we waived our claim to their leavings. The Mongol accounted for them by saying that they were the descendants of a certain fly which lays its eggs under the skin when the beasts are in bad condition.

Soon after noon we went on. I tried a lot of long shots without success, which was a pity since we were getting short of meat. We came to a tract of marshy ground above which a few terns swooped and chittered. To me, who am no great ornithologist, they looked very much like common terns; it seemed strange to find such birds 13,000 or 14,000 feet above sea-level. They are fairly common in the Sinkiang oases, 10,000 feet lower down.

After seven hours' walking I applied for another lift on the spare camel, but this time the Mongol, who was an ungracious sort of man, objected that we had only paid hire for the use of it on Borodishin's return journey.

Hoping to make him lose face, I told Borodishin to ask him how much he charged for half an hour; I fear the irony was lost on one who can have had only a very vague idea of what half an hour was, but at any rate I got my excruciating ride for the rest of the stage. In a cold and lowering dusk we halted at a place where there should have been grass; but the wind (according to Borodishin) had done away with it, and as fuel was also scarce we made a cheerless camp.

On the next day, which was May 23rd, a bad time was had by all. We left the Boron Kol, which here bends to the south, and marched north-west across an empty grey shelf of desert some 14,000 or 15,000 feet above sea-level, according to our maps. A few small troops of asses manœuvred, shy and curious, on our flanks, trailing neat little clouds of dust; their runs curved and intersected bewilderingly on the otherwise trackless ground. Again there was a head wind to pepper us remorselessly with dust, and we envied the marmots the burrows from the thresholds of which they whistled at us petulantly.

Greys trailed miserably behind the camels, dragging on his headrope; his condition nullified for me whatever compensations the march might have had. They would in any case have been few. The going was sandy, and an endless battle with the wind tired the body and irked the mind; the world for once seemed harsh. Shortly after noon we sighted through the dust-haze the range of hills for which we were headed; Borodishin and the Mongol, who because of the haze had had nothing to steer by, had been doubtful of their bearings and were much relieved when they made out a conical black hillock guarding the entrance to a valley. 'That's where the spring is,' said Borodishin. 'Only ten miles more.'

Three hours later we were entering the valley. Greys seemed to be on his last legs. I had to beat him to keep him moving at all, a thing I hated doing; it was not his fault that his strength had gone. The valley narrowed and we began to climb. I had a vague feeling that something was wrong; Borodishin was looking about him with perplexity and the

Mongol maintained a silence which might have been armour for a sense of guilt.

'Where's the spring?'

'A little further on,' said Borodishin; but his voice was uncertain.

Greys was dragging so hard on the last camel that I took the headrope myself and pulled him up the hill by main force with Kini whipping in; it was hard work at this altitude and at the end of a long march. We climbed slowly up to a little col and found the camels halted. 'We're lost,' said Borodishin. 'This is the wrong valley. I can't find the spring.' He was rattled.

We sent the Mongol up a steep hill on our left to spy the ground and meanwhile gave the animals a rest. A sudden hail-storm broke on a situation comfortless enough already. There was a little barley in the bottom of Greys' nosebag (he was a listless eater, these days) and I gave this to him and he revived slightly. The Mongol came down to report a small salt lake beyond the hill; but this landmark meant nothing either to him or to Borodishin, and we turned right-handed and slanted down to the foothills. For two or three hours more we marched and countermarched fool- ishly, establishing nothing save that the black hillock was the wrong black hillock. At dusk we gave it up and halted in a waterless gully; we had been going hard for nearly twelve hours.

This, I know, is my cue for tight-lipped heroics, for a grim portrayal of the agonies of mind and body; but, though our plight perhaps sounds serious on paper, in fact it was nothing of the sort. We were indeed lost, but only by a small margin; it was reasonably certain that we should be able to pick up our bearings next day. As for being without water, that was no serious matter on these chill uplands, and only really affected us because you cannot eat tsamba without soaking it and we had nothing else with us that we could eat uncooked. The whole thing only amounted to missing a meal at a moment when a meal would have been particularly welcome, and you can hardly expect to cross

Central Asia without occasionally experiencing inconveniences of this kind.

It was so great a luxury to have stopped marching that we did not feel very sorry for ourselves. We drank a little brandy and evolved a repulsive dish by mixing tsamba with melted mutton fat and Worcester sauce; empty though we were, we could not get much of this down. But we were dog-tired, and found reward enough for our exertions in the delightful process of going to sleep.

I awoke after it was light next day, horribly conscious of inner conflict between the brandy and the mutton fat. Kini was diligently scraping a layer of snow off the tent into the cooking pot; it looked as if there might be enough, when it was melted, for half a cup of tea all round. Borodishin and the Mongol were already out on a reconnaissance, and at eight o'clock they returned in triumph. The spring had been located. We were no longer lost.

Without waiting to melt the snow we collected the scattered animals, loaded up, and moved off. Ninety minutes' march brought us to the spring, beside which there was a recently evacuated tent-site. There was also a little grass, and we decided to lie up for a day for the sake of the horses. I was feeling queer and had a ridiculous suspicion that I had strained my heart the day before. We spent most of an uneventful day in our sleeping bags, for snow was falling and it was very cold. We dined sumptuously; noodles had never tasted better.

CHAPTER III

THE TURBANED-HEADS

Two more marches brought us to Issik Pakte. The first was a long one. All through a bitter frosty morning we slanted down from the hills. There was a faint track of sorts, and the bleached skeletons of animals which decorated it at intervals we viewed with an interest less academic than heretofore. A long stretch of sandy desert brought us to a marsh alive with antelope and asses. Greys had started well, but by the end of the march I once more had the heart-breaking task of thrashing him along; we only just got him into camp.

The camels were weakening, too, but we were now only a short stage from Issik Pakte and in the middle of the next morning we sighted the encampment. Half a dozen dilapidated yurts stood scattered on the shore of a small salt lake under the towering snows of the Karyaghde; beyond them a cluster of domed mud tombs were surmounted by tall poles from each of which a yak's tail drooped like a dark plume. We had seen no human beings, let alone habitations, for five days, and we felt very excited. The Mongol, raising a point of etiquette, objected strongly to my arriving on foot, so for the sake of the expedition's dignity I mounted poor Greys for the last time. Groggily, but full of hope and curiosity, the little caravan picked its way through the marsh towards the dwellings of a new race.

It is difficult, now, to remember what we expected of the Turkis; but from travelling with the Chinese, who are invariably contemptuous and invariably afraid of their neighbours, I am sure I looked – quite wrongly – for something formidable, for evidence of cruelty and of courage, in the men who came to meet us. Their appearance was certainly wild. They wore cloth coats lined with sheep's wool, cut less voluminously than the Mongols' robes; their feet were protected by crude moccasins made of skins, and their legs were cross-gartered like the legs of Ancient Britons. Some wore skull-caps, others fur-lined hats, and a few a kind of turban.

Their faces, blackened by exposure, were startlingly un-Mongoloid. Their straight or aquiline noses, their eyes which did not slant and some of which were grey, the whole set of their features gave us a momentary feeling of being almost back in Europe; we had both seen men not so very different from these in the Caucasian backwoods. Most of them were bearded, and two or three had reddish hair. The women up here went unveiled, though that is not the usual Turki practice.

Borodishin had been here before, and we were welcomed with a certain incredulity by his old acquaintances. We pitched the tent on a little island of dry ground beside the yurts and got inside it – for snow was falling – to await developments. Borodishin had disappeared into one of the yurts with the Turkis; we were agog with curiosity and could not help wondering why we had not been invited too, for it is usual to offer visitors at least a cup of tea on their arrival at your camp. The reason presently appeared; the Turkis had not got a cup of tea.

It sounds a small thing, but in its implications lay a threat to our plans and the prolongation of uncertainty. The Turkis had no tea, and no flour either, because for two years no merchants had come through to Issik Pakte from Sinkiang; ever since the outbreak of the civil war in 1933 the little community by the salt lake had been cut off from its only source of supply, and for many months now these people had been living entirely on the meat of antelopes and wild asses, washed down with red pepper boiled in water. Fate, in fine, was playing the same trick on us that it had played at Teijinar. We had travelled for three and a half months; we were, according to the map, actually inside the borders of Sinkiang; and yet for all we knew about the dispositions of the Tungans, on which our hopes of reaching

India depended, we might still have been in the Legation Quarter in Peking.

We were tired of blind man's buff, and we had reached a phase of the journey during which the game could no longer be played in an entirely carefree spirit; but retreat was unthinkable. Borodishin set about inducing the Turkis to provide us with a guide as far as the next inhabited place, which was called Bash Malghun and lay some ten or twelve arduous marches further west. The Turkis were afraid and none of them wanted to come; but Borodishin told them that we were very exalted kind of people – close relatives, as a matter of fact, of the King of England – and the prospect of being able to buy flour at Bash Malghun with the dollars they would earn from us was a powerful incentive. In the end two of them signed on.

Issik Pakte conformed to the Tsaidam tradition of belonging to one place, being situated in another place, and being inhabited by the people of a third. The map put it inside Sinkiang; but it was recognized locally as being part of the territory of the Teijinar Mongols, and the only visitor for the last two years had been an emissary sent up by the Prince of Teijinar who was pardonably curious to know if anybody still lived at Issik Pakte. The Turkis are a spineless race. Their civilization is based on the oasis, and the oasis is based on an irrigation system which makes its inhabitants less dependent on the climate than any other agriculturalists in the world. Although the annual rainfall in the Tarim Basin is very nearly nil, the snows on the mountains which surround it melt punctually every summer and the oases accordingly offer a life which is easy and not in the least uncertain. The Turki's only troubles are political.

With political troubles he is ill-qualified to cope. The oases in which he leads his aimless, devout, and unaspiring life are for the most part separated by tracts of desert, and accordingly impose on their inhabitants a parochial and disunited outlook. There has really been no need for the Chinese to put their immemorial colonial policy of *Divide et impera* into practice; nature has done it for them.

Nothing is more typical of the Turkis of Sinkiang than the fact that the only collective name by which they are known is the nickname of *Chant'o*, meaning 'turbaned-head', bestowed on them by their conquerors. They refer to themselves merely as 'Moslems'; they seem to have the minimum of racial consciousness, and although they form something like eighty per cent of the population of Sinkiang they are very easily ruled.

We stayed for two days at Issik Pakte. Greys, it was clear, could come with us no further; he needed a long rest and good feeding before he could take the road again. In the circumstances there was nothing for it but to exchange him for the best horse Issik Pakte could produce. This proved to be a little two-year-old mare. They fetched her in out of the marsh, and at first sight she seemed more amphibian than equine; she suggested, rather than resembled, a water-rat suffering from mange and malnutrition. Her hooves had not recently been cut and such patches of her shaggy coat as still remained to her were drably caked with mud. She had abnormally long ears and a general appearance of frailty and apprehension. She was not a patch on Greys, but we had to accept the bargain, whose unfavourable terms were negligibly modified when the Turkis threw in half one of the bricks of tea included in the wages of our guides. I took what consolation I could in their assurance that she would command a high price in stock-breeding circles in Sinkiang; a young mare like that, they said, would make an excellent mother of mules. I called her Cynara, for sentimental reasons.

Little else of note happened at Issik Pakte. In a patch of broken ground I did the first stalk I had had the chance of doing, and a long-range bombardment with the ·22 produced a couple of young orongo antelopes; this was very lucky, since we needed meat both for ourselves and for the return journey of Borodishin and the Mongol. Both animals carried the same subcutaneous parasites that we had seen before, but this time we could not afford to be nice. The bugs were ignored.

Insect life was regrettably to the fore on a second

occasion. Kini, who was doing some washing, got hold of my shirt and it very soon appeared that the bantering allegations which she had from time to time been making against me were all too well founded. I was lousy. Her total bag – totted up with what seemed to me unnecessary precision – was eight lice and one hundred and seventy-one nits, which are the eggs of lice. In vain I pointed out that the presence of these little creatures on my person was nothing to be ashamed of, since they had at no time caused me the smallest inconvenience; in vain I recalled the inns on the Chinese roads where it had been always she, and never I, who had attracted the attentions of fleas and bed-bugs. Kini enjoyed her triumph to the full, and I had to admit, if only to myself, that I had lost face.

We did a little doctoring, fried some more of what we always referred to as bread, and procured two wooden spoons in exchange for a few ·44 cartridges; parity in cutlery was thus achieved between Kini and me, and I ceased to be haunted by a fear that the teaspoon might get lost. We fingered for the first time some pale green lumps of hashish, called by the Turkis *nasha*; it is made in the oases from hemp and large quantities of it are, in normal times, annually exported to India. On the last evening a man came in on foot with a little news; there had been fighting between Charklik and Cherchen, but that was now thought to be over, leaving the Tungans in control of both oases.

This, as far as it went, was good. We had a great farewell feast with Borodishin and he talked far into the night of Annenkov, and guerilla warfare with the Bolsheviks, and the ruses that the Whites had employed to secure admission into Chinese territory. We gave him money and a few small presents, including a packet of a hundred evil-looking Szechwan cigars, some of which I had brought against the time when my tobacco should run out.

At dawn he left with the Mongol, riding back along the way we had come, hunched on his camel, eternally sucking at his long pipe, his sad loyal eyes staring across the empty lands before him. As I watched him go I tried not to think of the two grubby yurts at Teijinar, where the redshanks called, and he and Wang Sun-lin took it in turns to go out and fetch fuel, and nothing ever happened. We had got very fond of Borodishin.

CHAPTER IV

BIRTHDAY

Two hours later we started ourselves, in the opposite direction. The two Turki guides loaded the camels clumsily, using a different method with the ropes from the Mongol one, and the people of the place bade us (we assumed) farewell. As we rode off I had my last sight of Greys; he had his head in a nose-bag full of chopped wild ass meat and appeared to be finding cannibalism congenial. It was sad to leave him, but for both our sakes I was thankful that there would be no more marches on which I had to supply the motive power for him.

It was a lovely day. Cynara, cocking perplexed and ungainly ears, scrambled along with a nervous, eager gait. After two hours we came to three outlying yurts where lived the family of a rich man whom Borodishin had known on a former visit. The rich man was away, but his wife gave us a charming welcome. In a smoky yurt, its walls lined with consequential-looking chests, we played with squealing children and returned the stares of half a dozen rather pretty girls who appeared singularly unmindful of Koranic law. Although neither party could understand a word the other said it was a pleasant interlude, and our hostess produced unheard-of delicacies in the shape of three wild goose eggs and an onion – a real onion – which we gathered had come all the way from Charklik, a long time ago. With these, and some flour, she made a kind of batter cake which we ate with as much restraint as we could. When we said good-bye Kini took off a presents-for-the-natives necklace that she was wearing and gave it her. Then we rode on after the camels.

We overhauled them slowly, riding west along a sluggish lagoon of fresh or fairly fresh water which runs between the little salt lake at Issik Pakte and the much bigger one, called Ayak Kum Kul, which the map showed ahead of us. To the south we could see herds of antelope and asses and a few yaks. After a long stage we halted at a place where there were plenty of the colourless tufts of brittle vegetation, the size of sea-pink, which camels can eat and horses cannot. If it was going to be like this all the way the horses were in for a bad time, for we had been unable to renew our supply of barley at Issik Pakte and it was almost finished.

I had compiled, with Borodishin's help, a glossary of some twenty Turki words, and in camp we ran through this with the men, much to their amusement. One was an oldish man with a fierce dignity and an abstracted manner which cloaked, at first, his ineffectualness. The other, whose name was Tokta Ahun, was in his early twenties. There was nothing either dignified or abstracted about him. He was full-faced, surly, and ill-mannered, and he had a notable appetite. For many months he had subsisted on a diet composed exclusively of meat, and the sight of tsamba, flour, or mien went to his head at once. He knew – had been warned, could see for himself – that our supplies were scanty; but he never hesitated to demand, in tones not so much peremptory as menacing, a second and after that a third helping. I refused him as often as I could, but my command of his language was not such as enabled me to soften the blow with explanation, and – since not only our further progress but our lives depended on these men, who had no reason to regard us with sympathy and who could with impunity fail to do so – I did not dare to take the high and mightly line I longed to take.

The next day we rose at dawn, but the camels had strayed far in search of grazing and it was two hours before we started. While we waited, Slalom moved us to pity and alarm by appearing in camp chewing a bone; and later he was listless on the march. There was no wind, and the morning was all blue and gold. In the lagoon mandarin ducks swam, gilded, in the mirrored tranquillity of the sky; antelope, standing in the shallows to drink, observed with curiosity our slow approach, then broke and fled over the

207

southern bank, splintering their own reflections. On our right the rocky hills soared to uncompromising peaks. The quiet hot sunlight made us sleepy.

At noon the lagoon petered out, and we halted to load water in the little keg that had once (how long ago?) held Chinese spirit. Then on, till we sighted the eastern extremity of the Ayak Kum Kul and made camp beside it in the middle of the afternoon. The salt water mocked us and – much worse – flavoured strongly the brackish, muddy fluid which we dug out of an artificial water-hole in a scanty patch of scrub. The day became suddenly unkind; 'the usual bloody tempest' notes a jaded diary. It had been a long stage.

The next day was May 31st and my twenty-eighth birthday. I am, in ordinary life, less susceptible to anniversaries than almost anyone; great occasions leave me cold. But Kini and I were leading a life in which the component days were landmarked usually by meals alone; and just as its uncertainty drove us to superstition – to reading the future in the patience cards, to putting an embargo on the word 'India' – so its emptiness and monotony aroused in us the instinct – comparable to the instinct which makes people carve their names on trees – to as it were tie ribbons on to certain days, to seize any excuse for variegating the calendar. Three months since we left Peking, two months since we left Tangar, nine, ten, eleven months since one of us had started out from home . . . a brother's birthday, a date in history remembered by chance . . . thinner and thinner grew our excuses for infusing significance into this day or into that, and stronger and stronger, as the weeks dragged by, became our urge to infuse it.

In a way it was like our lust for news. 'Any news?' I always asked Kini when I came in from shooting. 'Any news?' asked Kini, if I rejoined the caravan after riding ahead or lagging behind. Of course there never was any; important or even amusing things hardly ever happened. But perhaps there had been something – some odd behaviour on the part of man or beast, a remark in an unknown language whose tone challenged conjecture – that was worth relating, examining, building hypotheses upon. The reader, who can tremble or rejoice with five continents between his first and second cup of coffee, may find this thirst for second-hand incident childish or incomprehensible; but the fact remains that we suffered from it.

The last day of May, at any rate, was my birthday; and this most fortuitous of circumstances had the power to make the world feel different. It had been like that when one was a child, but then there had been presents, privileges and exemptions, a party, candles on the cake, to bolster up the illusion. Now there was nothing more concrete than Kini's promise of a special dinner, with curry; and that, at dawn, was twenty miles away and more. But we had an extra ration of sugar in the breakfast tea, and when I started off on foot, leaving Cynara with Kini, I felt that queer elation to which, on this journey, we were both intermittently liable. I walked all day, resting every now and then to smoke while the camels caught me up. After two hours we halted to load water, scraping for it in the lakeside shingle at a place which the Turkis knew; it was strange to find fresh water – or as nearly fresh as made no difference to us – within six feet of what might have been the sea.

Then we marched on, between the melodramatic mountains and the lake which glittered with a vulgar, picture-postcard blue, for another seven hours. The sloping desert was as bare as your hand, and a hawk was the only living creature that I saw. At half-past four we halted in a shallow gully and made camp in a brisk little storm of sleet. Our sack of barley was now all but empty, and we mixed the dregs with tsamba which Slalom ate but Cynara, baffled as ever, could make nothing of; there was no grazing for the horses here. Kini cooked a great feast of rice and antelope and curry which more than resigned me to the imminence of old age, and we both thanked heaven that we were not celebrating somebody's birthday at the Savoy.

CHAPTER V

CASUALTIES

JUNE opened with a villain's smile. The first light showed us a still, bright morning and the too-blue surface of the lake unruffled. We were near the end of the lake, and after an hour or two halted to scratch up a last supply of the saline, gritty water underneath the shingle. I had a long shot at a mandarin duck silhouetted on a little promontory, but he fell in the lake and we lost him to a breeze which had newly sprung up. Leaving that place, we turned a little north of west, climbing up towards a low pass in the mountains on our right. We were not sorry to be done with that cerulean and redundant sheet of water.

The faint pleasure that one always feels at changing landmarks was short-lived. Within an hour's march of our watering-place things were going gravely wrong. First one camel, then a second, began to protest raucously and to drag on the head-ropes. Slow chaos overtook the caravan. Progress became jerky and sluggish, was more and more frequently interrupted by halts to shift the loads or to splice a broken head-rope. The head-ropes were fastened, according to the Mongol usage, to a wooden pin driven through the camel's nose; the other end was tied to the packsaddle of the beast in front. Any strain on the rope is naturally painful, and a camel must be very wild or very sick before he digs in his toes and jibs hard enough to snap it.

Snow, mixed with hail, came down to scourge us. We detached the weaker of the two camels and I towed him along while Kini flicked his hindquarters where the wool was coming off in expectation of a summer non-existent up here. For half an hour we struggled on like this; but it was no good. With a last apologetic roar he knelt down and nothing we could do would make him rise. There was nothing for it but to leave him – to 'cast him on the gobi', as the Chinese say.

The Turkis had two fresh and fairly lightly loaded camels with them, and to these we transferred his load and his pack-saddle. His sudden collapse was mysterious and could only be due, we decided, to bad water. All the camels had been well and marching steadily the day before, but both Slalom and I had shown unmistakable signs of being affected – though not greatly inconvenienced – by the water. In the circumstances I decided not to shoot the camel we were abandoning; for all I knew he might shake off the effects of bad water and recover his strength.

But it was horrible to leave him there, hunched, apathetic, and somehow shrunken, with the snow plastering his inexpressive face: horrible, as we rode away, to watch him dwindle to a small dark speck in a great naked sweep of desert. In our empty world the animals that served us, revealing their characters by tricks of temperament or gait, bulked almost as large as human beings. From now on the caravan marched under a shadow. The situation was not serious as yet, but the fate of one camel might be the fate of more and, remote though the possibility of disaster was, it was at least a possibility; we were a long way from anywhere. The other ailing camel was clearly on his last legs, and Slalom was losing strength. Under a lowering sky we crawled on up towards the pass, mechanically uttering the abruptly ended yell with which the Mongols urge their beasts. The sick camel moved with a faltering stride, roaring his grief.

Presently we made a short halt on a shoulder from which we got our last sight of the Ayak Kum Kul. The Turkis gave us to understand that no fuel was available for several stages to come, so we set about tearing up the little tufts which the camels ate and which had large, combustible roots; we filled several sacks and went on again. It was a chill, unfriendly evening. The great pinnacles of rock, the huge grey tracts of plateau between them might have belonged to another planet, a dead, ravaged star wheeling in the cold gulf of space. I thought of lawns, the quilted

211

tree-tops of a wood below a down, tangled June hedges . . . For it is a strange and terrible thing that the lady novelists are right, that young men in deserts do dwell with a banal wistfulness on sentimentalized, given-away-with-the-Christmas-number pictures of their native land, forgetting the by-passes, the cloudbursts, the sheaves of bluebells lashed to motor-cycle pillions, the bungalows and the banana-skins and the bowler hats.

Snow soon began to fall, and we made camp in a waterless gully about 14,000 feet up, after a trying march of nearly eleven hours. The sick camel knelt in his tracks, ominously making no attempt to search for grazing. We pitched the tent and cooked a meal and gave the horses a ration of tsamba with a little meat in it. The Turkis were depressingly rapacious and seemed blind to the fact that they were responsible for letting the camels get bad water. 'Afraid horses won't last long,' ends the despondent entry in my diary.

At dawn next day snow was falling again. The camels had wandered far afield, and while we waited for them to be fetched inaction bred misgivings. The sick camel still knelt where he had halted the night before. Despite his protests we put some menthol in his nostrils; but he appeared impervious to the reviving qualities which we believed this treatment to possess and registered only annoyance. The skeleton horses munched their tsamba listlessly. Snow-flakes vanished with a resigned hiss as they settled on the ashes of the fire.

At 8.30 we started, putting a nominal load of two light suitcases on the sick camel. When we got him to his feet he made water in prodigious quantities, and I hoped that this was a symptom of recovery. The way at first lay down hill, and for three hours I dragged him along, though so slowly that the other camels gained on us steadily and at the cost of so much exertion that to do a whole stage like this would clearly be more than I could manage. Then we began to climb, and though the slope was not a steep one it was enough to turn the scales. The camel knelt down. With superhuman efforts Kini got him to his feet again, but ten

212

more yards was the limit of his capacity, and he knelt again with an air of finality.

Sadly we took the suitcases off him and put them on to Slalom. The packsaddles we abandoned, and it was not till days afterwards that I cursed myself for not ripping them open and feeding the stuffing to the horses. The camel watched us move off with mercifully unemotional eyes.

We had now lost two camels out of four; but statistics are ever misleading, and our predicament was not as grave as it sounds. For one thing, our loads were much lighter than they had been; for another, there was room for a certain amount of freight on the two camels of the Turkis. So we did not as yet face the necessity of jettisoning some of our scanty and precious belongings, though already each of us was secretly drawing up a provisional roster of sacrifice.

After leaving the camel we climbed on up to a wide col beyond which a broken, rolling tableland stretched between a ring of 20,000 foot peaks, many of them capped with eternal snows. Cynara was going very lame but at least seemed lively; so we transferred the suitcases to her, for Slalom was weaker than he had ever been before. Only with one dragging and the other whipping could we keep him moving at all, and our pace was so slow that the camels were soon out of sight ahead of us. This increased our resentment at the Turkis and flavoured it uneasily with suspicion. They had already thrown away two camels as casually as if they had been half-smoked cigarettes; and, since they had with them in the loads most of our money and possessions, they might be expected to view with an even greater degree of composure the possibility of our being benighted.

The possibility was undoubtedly there. There was no trail of any sort for us to follow; we had only the camels' tracks to guide us and these, owing to the hardness of the ground, were often invisible for long stretches at a time. One of my eyes was out of action owing to a recrudescence of the trouble I had had in the mountains south of the

Koko Nor, and when I was in the lead, dragging Slalom, we went astray several times.

We struggled on in bleak uncertainty. Towards the end of the afternoon the tracks led us steeply down from the plateau by a dried-up stream bed; there were no signs of moisture, but here and there the tips of a few blades of grass braved the inclement air and raised our hopes. But when at last we debouched into a great dun valley there was no further trace of water or vegetation, and we could see the camels still moving tinily, two or three miles ahead.

Slalom, by this time, was very far gone. He no longer answered to the whip, and our advance had become a miniature pageant of despair. In front went Kini, bent almost double, dragging doggedly on the reins. Behind the tottering Slalom, I, also bowed, barged with one shoulder against his gaunt hindquarters; and behind me limped the little mare on whose burden of suitcases tattered hotel labels incongruously evoked palm trees and beaches, crowded streets and *confort anglais*. We moved at a snail's pace with frequent panting halts, for we had to push and pull for all we were worth and the altitude found us out. Each halt made it harder to get Slalom going again.

We crawled across the iron floor of the valley. The light thickened (with apologies to *Macbeth*, there is no other word for it) and the background to our exertions was suitably grim; the camels were far away out of sight and we were alone in a world where life had no other representatives. Dusk, even in cheerless weather, can be tranquil or romantic or just comfortably sad; this dusk was none of those things, but hard and drab and what's-the-use? like an early Monday morning in a city. We consoled ourselves with the reflection that we had not much further to go.

But we had. We expected to find the camels halted at the tail-end of the valley; but when, rounding a bluff, we got there we saw that there was no water, no grazing. They had gone on and – much worse – up, over a cruel little pass leading northward. In normal conditions it was nothing of a climb; but we were virtually carrying Slalom, and the last two or three hours would have been impossible if we had

214

not been going downhill. We were both very tired, and our elaborately facetious protests, our grin-and-bear-it grumbling, had become the most flimsy of façades because exhaustion made our voices hoarse.

Slalom, it was clear, was done for, would be no more use to us; but we could not leave him here. In the first place, there was no grass and no water and we were fond of him; in the second place, we had striven so hard all through the day to get him even as far as this that we were as it were obsessed, and could not tolerate the idea of failing to bring him into camp. So after a short rest we attacked the pass.

Somehow we manhandled Slalom to the top. I do not remember much about it, except that once, as we leant gasping on the horses, I noticed that Kini's face looked strangely drawn. It was no great feat, but we had had a long, hard day and (I think this was more important) there was no *certainty* beyond the pass, no promise of a fire and camp; we had no idea how much longer we were condemned to this Sisyphean advance. Anyone can spurt on the last lap; but we had no reason to suppose this was the last.

Nor was it. Night had almost fallen when we reached the head of the pass, but far down another valley we could just make out the camels, still moving; as we watched them they disappeared behind a bluff. Beyond the bluff a whitish streak showed dimly. Was it salt? Or was it snow, or a frozen river? We would have given a lot to know. To move at all was difficult; to move in the right direction would shortly be impossible, for by night the faintly marked camel-tracks would be indecipherable and night was nearly on us. Still, the next stretch was visibly downhill. We went on.

Our movements had become mechanical. Vaguely aware of jagged peaks softening and blurring around us, of a herd of pale orongo antelope all ghostly in the last of the light, we dropped down to the bottom of the valley. As other landmarks faded, the pale streak before us, a potential journey's end, grew more and more alluring and intriguing; our eyes were tired with staring, our minds with speculation, our hearts with hope deferred.

But of course it was all right in the end. Four dark shapes loomed up ahead of us; they were the camels, unloaded. We stumbled rather blindly into camp – a more than usually courtesy title since the Turkis had no matches with which to light a fire. For hours I had been marshalling my exiguous vocabulary into a denunciation of their conduct; but when the time came I abandoned it. Their knowledge that I was unacquainted with their language had never yet curbed their volubility, and I did not feel equal to coping with twenty minutes of expostulation in order to convey a bald and rudimentary rebuke whose cogency was unlikely to be felt. So we unsaddled in a chilly silence, fancying – rightly, I think – that we detected signs of shame in their demeanour.

The routine of pitching the tent was carried out stiffly: lifting boxes, hammering pegs, we moved in a numb and dreamy way. The white streak had materialized as ice partially covering a little river, and I took Cynara down for a drink (the horses had had no water for thirty-six hours and very little water – bad at that – for several days) but Slalom would not move. He stood in the firelight on the spot where we had ceased to push him, hanging his ugly but familiar head, visibly alive only because he was still on his feet.

We had been marching for eleven hours, with no food since dawn; but we were not hungry. We drank some cocoa and as it warmed our bellies felt a faint reaction, a kind of drowsy triumph. So far it had been an easy journey; to-day, for the first time, we had faced crisis of a sort without assistance. And though it was no great achievement to have dragged a failing horse a few miles further than seemed at one time possible, we were pleased that we had done our best by Slalom and we hoped that we had saved his life. In the friendly candle-light we grew complacent and forgot the rigours of the day.

CHAPTER VI

WE SAY GOOD-BYE TO SLALOM

THE river we had come to was called the Toruksai; in the summer Turkis from the southern oases visit it to wash gold. There was a little rank grass there, and we lay up all the next day, which was fine and sunny. The valley harboured antelope and I tried an expedition against them; but the glare was too much for my bad eye and I had to give it up almost at once.

Kini's acute sense of smell I have mentioned as a handicap in travel; but here it stood us in good stead. She went out to have a look at the surviving camels and caught a whiff of rotting flesh; it came from the Prime Minister's camel, originally christened The Pearl of the Tsaidam and now known as The Pearl for short. Kini brought him into camp and we took his packsaddle off; on the spine between the humps an ancient sore under the skin had reopened and was festering fast. We pegged his head down and with very little help from the Turkis, who were hopeless with animals, Kini doctored it despite his bellows. It looked a terrible place, but she made such a good job of it that it healed completely within a few days.

The Pearl was a noble beast. At first – misled by his pride and by Yanduk's reference to his 'bad heart' – we had misjudged him. His head, topped by a barbaric and assertive crest of wool, was handsome, and his forefeet were very much bigger than his hind feet, a sure sign of excellence. Gradually he lost his unruliness and mastered his dislike of horses, and in these hours of need he served us splendidly though he was daily losing strength. He was an individualist with a Byronic aspect – if camels can appear Byronic. Detached and sceptical, he seemed always to be something more than a camel: perhaps a prince unluckily metamorphosed. His surviving companion –

Number Two – had, as his name suggests, less character; but he was an honest, steady worker with a very long stride. We had come to feel affection, as well as solicitude, for both camels.

The only other incident that day was an attempt at rationing. The Turkis, in spite of warnings, still ate enormously, and supplies were low. I took the sack of tsamba and divided what was left in two; I also gave them a tin of melted mutton fat, which was our substitute for butter in mixing the tsamba. This, I told them, was all they would get. Tokta Ahun, who knew by now that we loathed him, received this announcement with ugly looks; the old man merely filled his bowl with an abstracted air.

Next day we went on. While we were having breakfast Slalom poked his mournful and ungainly face into the tent, snuffled apologetically, and began to lick a tin; it was almost more than we could bear. We got his nose-bag and filled it with a great feast of tsamba and meat and some wizened and revolting slices of dried apple that we found in the bottom of a sack; he ate it ravenously.

Then we loaded the camels and set off. Slalom followed willingly enough and Kini even mounted him to ford the river. But on the further bank he stopped and hung his head, and we saw, what we knew already in our hearts, that he would not do another stage. It was better to leave him there, where there was water and a little grass, than to drag him any further.

We called to the Turkis to halt and unsaddled him for the last time. He stood as still as a stone, the ugly shadow of a horse, alone in the sunlight under the encircling hills; he had served us faithfully ever since Tangar. The camels moved off and I followed them; Kini stayed a little longer with Slalom. I found that I was crying, for the first time for years.

We marched on round a rocky shoulder and turned north-west up a steep, narrow corrie where we surprised a herd of antelope; but I was unloaded and in the end bungled a long shot. We seemed to be climbing into a

218

kinder world. There were several little streams, and near the bed of each a few tiny but indubitable blades of grass; our sadness over Slalom began to wear off. We were working our way – slowly, on account of the altitude – towards a pass at the head of the corrie. Marmots, their red coats very gay in the sunshine, whistled defiance and perplexity, then scampered into their burrows with a curious flouncing gait. In the mouth of the pass I shot one. '*Abdan*?' I asked the Turkis, pointing to the marmot and then to my mouth. They shook their heads and laughed. '*Yaman*,' they said. The opinion of trenchermen so resolute and so omnivorous clearly carried weight; so the marmot occupies a unique place in the history of the expedition as being the only thing – barring a diseased antelope – which we shot but did not eat.

Beyond the pass we slanted down a long bare valley. It was a bright, warm day, my eye was better, and the little streams cheered us. We were picking our way round the northern slopes of the mountain range which our map called the Achik Kul Tagh, and in the course of the day we climbed three more steep passes. 'Camels go slowly and there is still anxiety,' notes my diary; but we did a long stage notwithstanding. We camped in a little pass beside a stream, on what would soon be turf. It was a pleasant place, and here we celebrated no less an anniversary than the Fourth of June; its significance, I fear, was rather lost on Kini, for my attempts to explain the connection between George III and fireworks at Eton were handicapped by the regrettable discovery that I had really no idea what the connection was; moreover, William Tell somehow got into the conversation and confused the issue badly. Still, we made a light but sybaritic lunch off a very small tin of crab which had been given me, seven months before, by the Japanese Consul-General in Vladivostock and which I had been carrying about Asia as a kind of talisman ever since. We amused ourselves by trying to imagine how one would set about explaining what a crab was to the Turkis, who had never heard of the sea and lived 2000 miles from the nearest bit of it.

In the evening I climbed a shoulder above the pass and did an abortive stalk after some antelope. The sun had gone and the great uplands had a very desolate air. But I felt gay and light-headed, and full of a conviction that I was invincible, that nothing was going to stop me from getting through to India. But even in this braggart mood, when success seemed so well worth achieving, I knew in my heart how sadly little the feat would be worth in retrospect – how easy it would all prove to have been, how many opportunities one would curse oneself for having missed. One's *alter ego* is at time an irritating companion.

Mine was powerless, however, to qualify the delights of the whacking great meal which we ate that evening in honour of the Fourth of June. We got out the brandy and the gramophone and played our three records several times and our favourite record over and over again; it was a saccharine and cretinous ditty called 'The Clouds Will Soon Roll By' which Kini had taken, when she first saw the title, for a musical fantasia on a meteorological theme. I can hear it now . . .

> Somewhere a robin's singing,
>   Up in a tree-top high;
> To you and me he's singing
> 'The clouds will soon roll by.'

It was a most reassuring kind of song.

I remembered the telegraphic greetings in facetious Latin which Eton on this day receives from far-flung alumni toasting her memory at dinner-tables from Peshawar to Patagonia, and wished snobbishly that I could send a wire from an address which could only be indicated in terms of longitude and latitude, and wondered how one would translate tsamba into Latin . . . At last we got into our flea-bags and fell asleep to the sound of running water.

Next day we did another stage of nearly nine hours. The camels moved lifelessly, and I began to speculate as to how much longer I could go on walking twenty miles a day. Kini distinguished herself by finding a sand-grouse's nest with three eggs in it, and when at last we camped beside a stream she mixed them up with a little flour and made a kind of omelette which was the most delicious dish of the whole journey. We had tasted no eggs – except the three wild goose eggs at Issik Pakte – for over two months, and this was a landmark in the history of the expedition.

The next day we did the longest march of the lot. We started soon after dawn. Cynara, who was in whimsical mood, refused to be caught and followed the camels at a wary distance. Distractions were so welcome on the march that at first we rather enjoyed trying to outmanœuvre her; but wide encircling movements, culminating in a sudden and invariably unsuccessful spurt, were an exhausting business and gradually we began to get angry. Cynara maintained an air of perfect innocence; she always loved to march with her nose under the tail of the last camel, and if we let her alone she would draw in close to the caravan. But if anyone, coming up stealthily from behind, made a grab for her head she would swerve away like a wing three-quarter and retire to the middle distance.

After several hours this became humiliating as well as tiring. Kini got up on one of the camels and made a lasso which she tried to drop over Cynara's head as she plodded demurely past, keeping her distance from me. But Kini had no luck, and finally we resorted to another method, which was to wheel the leading camel sharply round when Cynara was alongside the caravan and get her entangled in the head ropes. Thus, at last, we caught her after we had been marching for seven hours.

We had now dropped down from the shoulders of the Achik Kul Tagh and were slanting across a wide basin of desert towards a low watershed. It was dreary country, but at the watershed we came suddenly on a track of sorts. It was old and faint, but here and there camels' pads were marked sharply in what had been mud at the time of their passing, and occasionally three stones had been placed together for a cooking pot to rest on. The road, which leads presumably to Ghass in the Tsaidam, had obviously not been used for a long time; but these were the first traces of human beings we had seen for eight days, and we found them reassuring.

Beyond the saddle of the watershed we came into another long valley, flanked by very stark and rocky hills and dominated at the far end by a great snow peak; a dried-up water-course ran diffusely down the middle of it. In this, presently, we found a small spring. We had been going for nine hours and were fully prepared to camp, but the Turkis – I think because there was very little for the camels to eat here – insisted on pushing on. They said there was plenty of water further down the valley.

They were wrong. The water-course grew wider but no wetter. A mirage mocked us. Here and there there were traces of old camps, and near them water-holes had been dug; but the water-holes were dry.

We went on and on. The hours passed slowly. We crawled down that endless valley, a string of small, jaded automata under the dwarfing hills. Antelope, oddly luminous in the failing light, skirmished across the hard grey desert. The water-course here was half a mile wide, a skein of twisting little channels. Pricked, by the approach of night, out of the torpid, automatic routine of keeping pace with the camels, I made zigzag reconnaissance across the shallow stream-beds; not a trickle, not even a patch of mud, rewarded me. The Turkis, questioned, reaffirmed the imminent discovery of water in tones more and more perfunctorily optimistic; we knew them already for silly, ineffectual men and built no hopes upon their words.

Every man, provided that he does not raise blisters or other impediments on his feet, can walk in a day at least half as far again as he imagines. The muscles responsible for placing the left foot in front of the right foot, and the right foot in front of the left foot, do not tire quickly; it is the feet that count. My own feet are almost as little sensitive as hooves, and as the hours of march dragged into their early 'teens I had nothing to complain of save tedium, anxiety, and the staleness of sustained exertion. But water would have been welcome – doubly so when a keen north wind bore down across our line of march, sweeping the valley with a chilly enfilade. When night fell we were past talking, past hoping, past thinking. We moved numbly, each bounded in a nutshell of discontent.

At half-past seven we gave it up and halted, pitching the tent on a slope of stony desert. We had been marching, at a good pace for camels, for fourteen hours without food and with only two or three halts, none longer than five minutes; Kini had done the first seven hours – the most strenuous, because of catching Cynara – on foot. I got, during our seven months together, so used to regarding Kini as an equal in most things and a superior one in some that perhaps I have paid over-few tributes to (among other things) her powers of endurance. Praise, and especially praise in print, is an over-valued commodity, and I know that Kini has little use for it; nevertheless – because it is just as remarkable as any of the strange things that we saw – I should like to place it on record that, at the end of a fourteen hours' march in the middle of a hard journey (rising almost always before dawn, eating almost always a little less than enough), Kini went supperless to bed without, even by implication, turning a hair. The best that I can do in the way of eulogy is to say that I thought nothing of it at the time.

CHAPTER VII

GRASS, MEN, NEWS

THAT was a poor sort of a camp. The animals hardly bothered to nose the earth's iron crust in search of grazing. Men and beasts subsided gratefully into sleep, into oblivion of the necessity for another stage the next day and the day after that. Everyone was dead tired.

The Turkis, however, woke us at three. The star-lit world was silent and obscure, but a pot, incredibly, was boiling on the fire. There were streams in these parts that flowed by night and not by day, and one such, tardily revived by snow thawed, hours before, on distant peaks, had begun to plunge musically down the face opposite, rousing the elder Turki to unwontedly profitable action. So before starting we had tea to drink and – more important – to soak our tsamba in; we moved off on full stomachs, leaving behind us the horrid skeletons of my last pair of socks. From now on I walked or rode in boots alone; they were a pair of American field-boots, stricken in years and seamed with outlandish scars, but they fitted me so well that, although one sole was almost and the other quite worn through, I was never inconvenienced by the lack of socks.

It was a brilliant morning, presaging heat and thirst; but at the tail end of the valley we found water in the central stream-bed. The animals drank deep and moved more easily. We squeezed our way out of the valley by a narrow gorge in which we had to ford the river several times. Here there were rare flowers (the first of the year for us) like crocuses, and wind-flattened tufts of a plant resembling bell heather; 'much grass by our standards' says my diary, not meaning a great deal. We took a short cut, climbing up over a shoulder where shrill resentful marmots vanished abruptly underground.

The machine which worked my legs began to show signs

of running down. The Bactrian camel, as I have said before, marches at the more than reasonable pace of roughly two and a half miles an hour; but the Bactrian camel never stops, and if you keep pace with him you find yourself, after three or four hours, yearning for an excuse to take the weight off your feet and legs, to bend your back, to stop moving and sit down, if only for a moment. For days my pipe had provided this excuse. 'Catch you up,' I had cried, going to ground behind the shelter of a rock; 'I want to smoke.' To-day the formula was more often used than implemented. The pipe, the pouch – you dragged them out, of course; but the sun was warm, the rock behind you impersonated adequately an arm-chair, and immobility alone was so exquisite a sensation that you were loath to dilute it. Half of you watched the four camels and the little mare – a company, at first, of familiar, individual quad-rupeds but presently only a small dark blob which expanded or contracted sideways; the other half dozed, slipped swiftly out of High Tartary into other worlds and in them lived briefly on parole, a tethered but appreciative ghost. Your time was up very soon. The empty pipe, the inviolate pouch, you stuffed back into your pockets. You rose stiffly, picked up the ·22, blew dust from its breech, and went on.

You were walking fast now: the stride longer, the exertion greater than was usual. But the little caravan, a speck with all nothing for a background, kept its distance. You dogged it through a rolling desolation . . . After half an hour it showed a little bigger; but surely you should have decreased its lead by more than this small margin, surely you had not halted for so very long? By degrees it became a will o' the wisp; you felt that you were doomed to race against it and be beaten. You knew by now the technique for enduring long marches – how helpful is a train of thought, how it pays to have a half-remembered quotation, a half-worked-out idea, as iron rations for the intellect: something on which the mind can dwell, ignoring the body. But now it was too late for this; the inoculation would not take. Thoughts wheeled erratically inside your head, fleeting in and out of prominence like bats in a lamplit room; you could not concentrate. The mind could keep the body going, but it could not forget what it was at. No anodyne availed. You were aware of nothing save the caravan that flickered in the glare ahead of you. . . .

In the middle of the morning we came to Dimnalik. This place was dignified with a name on our map, and the Turkis had confidently predicted that we should find people living there. As usual they were wrong; there were no tents, no herds, only an empty sweep of hillside. '*Adam yok*,' said the old man in a pained voice; 'there is nobody.' We went on.

After marching for six hours we dropped down again to the river gorge and loaded water; then we pressed on for three interminable hours across a wide saddle of desert stippled with camel shrub, to camp in a sandy patch where we had to use old antelope horns to reinforce the tent-pegs. A little hail fell that was almost rain; we had lost a lot of altitude in the last two days. The Turkis said that we had only one more march to Bash Malghun.

For once they were right. On the next day, which was June 8th, a dogged, tedious nine-hour stage across a glaring desert brought us to a dried-up river-bed. We pressed through a belt of tamarisk beyond it and found ourselves miraculously translated to another world. Real grass grew, in substantial quantities, upon the ground. Flocks of sheep and goats pastured in sunlight which no longer irked our eyes by rebounding from the desert. A donkey brayed. We swooped down upon a little girl who was herding goats and by her were led towards a distant group of yurts and tents.

Half a dozen men came forward to meet us. Manners down here were courtlier than in the highlands at Issik Pakte, and we had quickly to adapt ourselves to the Turki method of greeting, in which each party takes both the other's hands in both of his, and then steps back, bowing slightly, and strokes his beard with a graceful, deprecating gesture; the clean-shaven must make the same gesture as the hirsute.

These men were less weather-beaten and nearer (as we

discovered later) to the average Turki type than the hunters at Issik Pakte; they looked a softer lot. While we unloaded the camels and pitched the tent they fetched the faded red cloth, called *dastakhan*, off which meals are eaten all over Turkistan; and soon, a little incredulously, we were tasting our first fresh bread since Tangar. There was also sour milk in a capacious wooden bowl. This, for the moment, was Paradise enow.

As soon as our guides had had time to communicate their scanty knowledge about our identities, place of origin, and destination, I began to inquire about the road ahead of us. To inquire was comparatively easy, since place-names, interspersed with the words for 'good' and 'bad', broadly conveyed the gist of my questions; the trouble started when the Turkis answered. They all spoke at once, in loud voices, and none of them seemed capable of conceiving that the world held human beings unfamiliar with their language. Politics and geography, prophecy and history – information of the very first interest and import-ance to us – poured out in a headlong spate of words, 95 per cent of which were gibberish to me.

Nevertheless, by sifting and repetition certain facts were not too conjecturally established. The Tungan armies were still in control of the southern oases; the fighting between Cherchen and Charklik, of which we had heard at Issik Pakte, was over; and public opinion at Bash Malghun saw nothing to prevent us from completing our journey to Cherchen, which was some six marches further on. The Tungans they admitted to be 'bad', and their estimate that we should have a favourable reception from the rebels seemed to me to be somewhat airily arrived at. Still, the news so far as we could understand it was good, and there was at least no question of our having to turn back yet. We settled down to enjoy a day's rest.

Our guides, especially the old man, played the tough backwoodsmen among these gentler dwellers at a mere 10,000 feet; they swaggered, gesticulated, ranted and domineered. Patients came to us from all over the scattered encampment; they included a blind man and a deaf man and an ancient with the aspect of John of Gaunt and swollen bones in his legs. He was pathetically insistent that we could cure him if we wished, and Kini gave him some ointment in the hope that auto-suggestion would do the rest; he embarrassed us by sending a present of rice in token of his gratitude. We gave a gramophone concert to the entire community, and delighted the children by lending them a cap-pistol, which was all we had with us in the way of side-arms. Life seemed very pleasant after the grim days behind us; 'I expect we shall look back on this camp as a Fool's Paradise', comments my cautious diary.

On June 10th we started on the last lap to Cherchen. For one brick of tea and five dollars we had secured a guide, and three donkeys to supplement the camels. The guide was an altogether charming man called Tuzun; his face beamed rosily behind a huge fluffy beard, and his whole manner and appearance suggested a favourite nephew of Santa Claus. We had traded matches, soap, and needles for rice and flour, and with some of the latter the women had baked us a supply of *tukach*, which may be described as the ship's biscuit of the desert. We had also been given a sheep. The gift was accompanied by many smiles and fine words, and followed, a few hours later, by a whining request for payment; but it only cost 1s. 3d. and this was the first item on our butcher's bill, so we did not grudge the money.

We loaded up in the middle of a jabbering crowd and moved off at ten o'clock. A very pretty little girl who had taken a fancy to me gave me a box of Russian matches as a parting present, and everyone was friendly and benevolent. After going for about an hour and a half we came to the residence of John of Gaunt, which was a kind of crater roofed over with felts. Here we lunched off bread and sour milk and antelope meat, noting for future use the Turki custom of rinsing the hands in water before a meal. John of Gaunt's legs were by no means better, and I thought that I detected a hint of disillusionment behind his hospitable manner.

At noon we went on, and soon left that little island of grass for desert tufted here and there with scrub. We were marching down the valley of the Cherchen Darya, the river which waters the oasis of Cherchen; its current at Bash Malghun had been crystal clear, but as we drew nearer to civilization the stream – perhaps symbolically – became ever muddier and more turgid. Tuzun was surprised, and more than a little shocked, by my refusal to ride one of his donkeys. Central Asia attaches a great deal of importance to your mount, and to go on foot is rank bad form; he found it incomprehensible that I preferred to walk.

The donkeys trotted demurely, encouraged from behind by a sound approximating to an angry sneeze; but they seized every opportunity to stray from the track and, what with our late start and our midday halt, we made a short stage that day. We stopped for the night at a hut which was half a dug-out; it was tenanted by a very poor but very hospitable old woman who gave us some delicious butter, our first and last for a long time. We pitched our tent next door, watched a herd of goats being tethered for the night in a long double file, and presently received an unexpected visitor.

He was a Tungan merchant bound eastward for the Tsaidam with a caravan of goods: a little slit-eyed Chinese Moslem with a jerky manner and a blue cloth tied round his head in pirate style. He was travelling by way of Ghass Kul to Tunghwang in Kansu, and Teijinar was his first port of call; he knew Yanduk and Wang Sun-lin, and we wished that we could write Russian so that we could give him a letter for Borodishin. He confirmed the news that we imagined we had heard in Bash Malghun; the Tungans were in control of the southern oases and hostilities with Charklik were over. He made apocryphal amendments. Ma Chung-ying, the Tungan leader, had gone to England; his place had been taken by Ma Ho-san, who had arrived at Khotan in an English aeroplane. All this, as we knew later and suspected at the time, was something less than legend;

but it added to the interest of our chronically conjectural lives, and we elicited also some useful financial pointers – the value in the local currency of a brick of tea, the potential market price of a camel. The scrap of unreliable gossip went to our heads and we felt ourselves at the hub of events, with our fingers on the pulse of Central Asia.

CHAPTER VIII

THALASSA THALASSA

Next day, before we started, we were paid a visit by the merchant's partner, who had a snub nose, smoked a pipe, and was therefore judged to be no Moslem. He was a less communicative man, but we bandied last night's rumours with him and expanded them a little. We had, by this time, an unbridled lust for news or anything that smelt of news.

The old lady who was our hostess gave us a stirrup cup of milk, and Kini bestowed on her in return a necklace of red beads which filled her with delight. We marched off into a still, hot morning, which was later marred by a head wind that filled the valley with a pale drab haze of dust. Shortly before noon we were joined by a lady with two donkeys, on one of which she rode; the other carried a light load of household goods, on top of which was more than firmly lashed a yearling child. This infant relished very little the delights of travel and lodged almost continuous protests; but its mother – a domineering person with a harsh, masculine voice – abused the donkeys so roundly that most of her offspring's cries were drowned. There was something Chaucerian about her as she jogged along with her veil flung back, exchanging full-blooded banter with the men.

We camped after a seven-hour march in the gorge of the river. 'Short stage men,' remarks my diary, rather contemptuously and altogether prematurely, of Tuzun and of an anonymous companion who had attached himself to us the day before. They were to live this comment down in the near future.

Dawn the next day was hazy and very tranquil. Cynara gave trouble again, and we did not catch her until after the march had started. The valley narrowed, and we found ourselves marching down a gully whose walls were pock-marked with smooth caves like the flanks of a Gruyère cheese. For the first and last time in the whole journey it began to rain quite hard; Kini fished a mackintosh out of her saddle-bag, and the sight of its dank folds evoked a vision of England, of jaded holidaymakers quartering their small island in search of sun and privacy. The baby's cries now grew feebler. Its mother had placed a cloth over its face and this, growing sodden, was in a fair way to stifle it; in normal climatic conditions the cloth was thrown back to admit the dust.

In the middle of the morning we left the river and took a short cut through the last range of mountains separating us from the great depression of the Tarim Basin. We followed a crumbling track up over a succession of steep and jagged passes; it was hard work, and both The Pearl and Number Two showed a deplorable tendency to stop and kneel down on the stiffest gradients. In a big corrie we met three men going up to Bash Malghun; of their talk I could understand nothing save that it appeared to be sensational and to concern the taking of prisoners.

At the foot of the last pass we halted for a short rest, then climbed it very slowly. I took charge of the camels, for on these narrow and vertiginous tracks the donkeys needed all the men's attention. The Pearl was moving stiffly and eyed the world with distaste, but when we reached the last razor-backed ridge it was pleasant to look back on the peaks massed behind us round the towering snows of the Tokuz Dawan and to reflect that from now on it would be all downhill. Below us, hidden by a dust-haze, lay the desert.

We plunged down sharply by the zigzag track into a tremendous gorge, a huge gash in the side of the mountain between whose high enclosing walls we marched with the unfamiliar sense of being shut in, of no longer having distances about us. At four o'clock we made camp near a little salty water-hole, after a good stage of ten hours.

The next day, June 13th, was a long one. Soon after dawn we moved off down the narrow, winding gorge, following a dried-up stream-bed through a succession of highly romantic grottoes. Presently it widened, and we passed clumps of flowering tamarisk at which the camels snatched greedily. Everything was deathly still; only a little bird from time to time uttered a short and plaintive song whose sweet notes echoed anomalously under those frowning cliffs. The silence, the tortuous and hidden way, made me feel as if we were engaged on a surprise attack.

After five hours we came to a place which both our map and our guides called Muna Bulak. But once more '*adam yok*'; the looked-for tents were absent, and there was only a little spring of very salt and brackish water. We filled the keg and went on for two more hours, debouching from the gorge into a huge desert of sand and piedmont gravel which stretched as far as the eye could see. The mountains with which for so long we had struggled at close quarters were relegated to a hazy backcloth.

At one o'clock we halted, cooked a meal, and wolfed great lumps of boiled mutton. The sun beat down on us savagely and we propped a felt up with tent-poles to make a little shade; this was a sharp contrast to the uplands. We drank a great deal of curiously tasting tea.

At dusk we started off again, marching north-west through a waste of tufted dunes. As the light faded the low patches of scrub took on strange shapes, became dark monsters which, as you watched them, moved; it was all very like that night-march with the Prince of Dzun. We were a long way from water and the men took the caravan along at a good pace. Presently we came out of the dunes into stark desert, as flat and naked and unfriendly as a sheet of ice. The camels were groaning with exhaustion and had to be tugged along. There was no landmark, no incident, to mark the passing of the hours; the stars looked down dispassionately on the small and battered company lunging blindly forward in the darkness. I whooped mechanically at the camels till my voice went. The Turkis were imprecise about our programme, and we wished that we knew how much longer the ordeal would last.

It ended at half-past one in the morning. We had done two stages of more than seven hours each and the camels were dead beat. They slumped down in their tracks and we unloaded and lay down in the lee of the baggage, refreshing ourselves with the dregs of the last brandy bottle and a little salt water. Then we slept, sprawling like corpses on the iron-hard ground.

After two hours Tuzun woke us. Feeling stiff and stale, we made tea with the last of the water, loaded up, and moved off. Sunrise showed a discouragingly empty world; even the mountains were already lost behind the dust-haze which is chronic in the Tarim Basin. We stumbled muzzily on, uncomfortably aware that it would soon be very hot.

Presently we heard a kind of roaring sound. Kini, who had crossed the Kizil Kum and claimed to know something of deserts, said it was the wind in some sand dunes we could see to the north. Happily she was wrong; another half-mile brought us to the lip of a low cliff beneath which a wide stony bed was noisily threaded by the channel of the Cherchen Darya. We scrambled down and watered the animals in a current that was opaque with yellow silt and looked as thick as paint.

Tuzun spoke hopefully of reaching Cherchen that day, and we climbed out of the river-bed for the last lap. The sun was well up now; the heat seemed to us terrific and was in fact considerable. The world around us jigged liquidly in a haze. Before long we hit a bad belt of dunes about a mile wide. The soft sand was cruel going for tired animals; once Number Two lost his balance and collapsed sideways, and we had to unload him before he could rise. When we struggled out again on to hard desert there was not much life left in any of us. We crawled on for an hour or two, but the sun was pitiless and at last Tuzun called a halt on a little bluff above the river.

Here we lay up for five hours, and I disgraced myself by drinking a whole kettle of tea while Kini was bathing in the river. She came back so glowing and self-righteous that in the end I went and bathed too, wallowing in the swift khaki water and speculating lazily about Cherchen. Our ignorance, our chronic lack of advance information, must be unexampled in the annals of modern travel. We had neither of us, before starting, read one in twenty of the books that we ought to have read, and our preconceptions of what a place was going to be like were never based, as they usefully could have been, on the experience of our few but illustrious predecessors in these regions. Cherchen, for all we knew or could find out, might be a walled city, or a cluster of tents, or almost any other variation on the urban theme. This state of affairs reflected discreditably on us but was not without its compensations. It was pleasant, in a way, to be journeying always into the blue, with no Baedeker to eliminate surprise and marshal our first impressions in advance; it was pleasant, now, to be within one march of Cherchen and to have not the very slightest idea what Cherchen was going to look like.

We enjoyed the halt. The felt gave very little shade, and a light wind that had sprung up coated our somnolence with half an inch of sand; but at least we were no longer moving, no longer pressing forward. We dreaded – passionately but surreptitiously, as children dread the end of holidays – the imminent beginning of another night-march of indeterminable length.

At four o'clock, though it was still vindictively hot, we began to load up. The skeleton camels – whose thick wool now appeared, and was, anomalous but who had had no time to shed it – knelt and rose again not without protest. With far-fetched prudence, fearing an examination of our effects like the one in Lanchow, I removed from my bundled overcoat, which came from Samarkand and should properly have clothed a cavalry officer in the Red Army of the Soviet Union, buttons embossed with the hammer and sickle. At half-past four we started.

Men and animals moved groggily; this was our fourth stage in thirty-six hours, and even Tuzun, who had started fresh five days ago, showed signs of wear and tear. Very soon we came into dunes again; the animals floundered awkwardly and the march lost momentum. The camels showed signs of distress; one of the donkeys was dead lame and another, from sheer weakness, bowled over like a shot rabbit on a downhill slope. A kind of creeping paralysis was overtaking the expedition.

We knew that we were near Cherchen, but there comes a point, while you are suffering hardship or fatigue, when you cannot see beyond the urgent business of endurance. This point we had reached. We might have been a month's journey from our goal, instead of a very few hours, for all the difference that its proximity now made to us. We could no more think than we could see beyond the next ridge of dunes; our reprieve, no doubt, had been signed, but we were still in prison. Our minds told us that this was the last lap; but our hearts and our bodies could take only an academic kind of comfort from the assurance. We were absorbed in the task of finishing a difficult stage.

The sun began to set. The donkeys tottered along very reluctantly, and the tired camels wore that kind of dignity which you associate with defeat; it was clear that we should not make Cherchen that night. Then, suddenly, from the top of a high dune, my eye caught a strip of queer eruptions on the horizon to the north-west; the sky-line, for months either flat and featureless or jagged and stark, was here pimpled with something that did not suggest a geological formation. I got out my field-glasses. . . .

It was like spying on another planet. The green of the trees, with the approach of dusk, had turned a soft and bluish grey; but they were trees beyond a doubt – a deep, serried phalanx, pricked here and there with the lance-heads of tall poplars. For all that we had been expecting a phenomenon, it was incredible; we had grown so accustomed to the life of nomads in an empty winter world that we had not bargained for so concrete, so delightful an intimation of spring and domesticity. The peaceful and luxuriant silhouette before us suggested a kind of life to which we had over-long been strangers.

It seemed not far away; but even if it was as near as it looked we could not reach it before nightfall, and I objected on principle to entering a community of uncertain temper after dark and on empty stomachs. So we dropped down into the river-bed and made camp in the mosquito-haunted

236

tamarisk. We pitched the tent by moonlight, and it was one of the best camps of the journey. There was running water to wash in, and just the right blend of anxiety and self-satisfaction – just the right feeling that something good had been done and something crucial was about to happen – to make us at once complacent and alert. Also we needed sleep, of which we had had only two hours in the last forty.

CHAPTER IX

BRAVE NEW WORLD

NEXT morning, exactly four months after leaving Peking, we entered the oasis of Cherchen.

For two hours we slanted expectantly across the wide and sprawling river-bed. We could not keep our eyes off the wall of vegetation which crowned its further bank. It looked extraordinarily dense, like the jungle. We could see as yet no signs of human life: only this opulent but non-committal screen, concealing what? Concealing, it was certain, the arbiters of the expedition's fate, the outposts of the rebel Tungan armies. What would they take us for? How would they treat us? We had plenty of food for speculation.

But as we came in under the trees we ceased to speculate. Wonder and joy fell on us. I suppose that the earth offers no greater contrast – except that between land and sea – than the contrast between desert and oasis. We stepped clean out of one world into another. There was no phase of transition; we slipped into coolness and delight as smoothly and abruptly as a diver does. One moment we were stumbling in the open river-bed, plagued by glare and a grit-laden wind; the next we were marching down a narrow path under the murmurous protection of poplar and mulberry and ash.

Trees lined the path, which threaded a patchwork of neat little fields of hemp and rice and barley. Men of gentle appearance in white robes lent on their mattocks to watch us pass. Here and there an acquaintance of Tuzun's came forward with a soft cry of '*Yakshi kelde*'; hands were pressed, beards stroked, curious glances thrown at us. Everywhere water ran musically in the irrigation channels. A girl in a bright pink cap, washing her baby in a pool, veiled her face swiftly at the sight of infidels. Low houses with mud walls and wooden beams stood under the trees round courtyards half roofed over; women peered, or scuttled into the shelter of their doorways. A cock crowed. . . .

A cock crowed. The familiar sound, unheard for nearly three months, asserted definitively our return to a world where men had homes; we began to think gloatingly of eggs. I think it was the sounds that were, for me, the most vivid part of a strange and unforgettable experience. The wind in the leaves, the gurgling water, a dog barking, men calling to each other in the fields – these noises, and especially the wind in the leaves, changed the whole texture of our environment, filled the air with intimacy, evoked forgotten but powerful associations. Then a cuckoo called, lazily; the essence of the spring that we had missed, the essence of the summer that we had suddenly overtaken, were comprehended in its cry, and I had a vision of lawns picketed with great trees, young rabbits scampering into gorse, a wall of ivy loud with sparrows: a vision that the cuckoo made oddly substantial, oddly near.

We wound deeper into the oasis in a kind of trance. The gaunt camels strode ahead; the little echelon of donkeys followed patiently. Cynara, with Kini up, stepped delicately, twitching her ears and blowing down her nostrils; she had never seen a tree before and was gravely disconcerted by these monstrous growths.

Presently, for no apparent reason, we halted at a poor house where we were welcomed by friends or relations of Tuzun, who installed us on a dais in their courtyard and brought us bread and sour milk and unripe apricots, our first fruit since March. Half a dozen women flocked, giggling, to stare at Kini, and held animated debate upon her sex. Tuzun, with touching courtesy, presented her with a rose. He was an extraordinarily nice man, two days before I had given him an iron fire-place for which we had no further use, and ever since he had carried it, with true delicacy, on his back, refusing to burden our tired donkeys with something that was no longer ours.

Among the men there was much talk of an *aksakal*. The

word means 'white beard' and may be applied to any venerable head of a community; there had, for instance, been an aksakal at Bash Malghun. But it is also the official title given to the local agents of the British Consul-General in Kashgar, one of whom had formerly, as we knew, been stationed in every important oasis to deal with matters affecting the interests of British subjects – mostly traders from India – in the Province. We hardly expected, after two years of bloody civil war, to find a British aksakal as far afield as Cherchen; nor could I discover whether the aksakal into whose hands they proposed to deliver us was a British aksakal or just a local worthy. Still, here was a ray of hope from an unexpected quarter.

The leaves rustled in the wind, cuckoos called, the women chattered, and I fell inadvertently asleep. At noon they woke me for a meal of mien and boiled vegetables like tasteless radishes; then we loaded up again, said good-bye to these kindly people, and set off for the aksakal's house. It was thought unseemly that one of us should walk, and a donkey was procured for Kini. When we had gone a little way a man stepped out from the side of the road and offered me apricots in a wooden bowl. Cynara, taken aback by such spontaneous generosity, collapsed on her nose in the dust; she had not yet found her feet in civilization.

Presently we came to another branch of the river-bed, which split the oasis with a wide shallow depression. As we left the trees the fierce sun gave us a faint after-taste of the desert. In the muddy stream little boys bathed noisily, and a big herd of camels was grazing in the green pastures on its banks; plump and naked, like foreshortened caricatures of prehistoric monsters, they were a great contrast to our shaggy, Rosinantine beasts.

As we splashed through the river I saw in the distance two horsemen making upstream at full gallop; to ride so hard in this hot noon was surely . . .

Then I knew. As though it was part of a story read before and suddenly remembered, I knew that they were riding to cut us off. As they drew nearer I made out khaki uniforms.

A moment later we were hailed in Chinese. We halted. Tuzun looked glum.

The Tungans thundered up showily: an officer and a private soldier with a rifle. But it was the horses, not the men, who at first monopolized our attention. Shining like seals, with thick necks arched heraldically, they towered over us, two splendid Badakshani chargers from Afghanistan. We had forgotten that there existed in the world horses so large, so sleek, and so well-fed. They took our breath away. We gaped.

But not for long. The officer, who wore a little film-star moustache and held himself well, was asking us our business and identities. Switching on my Chinese technique, such as it was, I answered in gay and deprecating terms.

Oh no, we were not Russians. That was wholly incorrect. I was English, she was French. My humble name was Learned Engraver on Stone,[1] hers was Horse of International Goodwill. Here were our cards . . . My affair was the affair of Extra-Special-Correspondent-Officer to the Newspaper - For - The - Enlightened - Apprehension - of - Scholars. A great English newspaper. Had the Before-born heard of it? (The Thunderer's echoes rolled, alas, but faintly here; the Before-born's face looked blank and unimpressed.) We had come from Peking, a most strenuous journey. Now we were going to Kashgar, and after that to England. Our business? Oh, we were on a *yu li*, we were expeditionary persons. . . .

The word *yu li*, comprehending so many of the lunatic actions of foreigners who go of their own free will to uncomfortable places Beyond the Wall, was always a strong card to play; the officer's face, though still suspicious, grew less perplexed. Had we the correct passports?

'Why yes,' I cried, 'certainly we have the correct passports.' I gave a merry laugh at the mere idea that our papers might be out of order. 'We're for it,' I thought.

'We will go to the bazaar,' said the officer. 'Your passports must be examined.'

[1] Fu Lei-ming and Ma Ya-na. The Chinese characters which form my name are stamped on the binding of this book.

'But we were going to the house of the aksakal . . .'

'It is not safe. There are bandits on the road,' replied the officer mechanically.

The hackneyed excuse, threadbare and transparent from much use by generations of officials, brought home to me more vividly than anything else that our destinies were once more in Chinese hands. Smiling blissfully, and making apologetic jokes about my vile Chinese and our disreputable appearance in so fine a place, we moved off. Except Tuzun, all the Turkis who had been with us had melted unobtrusively away. The private soldier rode with his rifle across his saddle-bow and his eyes on us.

'I suppose we consider ourselves under arrest,' I said to Kini.

Kini supposed we did.

CHAPTER X

RULE BRITANNIA

DEVOUTLY hoping that the populace would take our escort for a guard of honour, we rode towards the bazaar, which is, as we discovered later, the semi-urban core of every oasis. We noticed with surprise and alarm that our captors wore armlets bearing the blue star of the Kuomintang and the designation '36th DIV'.[1] These were Central Government insignia, and we had imagined that the Tungans were independent of Nanking, who had certainly proclaimed them rebels; if, as now seemed probable, they were or wished to be considered loyal, our lack of a Nanking passport might prove to be no joke at all. We began to feel more and more apprehensive.

Presently we came to the bazaar. In the streets, twilit under their awnings of matting, commerce appeared to be at a standstill; there were few people about, and most of the shallow-fronted shops were closed with wooden shutters. Kini's donkey created a diversion by bolting suddenly sideways through a doorway, a manœuvre which was happily not misinterpreted by the escort. A little further on we reached our destination – a small covered courtyard surrounded by little rooms like cells. They were all locked up, and there appeared to be nobody in charge. The place might have been an inn or it might have been a prison; it was very probably – judging by subsequent experience – both. Our gear was unloaded and stacked in the yard, and the animals were stabled. We were told to hand over our

[1] Thanks to a favourable report by Lo Wen-kan, who flew up to the Province as 'Pacification Commissioner' in 1933 (see *One's Company*, p. 208), the Tungan armies were officially gazetted as the 36th Division of the Army of the Chinese Republic; and when their leader, Ma Chung-ying, was outlawed he was not, as far as I know, deprived of his command. The Tungans' real relations with Nanking are analysed in the chapters that follow.

passports and stay where we were. The officer vanished; we heard him galloping down the street.

Meanwhile the news of our arrival had spread, and soon a sea of curious faces was surging in the gateway. Skull-caps, turbans, hats edged with lambskin bobbed up and down in efforts to secure an uninterrupted view of what in most cases were the first white people they had ever seen. An oily and unpleasant Turki, who claimed to be the inn-keeper, made himself officious and slightly thinned the crowd by calling for volunteers to sweep out a room. To a few Tungan soldiers and to some of the Turkis who spoke Chinese we divulged, in a non-committal and abstracted manner, our identities and place of origin. Tuzun, loyal but embarrassed, clearly disliked the turn events had taken. I myself was terribly anxious about the passports. The crowd eddied and murmured. Swallows skimmed in and out under the roof. A rumour started that the aksakal was coming. An hour passed slowly.

Suddenly there was a clatter of hooves outside. The crowd parted respectfully, the officer strode in and, to my inexpressible delight, handed back our passports.

'Correct?' I said. He nodded brusquely and was gone. Our most recent passport – the one so grudgingly issued in Sining – had been chopped with a scarlet seal.

It was unaccountable. The Chinese are most meticulous about official documents; though military headquarters in Cherchen might have been ignorant of the necessity for a special Nanking passport, they must have seen that there was nothing about Sinkiang on the paper they had visaed, which merely authorized us to travel to Chinghai. The incident was unparalleled in my experience of Chinese bureaucracy; nor could it be explained on the supposition that nobody at headquarters could read or write, for beside the seal there was a line of characters. We only realized how lucky we had been when further down the road we were more than once held up by officials who justly pointed out that we had no business to be in Sinkiang at all, and who were disposed to override the Cherchen visa. If we had met one of them in Cherchen I suppose we should have been turned back.

For the moment, however, fate had smiled and all was well. An ineffectual young man with large, romantic eyes introduced himself in bad Chinese as a member of the aksakal's household; we learnt not only that his master was on his way to greet us but that he was indeed the British aksakal. While we waited we drank tea and ate bread with the more consequential of the curious, feeling *blasé* and rather flat now that uncertainty was temporarily at an end.

Presently the aksakal arrived, riding a fine horse with a handsome saddle-cloth and accompanied by a servant who led a second horse. He was a tall, venerable Afghan with a dignified carriage and a shrewd eye, who saluted us respectfully and seemed genuinely pleased to see us. He talked through his nose in Turki, Hindustani, and Afghan, but unfortunately not in Chinese; however, there were plenty of interpreters available, and we gathered that we were invited to his house. Once more the animals were loaded. Kini mounted the led horse and rode off at a brisk pace with the aksakal: I followed more slowly with the camels, Cynara being incapable of such a turn of speed.

It was an hour's ride from the bazaar to the aksakal's house. The wind had dropped and the dusk was very tranquil. Doves called. White-robed figures were drifting homeward through the fields, and the confidential murmur of their talk echoed pleasantly in ears attuned to desolation. Firelight showed ruddily in doorways. Perches for birds, which the Turkis erect on poles fifty feet high, graced homes where life was no longer a grim affair, where there was room for gentleness. Everything was in the sharpest possible contrast to our long bleak struggles on the uplands.

At last we came to the large new house which was to be our home for several days. A wall surrounded a garden of apricot trees and vines, and over a gateway in the wall there hung – home-made, unorthodox in design, but infinitely reassuring – no less an emblem than the Union Jack. I dismounted, gave Cynara to a servant, and entered premises owned, in the last analysis, by His late Majesty King George V.

PART SIX

THE DESERT ROAD

CHAPTER I

DIRTY WORK

POLITICS are tiresome things at the best of times; and for the ordinary reader the politics of Asia are particularly tedious and distasteful. Their relevance to his own destinies is non-existent or at best remote; and though we know that all men are brothers and that the peoples of the modern world are knit together in a great web of sympathy and understanding, we still find it impossible to be deeply stirred by things that happen to those fellow-beings whose skin is of a different colour from our own. Moreover, the politics of Asia are richly encrusted with polysyllables scarcely pronounceable and so similar in their outlandish unfamiliarity that the ordinary reader has the greatest difficulty in distinguishing between a place, a political leader, and a prevailing wind.

But this book is called *News from Tartary*, and the news we brought back was political news. If so far as our journey had a serious object, it was to find out what was happening in Sinkiang; and in so far as it had any justification, it was that we were able, when we came back, to throw light on a situation whose secrets had since 1933 been guarded jealously and with success. I therefore propose, whether you like it or not, to amplify the brief sketch of Central Asian politics which I drew at the beginning of this book.

Always excepting the at present unfashionable Ruritania, Sinkiang is the last home of romance in international politics. Intrigue, violence, and melodrama have long been native to the Province; and their development has of late been directed by extraneous forces along lines that are not without significance. If it is untrue to say that at least four Powers are watching with the keenest interest the present situation in Sinkiang, it is only untrue because the present situation in Sinkiang is practically impossible to watch.

The Province is at the best of times difficult of access, being surrounded on three sides by mountain ranges whose peaks run well over 20,000 feet, and on the fourth side by the Gobi and the wastes of Mongolia. But physical difficulties failed to deter either Marco Polo, approaching from the west, or – before him – Buddhist pilgrims like Hsuan Tsang, approaching from the east; and since their day, thanks to the geographers and the road and railway engineers, the physical difficulties have notably decreased. But Sinkiang does not encourage tourist traffic; like Ruritania she is, unless you are very lucky, accessible only on paper. Her destinies are being worked out by methods, and towards ends, which their manipulators are the reverse of anxious to advertise. Things have gone far enough in the Province to make it no longer necessary to gloss over the identity of those manipulators by referring to them, in a hallowed euphemism, as 'the agents of a Certain Power'. The U.S.S.R. cannot hope to disown indefinitely her policy in Chinese Central Asia.

Sinkiang is bigger than France. It consists of the Tarim Basin – 354,000 square miles, of which a good half is desert – and of the more fertile valleys of Ili and Dzungaria, lying north of the eastern ranges of the Tien Shan. The population, which has been variously estimated but is probably in the neighbourhood of two millions, consists of Turkis (who form about seventy per cent of the whole), Mongols, a few Kirghiz and Tadjiks, Tungans, and small communities of Chinese merchants, administrators, and soldiers; there has also, since the Bolshevik Revolution, been a scattered colony of 'White' Russians who in the past two years have – as will appear – more than earned their inverted commas.

The name Sinkiang (Hsin Chiang) means The New Dominion; but China has curious standards of novelty, and she originally conquered the Province in the first century B.C. Her hold however was not at that time firmly established, and successive waves of conquest – Huns, Tibetans, Mongols under Chinghis Khan and Tamerlane – ebbed and flowed over territory which was for centuries important because it carried the overland route between the West and the Far East, the great Silk Road. In the latter half of the eighteenth century the massacre of over a million of the inhabitants celebrated the more or less definitive reassertion of Chinese rule, and in spite of recurrent rebellions throughout the nineteenth century, culminating in the temporary domination of Kashgaria by the adventurer Yakub Beg, Sinkiang formed part of the Chinese Empire during the last 150 years of its existence.

Great Britain's interest in the Province is obvious from a glance at the map. Sinkiang, bounded on the west by Russia, on the north by Outer Mongolia (to-day, for all practical purposes, an integral part of the Soviet Union), and on the east by Inner Mongolia and North-West China, marches on the south with Tibet and British India. For centuries Indian merchants have crossed the Himalayan passes to trade with Kashgaria; and any major infringement by another Power of China's sovereign rights within Sinkiang must of necessity be viewed with concern, both from the economic and the strategic point of view, in Whitehall and Delhi.

At recurrent intervals throughout the last fifty years such an infringement has seemed to some inevitable, to few improbable, and to none impossible. Suspicion of Russia's designs in Chinese Central Asia was at the close of the last century profound and widespread. It is reflected in the late Lord Curzon's speeches; it is reflected in at least one of Rudyard Kipling's earlier poems; and it is reflected, above all, in the proceedings of the Pamir Boundary Commission, which in 1895 called into being that buffer corridor of Afghan territory which separates the British and the Russian frontiers. At the close of the last century and the beginning of this, explorers of all nationalities, and officers on leave who visited Chinese Turkistan in quest of shooting, were, if articulate at all, alarmist; in their view, the annexation to the Tsar's dominions of this farthest outpost of the Chinese Empire was neither uncertain nor long to be delayed. They are unanimous on the point.

They had reason to be. The Trans-Caspian Railway, spanning the deserts east of the Caspian Sea, pointed directly at the frontiers of Sinkiang; and those frontiers were constantly being violated by military reconnaissance parties, only a minority of which took the trouble to disguise themselves as scientific expeditions. The Russian Consul-General in Kashgar furnished with a heavy guard of Cossacks, bulked much larger in the eyes of the inhabitants than his British colleague, whose official status was ill-defined and whose consequent lack of a uniform was a sad handicap on Chinese official occasions. The Chinese garrison of the province was a garish and Gilbertian force, existing largely on paper and on opium; travellers of all sorts returned from Sinkiang convinced that Russia, having spied out the land, was only waiting for an opportune moment to follow up her economic penetration of the Province with territorial annexation.

There can be little doubt that they were right. But the opportune moment was postponed by the outbreak of the Russo-Japanese War in 1904. Sinkiang was reprieved; but only, as it then seemed, temporarily. By the end of the next decade a graph of Russian influence in the Province would have shown a steady upward curve. Its climb was once more halted by extraneous events; Germany declared war on Russia and Russia had perforce to shelve her ambitions in Central Asia. Then came the Bolshevik Revolution and the Civil War. The Tsar's troops, in their long grey coats, at last entered Sinkiang in force; but they came as refugees, not as conquerors – the half-starved, typhus-ridden relics of White Armies who followed leaders like Annenkov and Dutov into what they painfully and slowly learnt was not to be a temporary exile. Some of them found their way down through Kansu to the coast; others remained in the province, forming precarious colonies of which the most important were in the Ili district. The Tsarist consular officials stuck to their posts until those posts lost the last remnant of diplomatic status; then they too faded from the picture. Russian trade had ceased altogether, and Indian merchants found their business with Sinkiang soaring to undreamt-of heights. But in 1924 the Government of the Chinese Republic recognized the U.S.S.R., the Russian consulates were reopened, and the inevitable process of Russian economic domination of the Province began again. It has continued ever since and is to-day virtually complete.

The year 1928 marked a turning-point in the destinies of Sinkiang. General Yang Tseng-hsin, the Provincial Governor, was assassinated, by whose agency it is not known, at a banquet in Urumchi. (The province's traditions of hospitality are all its own, and the death-rate at banquets is appalling.) Yang had ruled the Province since he was installed in office after the Chinese Revolution in 1912. His firm and strictly traditional methods had maintained peace, if not prosperity, throughout his tenure of office, and his policy of splendid isolation had preserved the Province, not only from the contaminating effects of foreign influence, but even from the impact of those ideas and tendencies which the Chinese Revolution let loose in its attempt to transform one-fifth of the human race from a Confucian race into a modern democracy. Yang's sixteen years in office produced a curious kind of time-lag in the history of Sinkiang, and the chaos since his murder is, in part, merely a tardy but logical reproduction of the distressing phenomena witnessed throughout the rest of China a quarter of a century ago.

Yang's successor was Chin Shu-jen, an official whose rapacity was insufficiently supported by administrative talent. In 1931 he illegally contracted a secret loan with the Soviet Government, and is at the time of writing serving a sentence of three and a half years' imprisonment in a Nanking gaol on this and other serious charges.

CHAPTER II

THE RED ARMY LENDS A HAND

CHIN SHU-JEN was succeeded by the present *tupan*, General Sheng Shih-tsai. Sheng was originally a commander of no great distinction in the North Manchurian Armies of the Young Marshal, and in 1932 was driven by the pressure of the Japanese invasion across the frontier into Siberia. Here for a time he and his troops were hospitably 'interned' by the Soviet authorities; but in 1933 they reappeared on Chinese soil at Urumchi, where Sheng, on the flight of Chin, took over the governorship of Sinkiang. The tupan is a man of about forty, who studied in Japan; he is said to be not without ability and is popular with his troops. It would, however, be a mistake to regard him as anything but a puppet of the U.S.S.R.

He arrived at a critical moment. His predecessor's misrule had fallen particularly oppressively on the Khanate of Hami, where a Turki insurrection had been stiffened by an invasion of their co-religionists, the Tungans from North-West China; the tungans were commanded by Ma Chung-ying, a very remarkable young man whose mysterious destinies I will discuss later. Urumchi, the capital of Sinkiang, was threatened.

Sheng Shih-tsai's seizure of power had been supported, if not inspired, by the Russians. Soon after it took place Colonel Huang Mu-sung (who in the following year was to act as the Central Government's Envoy to Tibet) was sent into the Province from Nanking with the large and hopeful title of Pacification Commissioner. His reception was not cordial; three of his staff were executed in his presence on a trumped-up charge, and it is legitimate to suppose that the official confirmation of Sheng Shih-tsai in office – which was announced on Huang's return to Nanking – was the price paid by the Central Government for its emissary's life.

Sheng did not at that time seem destined to enjoy for long a respectability so resourcefully acquired; he was beset by embarrassments. The Tungan-Turki rebel forces from Hami had been repelled with the utmost difficulty, thanks chiefly to a force of some two or three thousand White Russian mercenaries who had enlisted in the service of the Provincial Government; throughout 1933 the situation in all parts of the province was complex, lurid, and obscure, and seemed likely to remain so indefinitely. At least four major parties were in the field, and the pattern of their conflicts and alliances is bewildering, particularly in the south-west of the Province. In the north the issue was relatively clear. In December 1933 the Tungans and Turkis under Ma Chung-ying were investing Urumchi. Sheng's garrison – mainly White Russians and Manchurian troops – was no match for the Tungans, who fight as wantonly as weasels and whose Turki allies were crusading for their civil rights and their religion. Left to itself, the capital must have fallen.

But it was not left to itself. Earlier in the year Sheng had contracted a secret loan with the Government of the U.S.S.R., whereby (I believe) the Provincial Government received 500,000 gold roubles, a large supply of arms and ammunition, and several aeroplanes manned by Soviet pilots; in return for this the Russians secured a lien on certain of the natural products of Sinkiang. (They have, for instance, a monopoly of the valuable trade in unborn lamb-skins.) The riches of the Province are considerable, and wool, hides, sheep, and perhaps gold may be presumed to have figured in the agreement, whose less strictly economic clauses included, to judge by subsequent events, provisions for the construction of roads leading into the province from Chuguchak, Kuldja, and Irkishtan near Kashgar; the appointment of Soviet 'advisers' to key positions throughout the military and civil organization of the Province; and (perhaps) the eventual construction of a railway to link Urumchi with the Turksib.

In view of the existence of this loan, it was as natural that Sheng should appeal to the U.S.S.R. in his hour of need as that the U.S.S.R. should respond to his appeal. Early in January 1934 the Tungan forces beleaguering Urumchi were taken in the rear by Urumchi's creditors – a force of several thousand Soviet troops advancing from the west and supported by aeroplanes, armoured cars, and possibly light tanks. On the banks of the frost-bound Tutung River, thirty miles west of Urumchi, a battle raged for several days; but the Tungans' unskilled ferocity was no match for a mechanized foe, and the troops – who were all peasants from parts of China as yet but little inured to the blessings of modern civilization – were badly demoralized by gas-bombs dropped by the Soviet airmen. Ma Chung-ying withdrew in good order westward along the main road to Kashgar.

It may strike the reader as curious, even in these scrap-of-paper days, for the military forces of one Power to engage in hostilities on territory belonging to another Power without either Power saying anything to the other before or after the event. But Urumchi is a long way away, and there were no witnesses – no witnesses, at any rate, who could not be arbitrarily imprisoned like the two Germans and the Swede of whom mention has been made already. The illusions entertained by Europe concerning the ideals of the Soviet Union were preserved without difficulty from shock.

In Kashgar an 'Independent Moslem Republic of Eastern Turkistan' had meanwhile been set up. Its ideals were Pan-Islamic but woolly, its politics were anti-Nanking and anti-Soviet, its leaders were either mediocrities or adventurers, and it lasted about two months. It would hardly have been worth mentioning if it had not attracted at the time a certain amount of attention in the European Press. The sequence of events which brought it thus briefly into being is too complex to unravel here; it originated in a fanatical Turki insurrection in Khotan, inspired and led by three mullahs who shed an intolerable deal of blood to their

256

pennyworth of Pan-Islamic achievement. Throughout 1933 both the Old and the New City of Kashgar (they are about six miles apart) had changed hands repeatedly but seldom simultaneously; their successive conquerors, moreover, changed sides so often that it is profitless to fish for history in such troubled waters.

By the summer of 1934 Sheng Shih-tsai's authority was, thanks to Soviet aid, established firmly at Urumchi, and more or less firmly over the whole of northern Sinkiang. The focus of interest shifts westward to Kashgar, of which, and of Yarkand, Ma Chung-ying and the Tungan armies were by the end of June the undisputed masters. But the forces of the Provincial Government were advancing down the main road by way of Aksu and Maralbashi, and Ma put his troops at Kashgar in a posture of defence from which it is probable that further Soviet military assistance would have been needed to dislodge them. His men were confident and reasonably well armed. But it had been noticed during the past few weeks that their commander had been visiting the Soviet Consulate-General with greater frequency than mere etiquette demanded; the bazaar was full of speculations, the more sensational of which were fulfilled when on July 5th he suddenly ordered an evacuation in the direction of Yarkand and two days later, with a small bodyguard and without a word of explanation, took the road which leads over the passes into Russian territory. He travelled with the Secretary of the Soviet Consul-General, who happened, it seems, to be going that way himself.

The situation produced by Ma's departure has, broadly speaking, obtained ever since. The Tungan armies control the string of oases along the south of the Takla Makan, between and including Charklik in the east and Khargalik in the west; between Khargalik and Yarkand a kind of informal demilitarized zone separates them from their enemies. The rest of the province is under the Provincial Government of Urumchi. Sheng Shih-tsai's power rests, outwardly, on the Provincial Army, a force of some twenty to thirty thousand rifles, comprising Manchurian, Turki, and White Russian elements. The White Russian contingent, upwards of 2000 strong, is easily the best of the lot. The epithet 'White' must, however, be accepted with reserve; although most of the men entered the province as Tsarist refugees, each unit to-day looks to the U.S.S.R. for its orders as well as its arms. All ranks have been liberally diluted with Soviet agents; and since the fate of the Whites depends on the Provincial Government (which could, for instance, deport them back to Russia at a moment's notice), and since the Provincial Government is entirely controlled by the Reds, Tsarist sympathies are a luxury which they can no longer afford. A large part of the White Russian colony fled from Sinkiang during the civil war; those who stayed have had to change the colour of their politics.

At Urumchi, where Soviet influence is strongest and most apparent, Sheng Shih-tsai and the heads of the Provincial Government go through the motions of administration, and a 'People's Council', on which sit representatives of the various races included in the population of the province, provides a façade of democratic enlightenment and potentially breaks the ice for Sovietization. But – always excepting the Soviet Consulates at Kashgar and Urumchi – the only powers in the land are the Russian civil and military 'advisers'. Every department, every regiment, is in effect directed by a Soviet agent occupying a key position; the Province is run from Moscow. Communism of a sort is being preached (partly by renegade mullahs), but neither intensively nor with much success. The Turki schools, hitherto almost entirely religious in character, now perforce offer a rudimentary political training, and some hundreds of the children of officials are annually sent to be educated, free of charge, in Tashkent, thus providing their Soviet benefactors with an ideological hold on the rising generation in Sinkiang and (scarcely less valuable) with hostages against the docile behaviour of their parents the officials.

The Russians have opened a military academy and an aviation school at Urumchi. Confiscation of land and property takes place, but not – except in the case of shrine and school lands – systematically. Several of the wealthy Turkis who were unable to leave the Province during the civil war have disappeared or been imprisoned without trial; few of those who retain their lives and their liberty have managed also to retain their wealth. The chief instrument of internal policy is a powerful force of secret police, modelled on the G.P.U. and answering for its actions – like the G.P.U. – to none of the recognized authorities. The frontiers of Kashgaria are controlled by a much-dreaded band of levies, mainly Kirghiz, who are known as the 'Tortinjis' (the Fourth Regiment); most of this formidable rabble are citizens of the Soviet Republic of Kazakstan, across the border, and they are employed by the powers that be when the situation calls for a more than ordinary degree of violence and illegality. Of the powers that be – the Russian advisers – I know little at first hand. General Rubalkov, in effect the ruler of Kashgaria, is remarkable chiefly for his beard and his reticence; like General Bektiev, who in 1935 was commanding the garrison of 1200 Russian mercenaries at Maralbashi, he is ostensibly 'White'.

CHAPTER III

RUSSIA RACKETEERS

Moscow's ultimate aims in Sinkiang remain obscure, though that will not prevent me from discussing them. The most significant of her immediate aims is reflected by the persistent underhand campaign which is being waged by the provincial authorities against British interests. There are some 500 British Indian subjects resident in the Province. For centuries caravans have struggled over the 18,000 foot passes of the Karakorum, carrying merchandise between India and Kashgaria. In recent years the palmiest days of the Indian trade were the period immediately after the Russian Revolution, when, with competition temporarily paralysed, the annual volume rose to over ten million rupees. In 1935 our trade had shrunk to about a twentieth of that figure. This was partly due, of course, to the exceptionally chaotic conditions of 1933–34, but chiefly to an inevitable process – the economic domination of Sinkiang by Russia.

This process was greatly accelerated by the construction, in 1931, of the Turksib Railway, which flanks the frontier of the province at a distance, in many places, of only a few score miles; the pioneering glamour with which, in Russia, the completion of this line was sedulously surrounded faded very quickly, but in justice I must admit that on it ran the only train I have ever met with in the Soviet Union that arrived on time. The Turksib only serves to underline the inescapable geographical advantages which Russia enjoys in relation to Sinkiang. Compare the distances and the facilities for traversing them. By rail and road Moscow is less than a fortnight from Kashgar. The nearest railhead in India, on the other hand, is five or six weeks away, and the Himalayan passes are open for less than half the year. As for China, three months is fast going for a caravan from

Peking to Urumchi, and conditions on the lorry-route from railhead at Sian are adequately indicated in some of my earlier chapters.

In the circumstances it is not surprising that to-day every bazaar in the Province is flooded with cheap Russian goods and that several large trade agencies are maintained there by the Government of the U.S.S.R. For the last two years trade with China, by way of either Kansu or Mongolia, has been virtually at a standstill owing to the disturbances. Political interference has reduced trade with India to a trickle. The Russian goods, though plentiful, are of poor quality, and there is a constant though at present small demand for luxury commodities such as high-grade velvet, muslin, and cloth. This demand Russia cannot satisfy as yet, and in 1935, in her efforts to monopolize the market, she was actually importing British goods into the province via Moscow and Tashkent.

Other and less legitimate methods were being employed. Caravans from India were forced to pay duty three times between the frontier and Kashgar. All British traders, ingoing and outcoming, were subjected to countless inconveniences by the customs and police. This was the sort of thing that was happening: A merchant collects his caravan in Kashgar and applies for passports (formerly unnecessary) for himself and his men. Days pass. The British Consul-General makes repeated representations to the authorities, but by the time the passports are issued half the merchant's potential profits on the journey have gone in feeding men and ponies in enforced idleness. And he will be held up at least once more, arbitrarily, indefinitely, and without appeal, before he crosses the frontier into India. Meanwhile caravans entering or leaving Soviet territory meet with no bureaucratic obstacles of this kind and pay no duty.

British trade with Sinkiang is not, and never can be, of very great volume. But it has always existed and, given a chance, will continue to exist. The British Government has in the past been at some pains to protect the interests of its nationals engaged in this trade ever since Queen Victoria

261

sent a Mission under Sir Douglas Forsyth to the upstart Yakub Beg in Kashgar. British prestige stands high in Sinkiang and, trade apart, we should lose a lot of face in Eastern Asia if we were to give way before pressure which, as all Turkistan knows, is being brought to bear on our interests in Sinkiang at the instigation of a foreign Power and by illegal methods.

In the autumn of 1935, just after we had left Sinkiang, the British Government sent a Trade Mission to Urumchi in the hope of negotiating a commercial agreement which would put an end to anti-British discrimination. In September Sir Eric Teichman, the Chinese Councillor of the British Legation in Peking, set out across Mongolia with two lorries and half a dozen servants and reached Urumchi without serious mishap after an adventurous journey. There he was met by Colonel Thomson-Glover, our Consul-General in Kashgar. The British representatives were fêted effusively in Sheng Shih-tsai and his provincial authorities and were given a number of assurances which, if implemented, would have remedied completely the current abuses. The Mission then travelled on to Kashgar, and Sir Eric completed his journey to India (for he was going home on leave) by crossing the Himalayas as far as Gilgit in mid-winter, which would have been a remarkable feat in a very much younger man.

He travelled valiantly but in vain; or so it seems at the time of writing. Not one of the promises made by the Provincial Government has been kept; and protests to this effect are merely ignored. British trade suffers from disabilities as great as, if not greater than, those which oppressed it when we were in the Province; and the difficulties which beset Great Britain's representative in Kashgar have been cunningly increased. Russia, though she can have no valid motives for doing so, is bent on getting us out of Sinkiang.

CHAPTER IV

THE NEW IMPERIALISTS

To analyse, even conjecturally, Soviet aims in Sinkiang is not easy. It must be admitted that there is some reason to doubt whether those aims have been clearly formulated at all. The part which the U.S.S.R. is playing in Chinese Central Asia is being played behind the scenes. Her activities are clandestine; they are publicly disavowed by Moscow and not more than barely suspected by the world at large. It is natural in human beings to fear the unknown and, fearing it, to overestimate its power, as well as its will, to harm. Anyone who works behind the scenes is *de facto* assumed to be working, with abnormal efficiency, on some deep-laid plan. This may be so with Russia; but in the Soviet Union plans, however deep-laid, have a tendency to produce results surprising to all concerned, and a policy directed by a highly centralized, half-trained bureaucracy and developing in the territory of a foreign Power may be less darkly potent than its cloak of secrecy suggests. I have a strong suspicion that Russia does not really know what she is up to in Chinese Central Asia, and that her activities there are guided, to an even greater extent than Japan's activities in North China and Mongolia, by opportunism.

She has secured almost complete economic domination over a territory which is larger than France and parts of which are very rich. Sheng Shih-tsai and the Provincial Government at Urumchi are her puppets, and through them and through her agents she in effect exerts political control over more than four-fifths of Sinkiang. What more does she want?

She has not, as a matter of fact, got very much, though it sounds a lot. Official trade returns, which only show monetary results, do not give a clear picture of the situation; the provincial bank-notes are practically worthless, and a substantial proportion of Soviet-Sinkiang trade takes place by a process of large-scale barter. Nevertheless, the official figures are interesting. They show that in 1933 – the peak year – the volume of Russian trade with Sinkiang was just under thirty million gold roubles; that in 1934 it had shrunk, presumably owing to the civil war, to a third of that figure; and that, even at its high 1933 level, the Sinkiang trade represented only 3·5 per cent of Russia's total foreign trade.

The commodities with which Sinkiang supplies the U.S.S.R. are useful but not indispensable. Moreover, the trade returns do not tell the whole story, or anything like it. Invisible exports from Russia are a large item in the accounts; they include the cost of maintaining two heavily staffed consulates and several big trade agencies, as well as lavish expenditure on the manifold activities which come under the heading of 'secret service' – agents' salaries, bribes to the agents of agents, and so on. In 1935 there could be little doubt that Russia was spending more on Sinkiang than she was getting out of it.

It has been suggested – more loudly in Japan than elsewhere – that the people of Sinkiang will in the near future be seized with an uncontrollable desire to declare themselves an Autonomous Soviet Socialist Republic, and as such will be graciously accorded the privilege of affilia-tion to the U.S.S.R. This card would be an easy one to play, but does not at the moment look like a trump. The spreading of Communist doctrine does not appear to figure prominently on the Soviet agenda in Sinkiang; the whole affair is being managed – not, like the Communist move-ment in China, by the Comintern – but the Foreign Office in Moscow. Propaganda is not intensive and there are few signs that the ground is being broken for Sovietization.

Moreover, the wisdom of emerging, in however altruistic a guise, from behind the scenes is questionable at a time when the U.S.S.R. is wooing world opinion and the Soviet delegates at Geneva are all dress shirts and enlightenment. The Japanese in particular are highly suspicious of Russian designs in a region towards which their own Mongolian ambitions are drawing them, and any overt consolidation of the Soviet position in Sinkiang might provoke Japan beyond endurance, which in 1935 was the last thing Russia wanted to do. By bringing her activities in Sinkiang to a head and publicly labelling the result with a hammer and sickle she would incur the responsibility of answering awkward questions at home without effectually increasing her power in Central Asia.

The situation as it stood in 1935 ought to suit Russia well enough for a time. She can do, and does, almost as she likes in Sinkiang. The Nanking Government, partly as a result of blackmail and partly to save its face, has confirmed Sheng Shih-tsai in office as Governor of the Province; his most unconstitutional actions can incur no severer penalty than a volley of telegraphic rebukes, and to these he has already shown himself blandly impervious. At a more opportune moment Nanking might reassert her authority over Sinkiang by force; but in 1935 the military energies of the Chinese Republic were monopolized by a running fight with the Communist armies, and under the pressure of Japan's steadily increasing truculence the Central Government had scant opportunity to devise and undertake an expensive side-show in the Central Asian deserts. Russia had a free hand.

I have tried to show how she was using it in 1935; but the situation then obtaining was too unreal to endure indefinitely, and once more we come up against the riddle of her ultimate aims. In Tsarist days the bogey of a Russian military threat to India loomed large to the more romantically minded British statesmen. But even in the unlikely event of the U.S.S.R. being minded to invade India it is apparent to all who know the Himalayan passes that they could be held by a handful of men. Moreover, conditions on the two bottle-neck routes between Sinkiang and India are such that the infiltration of undesirables for propaganda purposes can be checked without the slightest difficulty.

Control of Sinkiang would, on the other hand, give Russia direct contact (for what it is worth) with the uninhabited 20,000 foot uplands which form the northern bastions of the Tibetan Plateau, and it would be possible for Buryat or Outer Mongolian agents to reach Lhasa with the Mongol pilgrim caravans which annually march southward from the Tsaidam. But I hardly feel that anxiety to swell the serried ranks of gods at Lhasa with a few busts of Stalin can be taken as a guiding motive in Soviet foreign policy.

No; it seems probable that the Kremlin's readaptation of the old Tsarist policy in Chinese Central Asia is less purely expansionist than the original. Russia, though she may contemplate in the future more distant and ambitious objectives, is at present jockeying for position *vis-à-vis* Japan. Japan's triumphantly illicit progress through Inner Mongolia is turning the flank of Outer Mongolia and will soon bring her influence up against the frontiers of Sinkiang, which in 1935 was probably the only corner of Chinese territory where her agents were not at work. Moscow could reasonably argue that Soviet 'advisers' at Urumchi to-day are the alternative to a branch of the Kwantung Army's Military Mission tomorrow. Strategically, Sinkiang is not of the first importance in a clash between Japan and Russia – unless of course it were controlled by the former; but the roads which are now being built to Russia's orders, the airfield at Urumchi, and perhaps eventually a railway connecting that city with the Turksib, will enhance its value in the event of war. Of far greater significance, however, is the fact that Sinkiang commands the main avenue into North-West China.

The north-western provinces of China, though much more than nominally controlled by Nanking, are remote from her direct influence and will be still further isolated by Japanese expansion into North China. With Sinkiang as a base, Communist doctrine in time of peace, and Soviet troops in time of war, could follow the Old Imperial Highway into Kansu, to the confusion of Japan and the further confusion of China. In 1935 the Chinese Communist Armies operating in Szechwan and the Tibetan borderlands were reported to be making for Sinkiang. Such reports should be treated with reserve. Hungry and not certainly controllable hordes of soldiery, however staunch their Marxism, would not at present be welcomed by the Soviet authorities in a Province which is already overmilitarized and where mutinies of unpaid troops are of regular occurrence. Moscow does not want her stormy petrels to come home to roost; she would, one imagines, prefer to keep them elsewhere in Chinese territory and to resume, as opportunity arises, those supplies of arms and money which were interrupted in 1931. This might be done from Sinkiang.

Whether her object be mischief-making or self-defence (it is presumably, in the last analysis, both) the value of Sinkiang to Russia lies in its situation *vis-à-vis* North-West China. And now the Tungans come into the picture. The Tungan armies, as I have said before, were in 1935 established in the oases south of the Takla Makan on a line extending from Charklik to Khargalik. Their effective strength is probably in the neighbourhood of 15,000 rifles, but they could put into the field a very much larger force of auxiliaries armed with swords. About 80 per cent of the regular troops are cavalry, extremely well mounted; there are several machine guns and a few light cannon. The units are officered by Tungans, but in some a majority of the rank and file are Turkis. The Tungans, who are born fighters, keep their troops intensively trained and undoubtedly constitute the most formidable fighting force in the Province.

In 1935 the rebel armies were commanded by Ma Ho-san, an energetically young man of twenty-two, with his headquarters at Khotan. His diplomatic position was somewhat anomalous. He proclaimed his allegiance to Nanking and, in the absence of telegraphic or postal facilities, had sent an emissary to the Central Government, 2000 miles away, reiterating his loyalty and asking for assistance (which he will not get) in his struggle against Soviet influence. Although the Tungans are unlikely to be reconciled to the Provincial Government, their defeat before Urumchi shook their morale, and the

Soviet aeroplanes and gas bombs in particular had a demoralizing effect. But Ma Ho-san was vowing vengeance against Sheng Shih-tsai and his Russian backers, and had already worked out the strategy of his next campaign.

Meanwhile the future of the whole Tungan cause remains uncertain for a reason already referred to. Ma Chung-ying, the twenty-five-year-old leader of the original Tungan invasion and half-brother to Ma Ho-san, was blandished across the Soviet frontier in 1934 and has not re-entered Chinese territory since. From Moscow he corresponds at intervals with his half-brother at Khotan, and the contents of his letters are sufficiently reassuring for extracts from them to be read out to the troops; exactly how spontaneous these effusions are it is of course impossible to judge, but at any rate they are signed with his personal seal. The form of internment to which he is being subjected by the Soviet authorities includes an honorary commission in the Red Army and the uniform of a cavalry officer. Khotan expects him to return.

Whether he will or not remains to be seen. At present he is being kept in Moscow as a kind of hostage-cum-stalking-horse through whom, if Tungan sympathies cannot be won to the Soviet cause, Tungan antipathies can at least be kept in check. What promises lured him into Russia nobody knows, but his personality certainly deserves a more active role than that of hostage. His face is great thoughout the Moslem communities of North-West China. In addition to Ma Ho-san, Ma Bu-fang, who has already figured in this narrative as the Military Governor of Chinghai, is his half-brother, and in 1935 an embassy from Ma Bu-fang visited Khotan under sealed orders. There is the makings of a formidable Moslem triumvirate in the three Mas.

At present Sheng Shih-tsai makes an admirable puppet at Urumchi; but the time may come when Russia needs something more positive than a puppet to further her designs, and then, it may be, Ma Chung-ying will return from exile. The standard of Moslem revolt has often been raised, with bloody consequences, by the Tungans in North-West China; and if Russia wants it raised again she may congratulate herself on having secured the services of the best of all possible standard-bearers.

CHAPTER V

CHERCHEN

SUCH was the abstruse and uncertain situation into which we had, not without difficulty, plunged.

Cherchen – except for Charklik, perhaps the most isolated of the oases bordering the Takla Makan – was once used by the Chinese as a penal settlement; to us it suggested, not Devil's Island, but the Promised Land. We spent five days there, lodged on a wilderness of carpets in a room which had something of the decorative impermanence of a film set. On the evening of our arrival we received from the local commander of the Tungan garrison a present of four chickens and a basket of eggs; these laid for ever the ghost of our anxiety. We ate a huge meal of eggs and slept – a little uneasily for all our fatigue – under the obscurely irksome shelter of a roof.

A sedentary interlude ensued, freely punctuated by meals and, between the meals, by snacks. There was usually food of some sort within reach – flat rounds of bread, or lumps of Russian sugar – and, except during short post-prandial periods, we could not keep our hands off it. All the accumulated hunger of four months revived and shamed us. Bestial still in this respect, we grew refined in others. We washed extensively, and I shaved, and Kini cut my hair with all the usual feminine enthusiasm and much more than the usual feminine skill. Sitting at a rickety, anomalous, but thoughtfully provided table, we wrote home letters which were no longer letters of farewell; smug if not vainglorious in tone, they predicted our return in three or four months' time. They were the sort of letters that anyone who wished us well would have been delighted to receive after so long a silence, but unfortunately they were intercepted – I do not know by whom – and we beat them back to Europe with three weeks in hand. They read very sillily in London.

One of our five days in Cherchen was devoted to official visits. There appeared to be two officers concurrently holding the title of Ssu Ling, or Commander-in-Chief, and we called impartially on both of them, consuming huge quantities of tea sweetened with Russian sugar and smoking Russian cigarettes. One Ssu Ling – said to be a Tibetan and probably in fact a half-caste – was a vague, willowy man with a little moustache who appeared to cut but little ice. The other was an effective, disillusioned young officer with a cruel incisive mouth, very staccato in his speech; he received us on a carpet-covered dais in an un-Chinese yamen, haunted by lounging soldiers whose grubby white undress uniforms were crowned incongruously by flaccid sun-hats. We called also on the civil authority, a kind of mayor who was, as in most of the oases, a Turki; he was out, but a captive lynx, graceful and *farouche*, paced an enclosure in his courtyard and stamped the visit on my memory.

The bazaar, as is usual in Sinkiang, was only busy on one day in the week. (Bazaars were a recognized landmark in the calendar. 'Stay till the next bazaar,' the aksakal was always urging us.) While we were there the market was sluggish. Half the shops were closed, for a military occupation had strangled commerce with arbitrary seizures and exactions. The few shops that were open were booths like shallow cupboards, whose shelves were littered with cheap Russian goods, negligibly diluted by Japan, Central Europe, Manchester, and India. Except that it was (being remote) ill-stocked, the Cherchen bazaar offered a fair reflection of international trade rivalries throughout the Province: Russia first, and the rest nowhere.

We fell with avidity on the shreds of rumour and gossip that were current in the cool courtyards and the little dark rooms. A kind of independence movement had just been suppressed at Charklik and more than a hundred people executed; the family of the Turki leader had been sent to Khotan as hostages. An embassy of eleven men had passed through on its way from Sining to Khotan, travelling the desert road via Tunghwang. A photograph of the mysterious Ma Chung-ying, with Russian writing underneath, was in circulation somewhere. Hami was not yet wholly under Soviet influence . . . We had been so long starved of news that we devoured and digested these abstruse and unreliable scraps with the greatest possible zest.

The aksakal was a charming and considerate host. Though he was five weeks' journey from Kashgar and had never, in all his long life, seen any of the Consuls who had been successively his superiors, and though he had never set foot on British soil, he was full of a snobbish but touching loyalty to the Empire whose interests he served. Of the very few white men he had met the one he liked best to talk about was Ishtin Sahib, a superhuman figure whom, after initial perplexity, we identified as Sir Aurel Stein. All through the southern oases this great explorer is still spoken of with respect and admiration.

We discovered that we needed rest; but we did not get very much. The wonders of our medicine chest were unluckily bruited abroad, and almost from the moment of our arrival we had to cope with an unending stream of patients. It started with no less a person than the more important of the two military commanders. Braying trumpets heralded his tempestuous arrival at the head of a troop of horse. They swept up jangling in a cloud of dust, and the whole bodyguard came in to marvel at our typewriters and the little gramophone. They were heavily though heterogeneously armed and had brought with them, for purposes of pomp, an old and portly machine-gun on a pack-horse.

Their rifles were interesting, as indeed were all unrudimentary possessions in this ill-provided part of the world. Here everything that was not of local manufacture had a history behind it, a long itinerary and an outlandish pedigree of owners; you could weave romance for hours on and round a tattered jacket of European cut or a tin bearing the name of a firm in a distant city.

The Tungans' weapons were a motley lot. One was a Winchester ·303, an old sporting model and clearly the legacy of an expedition. There was an ancient Japanese service rifle, several Snyders, a German rifle (1890), and a Lee-Enfield from the Indian frontier very approximately dated by the initials VR. But the most intriguing of all was a Remington marked 1917 and stamped clumsily with the double eagle of Imperial Russia; I saw these hybrid weapons elsewhere in Sinkiang[1] and presume that they were supplied by the Americans to White forces during the Siberian intervention.

The Tungan commander was suffering from rupture; we could only give him some ointment and hope for the best, but several of the bodyguard were successfully dosed and disinfected. After they had clattered off, trumpeting erratically, the commonalty began to invade us. For four out of the five days we were in Cherchen we had hardly an unbroken hour of leisure. Beseeching and diffident they came. There would be a delay while someone who spoke Chinese was sent for, then the familiar catechism would start: 'What sort of illness? Head? Legs? Belly? Is it or is it not the hot-cold illness? This illness, how many years? Can you sleep? Can you eat? . . .' and usually after a certain amount of prodding on our part and whimpering on theirs, the reluctant formula, dashing their high hopes, 'For that kind of illness we have no oil.'

Occasionally there was an obvious malingerer, more occasionally there was a droll, and once we were visited by the young wife of an official who was every inch the *malade imaginaire* with the grand manner – smoking cigarettes in a long holder, contrasting her home in Peking with the barbarous rusticity of Cherchen, smoothing her sheath-like dress with delicate fingers while she squatted on the carpets. But mostly it was a grim business. There was no doctor in the oasis, no doctor (it was said) nearer than the Swedish Mission in Yarkand, more than three weeks' journey to the west. We were their only hope, and in nine cases out of ten we could do nothing for them. Their eyes reproached us.

[1] They are also, according to Mr G. N. Roerich, to be found in North Tibet.

Old men, bowed or limping, rehearsed in quavering voices the long history of their ailments. Children with frightful skin diseases endured Kini's ministrations with uncomprehending apathy. Veiled women in timid, anxious twos and threes, wearing black robes frogged heavily with green across the front, offered the wasted, featherweight bodies of their infants and wept when we shook our heads. One, when we called her forward, drew back her veil and revealed, not a face, but a raw, featureless expanse of flesh; they explained that she had fainted and fallen forward into the fire two days before.

The worst of it was that they would not believe that we were powerless, that our scanty and depleted stock of medicines did not contain a panacea for all ills. They wept and whined and went away thinking us cruel or miserly or both. To those with malaria we could at least give quinine, and to those with sores disinfectant and hygienic advice; but the great majority were beyond the small scope of our knowledge and supplies. Thus arose a problem. Was it fair to raise their hopes by giving them some quite irrelevant pill (for as long as they got something they went away content)? Or would their eventual disillusionment be crueller than a blank refusal on the spot? In the end we decided that there was probably no harm in giving them a longer lease of hope, and doled out to all comers little packets of four or five Jintan pills. Jintan is a Japanese product, very popular in China and potent (according to the advertisements) against the whole gamut of disease; the pills, silver in colour and microscopic in size, appear to be harmless. Twenty is a minimum dose, but we only had two small bottles; so our little packets had a purely symbolical value.

CHAPTER VI

THIRST

MEANWHILE preparations for the next stage of our journey were going forward. Animals had, according to a custom universal throughout Sinkiang, to be procured from the mayor; ours had been ordered, and the date of departure was fixed for June 19th. The rate of hire was a cheap one, since silver was at a premium and for one dollar you could get between twenty-five and thirty of the local notes, which were printed in Khotan on coarse paper.

Aziz was the name of the man who was in charge of the animals and who would guide us. He was an obsequious and ingratiating Turki, neither particularly efficient nor particularly honest, but recommended by his command of bad Chinese. He always addressed me, in a whining suppliant's voice, as '*Ta jen*', a polite term much used in the Moslem parts of China; it means 'Great Man'. He wore a black three-cornered hat and a rusty bottle-green coat tied round the waist with a scarf which might have been a dirty tricolour; thus clad, he looked, as he slouched along, like a minor and unsympathetic character in a play about the French Revolution.

I told him we were leaving on the 19th, and he promised to make the necessary arrangements. But on the evening of the 18th he came cringing to announce that he had been unable to buy maize for the donkeys; he was a Charklik man, he said, a stranger in Cherchen, and nobody would sell him what he wanted. Would the Great Man be so good as to postpone departure for one day . . .?

The Great Man had no choice but to do so; but by the afternoon of the following day Aziz was still tearfully maizeless. I abused him, gave him my card, and told him to go and get what we needed from military headquarters.

This plan worked, and on the morning of the 20th we were ready to start.

With the greatest difficulty we had prevailed on the old aksakal to accept a pair of field-glasses (second-hand), an electric torch, and a fountain pen in return for his hospitality. He was a kindly and a charming man, and it was with real regret that we said good-bye to him in the last pool of shade on the edge of the oasis. Then we rode out into the desert, where the heat came up and hit us like a wind.

We had meant to sell Cynara and the two camels in Cherchen, but though we were not asking much for them we found no purchaser; so we decided to take them with us, unloaded, as far as Keriya, which was the next important oasis and where the tone in transport animals was reputed to be firmer. On the march they were led by Tuzun Ahun. This aloof, silent, and apparently prosperous young man – who is not to be confused with the Tuzun from Bash Malghun – had been attached to us by the Cherchen authorities, in what capacity we were never able to discover. He made it clear that he led the camels, not because it was his duty, but as a favour to us; and at halts he never helped with the animals or the loading. He rode a dun stallion, richly caparisoned.

Four donkeys carried our effects, and a fifth carried Kini; we had only been able to secure one horse. He was, however, a very good horse by our standards – a showy chestnut stallion with Afghan blood in him who looked rather like most of the horses that you see performing prodigies on the films. I bagged him unscrupulously from Kini, and found it a joy to have a mount so full of vigour and so easy in his paces. Alas, I only had him for one day.

All we knew about the stages ahead of us was that there were nine of them before you reached the next oasis, and after that three more to Keriya, where there was another *aksakal*. June and July are not good months to travel the Takla Makan, and we had a certain dread of the desert. At first, however, it seemed less naked, though not less desolate, than we had expected. The great writhing dunes

276

were plumed here and there with desert poplars (*P. varifolia*), a curious tree which, as its Latin name suggests, bears two quite different kinds of leaf. This was better than the stark gobi through which we had reached Cherchen.

Things, however, went unprosperously on the first day's march. Tuzun Ahun – like all Turkis cruelly careless about animals – went off with the two camels at what was, considering their condition and the great heat, an outrageous pace; and it was difficult to slow him down without offending him. Then, about a mile out of the oasis, we fell in with a little party of Turkis who were seeing each other off, and those who were going our way attached themselves to us. They consisted of an elderly man with a little son, a large, stupid woman, also with a little son, and a crude young man with a pock-marked face, whose ungovernable passion for song found expression in a deplorably limited repertoire. They were, to say the least of it, dull people and we had no wish for their company, which became still less welcome when we discovered that Aziz was serving them as well as us. He had made the arrangement without telling us, and had appointed a rendezvous outside the oasis so that the aksakal would not know that he had, so to speak, taken on extra passengers without permission. It was a small matter, but we resented such sharp practice; and we resented still more the delay consequent, every morning, on Aziz having to catch and load all their donkeys as well as all ours.

It was a grilling afternoon and we were not yet broken into the heat. The warm contents of our two silly little Japanese water-bottles from Peking were soon consumed, and we knew that we had in us the makings of a great thirst. Towards the end of the march it matured, and visions of iced lager danced, as they were often now to dance, before our tired eyes. At last we left the dunes for a shallow basin of caked mud in which grew beds of reeds. First at one water-hole, and then at another we tried to slake our thirst. It was not easy. The water, scooped out of little artificial craters, was richly and variously flavoured; but salt predominated. Insects skated between the suds of

277

scum upon the surface, and in the brackish depths some form of life was mysteriously active.

Of course no self-respecting expedition would have touched water like this without boiling it. But on a journey such as ours was there are only two possible policies: either you must take every precaution, or you must take no precautions at all. Thus far we had followed the second policy with success; and the first was in any case contrary to our natures. It was only when we reached India that we realized the enormity of our offence, the width of our breach with expeditionary etiquette. '*What!*' they cried. 'You drank at water-holes! You ate the food in the bazaars! You never wore hats! . . .' And they looked at us with that mingled disapproval and envy with which you look at a man who picks a horse with a pin and wins a lot of money.

At dusk, after a long stage, we reached Ketmo, which consisted only of the place-name and an untidy hut of mud and wattle. This was split up into two or three compartments, and we found ourselves installed in that which contained the cooking fire. Here, sweating, we drank mug after mug of tea in which salt and sugar waged an unappetizing war. Outside, the first violent episodes in a long-drawn-out romance between Cynara and the chestnut stallion were noisily taking place. We ate a little bread and lay down on the felt to sleep, feeling sticky and jaded. Mosquitoes pinged and zoomed. The Turkis gossiped tirelessly. We sighed for the little tent and the cleaner desolation of the uplands, and presently fell into an uneasy coma. This was soon interrupted by an outbreak of eroticism among the donkeys, who charged braying and kicking round the hut; so that in the end we got less than two hours' sleep.

At 2.30 we gave it up and made some tea. Two of the donkeys had vanished in the direction of Cherchen, and it was six o'clock before they were brought back and we could start. Kini had been very stiff the night before, and it now appeared that she was suffering from lumbago, a legacy of past ski-ing seasons. From now on, therefore, she rode the stallion and I a donkey. The lumbago was no joke.

A succession of ten-hour stages in great heat is something of an ordeal at the best of times; but Kini rode day after day in agony without complaint.

From Ketmo we crawled on through country of an infinite monotony to Akwai, where there was more bad water and another dilapidated hut, and where Kini forced herself to make an omelette. Our thirst was becoming gradually less unmanageable, but we still consumed with relish an astonishing amount of nauseous tea. The chatter of the Turkis in the hut drove us to sleep, among mosquitoes, in the sand outside.

The next day we were up before 3 and off at 4.30. Kini's lumbago was worse; she had sometimes to dismount and lie down, seeking a respite from the motion of the horse. We slogged on through reed-beds, across great terraces of hard white mud, into deep sand between towering pinnacles which the wind had built round growths of tamarisk. By the middle of the morning the heat was cruel, but we were getting used to it. After ten and a half hours' going we reached Chingalik, where there was a relatively solid and substantial hut.

But the hut was occupied already by an east-bound party of Turkis, so Kini and I decided to pitch the tent. We put it up rather insecurely, for the tent-pegs had no grip in the loose sand; then we lay down inside and tried to cool off. There had been a little breeze from the west all day, and when this strengthened and came stealing under the flap we were pleased. But presently the daylight took on a coarse yellow tinge, and to the west a strange dun-coloured wall was spreading across the sky. 'The *buran* is coming,' said the Turkis.

It was on us more swiftly than we had expected, and the tent was almost carried away. Cursing, with eyes half-shut against the flying sand, I feverishly reinforced the windward side of the tent with our sacks and boxes. The wind screamed; the world was cloaked in a premature twilight. In spite of all our efforts, draughts wriggled under the weighted tent-flap like snakes and everything inside was coated with half an inch of sand. Sand got into the boxes, got into our sleeping bags, got into our eyes, mouths, ears, and noses, stuck to our sweaty limbs. 'It can't go on like this for long,' we said. But it did.

Although we were not hungry, we needed a meal. I staggered out into the trumpeting world and queued up for the cooking fire in the hut. Here things were worse than in the tent, for the hut faced west and was being mercilessly enfiladed. However, with the help of a kindly man whose face was wholly and startlingly deficient in a nose, I boiled some mien and some dubious mutton, and off this, liberally seasoned with the Takla Makan, we dined grittily. Then we lay down to sleep under accumulating coverlets of sand.

CHAPTER VII

SUCH QUANTITIES OF SAND

NEXT day the wind had dropped, and we started off soon after seven feeling stale and grimy. Throughout all these stages we were worried about the camels. Number Two's nose-peg had rubbed raw the flesh through which it was driven and a small malignant cloud of flies hung always round his head. The Pearl was even worse off. At Cherchen, with the packsaddles off him, he had reopened the sore which Kini had effectively healed at Toruksai, swinging his head round and probing it with the sharp point of his nose-peg, and in the red unwholesome crater the flies had laid their eggs. Both camels' sores were now full of white loathsome worms, and we reproached ourselves bitterly for allowing, by negligence, our faithful servants to suffer thus. The Turkis, who habitually and cheerfully work their animals until they cannot move for galls, could not understand our concern. But those stinking, crawling little wounds irked us all the time. Neither of us was a sentimentalist, but the two scraggy beasts had displayed – in our company and for our benefit – a kind of stolid heroism, and in this sweaty desert we felt for them that sympathy which binds all exiles together. If any of our oasis-born fellow-travellers had suddenly died, we should have been only perfunctorily shocked; the camels' welfare was a different, a more personal matter, for they had been with us for a long time and they came, as we had come, from the hills.

Cynara, on the other hand, seemed quite content. Her ribs stuck out sharply from her moth-eaten flanks, but we had never known her otherwise than thin and she scrambled along beside the donkeys with the air (which children sometimes have) of being eager and abstracted at the same time. She was definitely flirting with the stallion, and her suitor was in sad case. He was a laggard if she was behind, and all too impetuous if she was in front. When we halted he was off his feed, and their reciprocal neighs echoed forlornly across the desert. The stallion got thinner and thinner.

On the day after the sand-storm, which was June 23rd, Kini's lumbago was worse than ever, and for the first time on the journey I found myself deliberately making conversation, forcing the talk, with a view to keeping her mind off the pain. After five hot hours we came to a water-hole where the Turkis suggested camping; but I was against it, and we compromised with an hour's rest. Then we went on, to halt at four o'clock at a place called, as nearly as we could make out, Shudung.

Here there had once been fields, as the old furrows and the brushwood hedges testified. Two or three mud houses stood in a scattered growth of tamarisk and poplar, and the tall, gallows-shaped perches for birds that we had seen in Cherchen struck faintly the note of civilization. We were billeted in a cool mud-walled barn with several chambers. It was good to get out of the heat.

But the camels were on our consciences. We brought The Pearl and knelt him down and roped him as well as we could round the knees; then Kini started on his sore with disinfectant. No surgery was possible, for we had not the Mongol skill to make the ropes a strait-jacket, and at the touch of Kini's knife he struggled free and rose roaring to his feet. But we mixed our strongest disinfectants and bombed the worms with them. The tubular white heads came periodically up out of the flesh for air, and when they came we dosed them vindictively. The Pearl kicked and spat but was very good about it on the whole; and, though we had little faith in this treatment at the time, it worked. Within a few days the vile worms had gone. It was a real triumph for Kini. She was dog-tired and in some pain; and she thought she had almost no chance of doing good. But she forwent a needed siesta in the shade to do a job which would have made most women sick.

I boiled some rice and meat, but neither of us was

hungry, so we kept it for the next day and it went bad in the night. It was things like this that made us resent the desert, and the heat, and always being sticky, and regret the rigorous but unshoddy uplands from which we had come. It was curious, but the two things we missed most on these interminable stages were hunger and uncertainty. Hitherto the dullest, longest march had had, in the evening meal, a goal which grew more and more desirable as the hours wore on; both tedium and fatigue could be kept at bay by serious and prolonged discussion of the menu – should we boil the meat or make shasklik with it, was mien more satisfying than rice? We used to go through ecstasies of anticipation, and the meal, when at last it came, was never a disappointment. But now there was none of this; salty tea and the hard, biscuit-like bread was all we had a stomach for, and from the spare routine of our life something valuable had been lost.

As for uncertainty, that was a loss too. We were now virtually sure that we should reach Kashgar and thence go on to India. And although on paper a journey through territory held by rebels who have as much blood on their hands as anyone in China may sound a hazardous and enthralling affair, in practice it was nothing of the sort. Our future no longer provided those cues for speculation, those endless permutations of contingencies with which it had formerly been so interesting to juggle. Chimerical strategy, based on long-range surmises, no longer gave useless but stimulating employment to our empty minds. We felt that the game had been won at Cherchen; we were playing, with little zest, the bye.

At Shudung two donkeys strayed in the tamarisk and we did not leave till 1.30 the next day. After much desultory bargaining I had exchanged Cynara for a good-looking donkey belonging to the young man who sang; much solemn handshaking and many professions of good faith sealed the transaction, but the donkey, which I now rode for the first time, belied its looks and collapsed repeatedly beneath me. The craven Aziz, who had sponsored the exchange, grew terrified at this, and sought to placate my wrath by promoting me from Great Man to Great and Good Man. I told him to cancel the bargain, and this, in spite of grumbling by the troubadour, was done.

From Shudung we marched on to Endere, where two or three wretched houses overlooked a muddy river in a gully. We arrived well after dark. Sword hilts projected from the saddlebags of four fine horses in the courtyard; their owners, an east-bound patrol of Tungans, were already asleep. We got the room next to them and made cocoa and I did my best to massage Kini, who had been in agony all day. Before we went to sleep our minds suddenly kindled, and in the candle-light we had a little spurt of foolish talk and reminiscence which banished for a time the desert and made our poor billet seem a pleasant place.

It was hotter than ever next day. We trailed wearily across a hard grey oven of desert, racked with thirst. Some of the Turkis had pumpkin gourds of water, but these were soon drained of their hot and smelly contents. The march was an ordeal for Kini, and her plight was not improved when jealousy flared up between the stallions and Tuzun Ahun's lashed out and caught her on the shin. It was a terrific kick and Kini's stoicism was shaken for a moment.

At last, towards dusk, we came to a water-hole where we sluiced down muddy water and then brought it up to the animals in wooden bowls. It was salt, but we couldn't drink enough of it. Another hour's march brought us, at seven o'clock, to a mean hut where we halted for the night. Once more we were too hot and tired to eat.

We slept for a few hours and moved off again at 4.30. A sandy, uneventful stage, during which one of the Turki boys picked up a little snake, the only one we saw in the Takla Makan, ended before noon at Yartungaz, where a house stood on a bluff above another yellow river crawling down from the eternal snows to lose itself in the insatiable sands. The people here were courteous and kindly; they gave us apricots and we gave them iodine and sweets. We had some sleep and a meal of lapsha, both of which we needed badly. It had been arranged that we were to continue the march when it got cool, but at dusk I discovered that this plan had been quietly shelved. I made a fuss, but neither of us was really sorry, and we slept like logs on the ground outside.

The next day, our eighth on the desert road, we forded the river at dawn and marched through slightly less ungracious country covered intermittently with a kind of pampas grass. After seven hours we reached Yangi Darya, and found the stage-house occupied by a Tungan officer in command of ten men. They were an escort in charge of hostages taken during the fighting at Charklik – two women and a little boy belonging to the Turki chief of the insurgents. They had been brought to Tungan headquarters at Khotan and now – by an act of clemency little characteristic of their captors – were being restored to Charklik. The officer, who spoke with feeling, said that the women had 'bad hearts' and made a nuisance of themselves, but that the little boy was of a good spirit and would fight well when he grew up.

After days of commonplaces in pidgin Turki, we were delighted with the chance of conversation. The officer, suspicious at first but later affable, spoke a little Russian, and we talked agreeably with him for some time, regaling ourselves with tea and fresh bread and sugar from his saddlebags. He had been present at the battle of the Tutung River, when in January 1934 Soviet Russian troops entered Chinese territory and marched to the relief of Urumchi, which must else have fallen to the Tungans. On him, as on all the soldiers we spoke to, the Russian aeroplanes and gas bombs had made a deep impression. 'When we get aeroplanes,' they were always saying, 'we shall win.' They did not say where the aeroplanes would come from.

Of this man we inquired, as we had inquired all along the road, for news of Ma Chung-ying, the young but redoubtable leader of the Tungans, of whose whereabouts we were at that time still uncertain. The officer discreetly admitted that his commander-in-chief had gone on a *yu li*, an expedition to foreign parts. He clearly did not know what had happened to Ma, and we did not press him further, for he would have lost face.

At four o'clock, when it was getting cool, we said good-bye to the slatternly but cheerful soldiers and moved off again, to halt after dark in a patch of reeds and scrub. As a camping ground the place had little to recommend it, but we were within one march of the oasis of Niya and the worst stretch of the desert road was behind us.

CHAPTER VIII

A CUCKOO-CLOCK IN KERIYA

On June 28th, burnt and bloodshot, we entered Niya. The trees of the oasis produced a paler repetition of the delight we had felt on entering Cherchen; and it was more than pleasant to take our ease in the cool roofed courtyard of the caravanserai. The Shang Yi, a Turki dignitary of stately port, visited us, a large astonished crowd witnessing the interview. We were given bread and sour milk and apricots, and we got a tub of warm water and made a semi-serious attempt at washing.

The two camels were very weak. They were marching without loads, but they had not yet shed their winter coats and the desert did not suit them. In the inn stable they refused their fodder; they had never before eaten vegetation which was not growing in the ground and they did not know what to make of these rich green bundles. So we decided that they must be given a day's grazing at the edge of the oasis. I did not want to lose time in Niya, so I arranged with the Shang Yi to have them and Cynara sent on after us to Keriya, where we planned to rest for a day or two. Thanks to Kini, The Pearl's sore was clean and healing fast; but Number Two still had worms in his nose, and we doctored the place with pepper, which was locally considered a sovereign remedy.

Emissaries from Tungan headquarters were commandeering camels in the bazaar, and in connection with this (in exactly what connection I never discovered) ten of the citizens had been arrested. There was no prison and they were confined in the caravanserai. So, accordingly, were we, since the big gates at either end of the inn yard had to be locked on guilty and innocent alike. But the loss of our freedom had its compensations, for it saved us from sightseers, and that evening, as the light died slowly, this courtyard in a forgotten corner of Tartary was a very tranquil place.

At dawn next day Aziz was calling me Great and Good Man again, so I knew that there was mischief brewing. Sure enough, the Turkis were on strike, demanding a day's rest in Niya; but the race has an inner core of softness, the accumulated heritage of oasis life, and I took a strong line with success. So we moved off at seven o'clock, leaving the cool friendly trees for a long tract of scorching desert.

The road here was more travelled than it had been and was marked with cairns. Just outside Niya we passed a cart drawn by an ox; it was exactly three months since we had seen our last wheel in Tangar, and I wondered how many of our contemporaries in Europe had ever got away from wheels for a quarter of a year. Further on there was an abandoned donkey, his back laid hideously open with galls; as we went past he staggered to his feet and stood there unsteadily, looking after us. The Turkis are completely heartless with their animals, whose breakdown is accelerated by callous neglect. From now on we often saw these wretched little beasts which had been left to die.

In the evening we reached an inn or post-house hidden in the sudden gully of a little stream. Kini had ridden ahead on the stallion (her lumbago was much better now) and I found her drinking tea under a big mulberry tree in the courtyard with a Tungan officer of sly and ruffianly appearance. This man was also in charge of prisoners, and in another corner of the yard five boyish-looking soldiers with gyves on their wrist were fraternizing with their captors. They were mutineers on their way to be court-martialled at Khotan; the fate in store for them was certainly unpleasant and possibly terrible, but the Tungans are Chinese and the atmosphere of the whole party was amicable and gay. Later, in Khotan, we saw the prisoners being marched into the yamen at military headquarters. Then indeed their demeanour was different, for there were people looking on and the conventions had to be observed. The mutineers were hang-dog, apprehensive, and abased; the escort – who a few days before had been catching vermin which their shackled charges could not reach – strode with stern, set faces and a terrible air.

We spread our felt on a little platform under the mulberry tree. It is always nice to sleep under a tree, and we were well pleased with our quarters. But in the night the *buran* came drumming over the desert, and a sticky barrage of fat white mulberries rained down on us, making squashy spots to which the flying sand stuck grittily. Sleepy and ill-tempered, we scraped ourselves and took refuge in the house. The roaring world was twilit, and we were storm-bound until the middle of the morning. This was the last day of June.

Then we went on, crawling timelessly across hard, dune-flecked desert, where tall wickerwork baskets, filled with stones and painted red, marked the track. For eleven days now I had ridden on a donkey and I was getting tired of it. There is something about a donkey which keeps your mind and spirits earth-bound. On a horse, on a camel, even on a yak, your imagination soars without much difficulty; you are never for very long impervious to the romance of the road, such as it is. But the donkey, though perhaps on some beach of your childhood it provided an adventure which made you as breathless as your nurse, is a sublunary mount for the adult. Its mean stature, its demure and patient aspect, above all the tripping rhythm of its gait – all these combine to take the gilt off the golden road. After a few days on a donkey you come to see life from the ignoble, the unstimulating viewpoint of a sack of potatoes.

But ordeal by ass was almost over. That night we reached a green outpost of the big oasis of Keriya and were met by an emissary of the British aksakal who wore on his bosom a little Union Jack and a certificate of his nationality written in three languages. We were given a good room in the caravanserai, and the next morning, after a breakfast which was the less hearty for the pathetic intrusion of a woman with an infant dying of diphtheria, we took to the desert again for the last stage to Keriya.

Kini's stallion was sick and lay down in the road no fewer than fifteen times; but we had not far to go. We met a small, suspicious, and ill-mannered contingent of Tungans escorting a caravan of plump, hairless camels; they took us for Russians and for a moment it looked as if we were in for passport trouble. But after an exchange of discourtesies they passed on, and presently we came to the edge of the oasis. As we approached the bazaar our fellow-travellers broke off and departed to their various homes; nor were we sorry to see the last of them, for the woman was a dull, greedy thing with an aptitude for cadging, and as for the troubadour, his harsh songs were a burden and a bore.

The gateway of the aksakal's house was draped in our honour with large home-made Union Jacks of similar but by no means identical designs. Rholam Mohammed Khan welcomed us in a little room which contained more of civilization than we had seen in three months' travel. There was a gramophone with Russian records in a variety of languages; there were oil-lamps from Tashkent, and an umbrella, and even a cuckoo-clock. This flotsam from the West created a homely atmosphere, pleasingly flavoured with incongruity.

The aksakal, a shrewd, humorous Afghan who spoke a little Chinese, was the kindest of hosts. We revelled in fresh bread and sweets and tea and gossip, and decided to stay a day in Keriya. It was a very full day. We were woken in the morning by the dulcet though redundant clamour of the cuckoo-clock which the aksakal, loath to rouse us by summary and disrespectful methods, had put into full cry. We breakfasted off jam made of roses and set out on a round of official calls.

Outside the military commander's yamen Tungans in white undress uniform were playing handball. A sentry took in our cards and in due course we were received. The commandant of the garrison (which numbered more than 2000 men) was a thick-witted, brutal-looking man; but his second in command was a shrewder fellow, and there was also present an astute young man from Ningshia, who wore his hair long and did not look like a Moslem. He alone of the three was literate, and he read out our passports in the modulated sing-song which Chinese actors use on the stage.

He had recently been posted to Keriya from Khotan, and when the courtesies and explanations were over we began to ask for news of the Tungan capital. Inevitably but tentatively the talk drifted to Ma Chung-ying. Was it true, we wondered, that the commander-in-chief was absent in foreign parts? We had heard so many conflicting rumours. . . .

It was by no means true, said the young man, whose name was Chang; the Little General (Ma's nickname among his troops) was even now in Khotan.

We expressed our pleasure at this news and our hope that the great man would be willing to receive us.

'Alas,' replied Chang, 'that will not be possible.' And he went on to explain that Ma, although he was transacting all the business of civil and military administration, was living incognito in Khotan; he would certainly have no intercourse with strangers.

An army which cannot account for the whereabouts of its commander-in-chief loses face, and Chang's fairy-tale was a blow struck for Tungan prestige. We were therefore careful to conceal our incredulity, and after a due quantity of tea and sweets had been consumed the interview came to a harmonious close.

CHAPTER IX

REBELS DON'T CARE

AFTER that we called on the mayor, a large man with an air of duplicity about him. A certain apprehension underlay his manner; this was almost always the case with the Turki officials we met in Sinkiang. He would have liked, he said, to leave the province and go to India, but the Tungans would not let him.

There was no doubt that Tungan rule lay heavily on the oases; the Turkis were groaning under the weight of other people's military ambitions. Almost all the activity that was going on was going on for the benefit of the garrison; the donkeys trotting in from the outskirts of the oasis with loads of fodder or of fuel, the men who were levelling a new parade-ground – these and other signs of forced labour abounded. Both farmers and merchants were victimized by exactions. On the day we were in Keriya the Tungans commandeered, without paying for them, no less than 6000 eggs, 300 measures of vegetable oil, and 140 bricks of tea; these they beat up and fed to their horses. We heard that they used to do this once or twice a month to make a change in the animals' diet of maize, which fattened without strengthening them.

We lunched off pilaffe and sour milk – our first cooked meal for two days and our last for several more – at the aksakal's country house outside the bazaar, which stood in a delightful garden. Kini, but not I, was allowed to visit his young wife, whom she reported very beautiful but averse to being photographed. Then we went back to our quarters, where we found gifts from the civil and military authorities – two sheep, six packets of sugar, and four bottles of Russian eau-de-Cologne. The commandant's generosity had exceeded the mayor's to the extent of two packets of sugar.

The latter dignitary had promised us animals for the next day. But horses, thanks to the garrison, were scarce in the bazaar, and in the evening Aziz came tearfully to tell us that, although he had only contracted to take us to Keriya and was exceedingly anxious to return to Cherchen, he and the worn-out stallion had been pressed into our further service by the authorities. I explained the injustice of this to the aksakal, who promised to put it right and narrowly escaped having his feet kissed by Aziz.

The glib Chang also called on us, and we played the gramophone and discussed, not without superficiality, the destinies of China and the personalities of her rulers. There also arrived a smooth-spoken merchant, who after some bargaining took Cynara and the camels off our hands for the price of one thousand of the local notes. This sounds a lot, but was in fact equivalent to only thirty dollars (Mex.) – about £2.

Before we started next day I went to have a last look at the animals. Cynara, *désorientée* as ever, stamped nervously and twitched her ears when I stroked her scraggy neck. Number Two was standing moodily in a dark corner of the stable, but The Pearl was kneeling in a patch of sunlight. He looked extraordinarily shrunken; the wool was coming off his flanks in patches and you could see the folds of empty skin. But his crested head was high, and his dark Byronic eyes still looked at life with more than a camel's contempt. There was, for me, something gallant about these ragged and ungainly monsters; they had been through a lot with us, and it was good to know that their long labours were over for the present.

We moved off at eleven next morning, after a certain amount of fuss and a great deal of photography. The aksakal put on his best clothes and posed on a chair in the courtyard with his assistant behind him. The assistant was a raffish but charming Afghan who, with his Hom-

293

burg hat tilted wildly, his defiantly folded arms, and his over-truculent stance, looked exactly like a wag in a house-party snapshot.

He and the aksakal rode with us to the edge of the oasis, where we parted with regret. Then – still accompanied by Tuzun Ahun, whose orders were to deliver us in Khotan – we went on all day through scrub and reedbeds. The mayor had not done well by us. The four donkeys were the merest shrimps and, though Kini had a sturdy bay, my white horse was a crock. Like a fool I had not supervised his saddling, and before the stage was half over I discovered that his back was a mass of old galls. So I did the last three hours on foot, dragging the wretched animal behind me.

I found the others, after dark, in an inn at a place called Karaki, where no food of any sort was available. Next day we started early. I abandoned my horse and did a grilling nine-hour march on foot; part of it was through sand, which was heavy going and from which the heat struck up through the worn soles of my boots into my sockless feet. We broke the stage at midday in a little bazaar where the headman gave us bread and sour milk, after consuming which we fell rudely and incontinently asleep.

At noon, when we went on, the heat was terrible. I stopped in another little bazaar to wait for the donkeys to come up. Here a woman was selling ice, which they collect in the winter and store underground; it was profusely seamed with what I hoped were only alluvial deposits, but beaten up with sour milk it made a delicious and refreshing drink. A large crowd watched the slaking of my thirst, a lengthy process. Though they had seen no foreigners before they knew what foreigners were; and they could not conceive how it came about that a foreigner demeaned himself by travelling on foot.

Farther on we met half a dozen Tungans in charge of a herd of camels. Two of them were driving the wooden peg through the nose of a young camel (this is done when the beast is three years old) and we stopped to watch, never having seen this before. An officer appeared and asked if we were Russians. We said we weren't, but he seemed not wholly satisfied and – wrapping up a command in hospitable words – insisted that we should come to his headquarters and drink tea. So for an hour we squatted in the shade, nibbling bread and explaining, in sentences which had long ago become mechanical, who we were and whence we had come. In the end his suspicions were allayed, and we went on.

Towards dusk we came to Chira, a fairly considerable bazaar. I dragged myself along, too hot and tired to care that I was losing face by travelling on foot. Just outside the bazaar there was a parade-ground, equipped, as all the Tungan parade-grounds were, with a hundred-foot-high wooden tower on which scaling parties might rehearse their assaults (though heaven knows there are few enough walls of that height in the Province). From the summit of this tower an officer with a megaphone was drilling two or three hundred cavalry. The fine Badakshani horses were divided, in the Cossack fashion, according to their colours – one troop of greys, one troop of blacks, and so on. The drill consisted of making your horse lie down and taking cover behind him.

This manœuvre was carried out with remarkable precision and efficiency, and I stopped for several minutes to watch it, standing in a timid crowd of Turkis and relishing the golden sunset light, the plunging horses, the barked commands, the distant sound of bugles. When I moved on along the edge of the parade-ground I was spotted from on high. There were shouts from the tower which I knew were meant for me, but I ignored them and it was not until two panting orderlies were on my heels that I turned and registered polite surprise.

They led me back. We picked our way between ranks of chargers disposed in most of the heraldic attitudes between rampant and couchant regardant; there was a strong suggestion of a circus in rehearsal about the whole scene. When we reached the foot of the tower the officer shouted (but not to me) an order; and a man who looked like a sergeant left the ranks and addressed me in Russian. I judged it prudent to conceal my knowledge of this language and said facetiously to the bystanders 'What kind of aboriginal speech is this?' The feeble sally got a laugh, and in China once you have got a laugh the battle is half over.

The officer on the tower asked me, in loud and peremptory Chinese, if I was a Russian. Mimicking as best I could his overbearing tones, I replied that I was an Englishman. Had I a passport? Yes, of course; 'passport have not, this remote place what manner arrive?' (The audience was with me, now.) The officer said he wanted to examine the passport. I replied that when I had reached my inn, and washed, and drunk tea, I would be glad to show my passport to anyone; at present I was hot and tired and dirty and in no mood for affairs of this kind. In the end, after further exchanges on these lines, I was allowed to go. I felt – though one can never be sure – that I had not lost face; and as I walked away through the lines of sprawling horses (it all looked, in the dusk which had now fallen, like a mass meeting of performing seals) I remembered the Private of the Buffs and felt complacently Newboltian.

Our inn in Chira was grubby and unspacious. Flies, which now played in our life the baleful part formerly allotted by an inscrutable Providence to mosquitoes, abounded. But there were compensations. Although no one came to inspect our passports, two or three soldiers sauntered in and sought our company with an alacrity which suggested that they were not altogether off duty and which made us guarded in our speech. One of them spoke Russian well, having been born in Frunze in Russian Turkistan, whence he had escaped with difficulty three years before. From him it was that we first learnt that Ma Chung-ying corresponded periodically with Khotan from Moscow, and that his letters were sufficiently cheerful in tone for passages from them to be read out to the troops. From this man we also heard of that photograph of Ma, taken in Russia, of which there had been talk in Cherchen. We became very curious to see it.

Our miserable donkeys from Keriya were played out and I needed a horse. So early next morning I called on the mayor, who for once was not a Turki but a shrivelled, old-style Chinese from Honan. He was a man of great affability, and by harassing his underlings I saw to it that the promises he made to me were kept. At noon our luggage left on four fresh donkeys, and soon afterwards a good white mare turned up for me. We delayed until the worst of the blazing heat was over, and took the road again at 2.30.

A thirsty desert stage brought us to Baishtoghrak, or the Five Poplars, where water was available. But we pressed on into the dusk, riding, a little too much at random, through a maze of dunes. The track was only a faint dappling in the sand, and when night fell the uniform drab silver on which our horses trod was full of unpredictable gulfs and unpredictable ascents. The young moon shone feebly in a haze.

Presently lights winked on the horizon, and in spite of the muffling sand we were aware of the approach of horsemen in large numbers. Laughter and bursts of song and the jingling of accoutrements guided our uncertain and over-imaginative eyes to discern at last with assurance black floods of movement on the star-lit dunes. One by one, four east-bound squadrons of Tungan cavalry rode past us, making a rent in the dark silence with electric torches and with talk. Each of them hailed us; but Kini and I shunned the questing eye of the commander's torch and let Tuzun Ahun answer for the party in Turki. This was neither the place nor the time for an excitable inquiry into our credentials.

At 10 o'clock we reached, roused, and invaded a solitary post-house by a well, where we drank some tea and fell asleep in the courtyard. Six hours later we were up again, and after a stage of three *potai* over the sheerest desert we rode into the oasis of Lop. The *potai* as a measure of distance we had been familiar with ever

297

since we left Cherchen, but it was about now that we began to see the concrete reality behind the Chinese word. The track was marked at intervals of about two and half miles by little solid turrets of dun brick; these are the milestones of Chinese Turkistan. Some were crumbling and some complete, but they all provided a welcome relief in a landscape which was little more than the simplest of geometrical expressions.

CHAPTER X

KHOTAN

WE hoped to reach Khotan that night; but in Lop we needed fodder for the animals and this could only be obtained from the authorities. The mayor was out and the shrewd old-fashioned Chinese in charge of his yamen was very properly alienated by my vagabond appearance – dirty shorts and Red Indian face and knees and arms. But I took his rebuffs coolly and, after referring to my friendship with several men of consequence in Khotan, I not too ostentatiously wrote down his name and rank; then I made as if to leave him, my demeanour expressing well-bred regret at such churlish treatment of a foreign traveller. This mild and oblique intimidation shook his nerve, and before long we got the fodder.

While the animals ate, we fought off the flies in a poor inn. An itinerant Tungan patrol was also quartered there; there was something medieval about the spectacle of its commander – the overweening sullenness of his face enhanced in sleep – being fanned by a pretty Turki girl lest the flies should disturb his rest. One of his men (the noun is a courtesy title, for he was very young) poured out his woes to us in a low voice. He had been pressed into the service of Ma Chung-ying three years before, hated a soldier's life and the company of soldiers, and yearned to see again his family in Tunghwang. There must be many in the Tungan armies like him.

We went on just before noon. The desert was ended, though the main oasis had not yet begun, and it was a green world through which we rode. As we approached Khotan Tuzun Ahun spoke darkly of a great river in flood, urging us to spend this night on the hither side and enter the city early next day when the waters, which are swollen towards noon by the melted snows, would be low.

But we were not to be gainsaid a goal so nearly reached, and eventually, leaving Tuzun to bring on the submersible donkeys next day, we forded the Yurungkash. A ferry of sorts was being operated, but would not accommodate horses. So at last, after much frothy argument about unsaddling and a great display of ineffectiveness by all connected with the ferry, we rode into the first arm of the turgid yellow stream. Twenty minutes later we floundered out on the further shore; I had been almost completely immersed, and our sleeping bags (on which, in the Turki style, we rode) were soaking, but neither of us was any the worse for that.

A heartening reception awaited us. The British aksakal's assistant – a young Afghan with a terrifying squint – accompanied by a Turki-Chinese half-caste called Saduk, who wore a mackintosh and the grey-green-yellow complexion of an opium-smoker, received us almost obsequiously. The aksakal, they explained, was away, but his house was at our disposal; and in their company we rode into the bazaar.

Past a parade-ground, fitted with the usual paraphernalia of siege. Past a dead horse, whose throat had been cut after his collapse so that the meat would not be useless. Past several mosques – larger, more solidly picturesque than heretofore – which, though they did not prevent Khotan from suggesting a film set, at least made it suggest a more careful, expensive, and permanent film set than the other oases. Past a surprising number of Union Jacks flown – an effective talisman – outside the premises of British Indian subjects in the bazaar. And at last into a long courtyard full of bales and cases from India, at the end of which steps led up into the aksakal's garden.

In the middle of the garden, under the susurrant mulberry trees, stood a pavilion without walls which looked exactly like a bandstand. In this we were lodged; there was a minimum of privacy and a maximum of flies, but at least it was cool. Tea and sugar, sweets and bread. Foreseen questions and familiar answers. But we had reached Khotan, and if it did not feel as stimulating as the headquarters

300

of a rebel army in Central Asia might be expected to feel, it was incontestably a major milestone in our journey. We ate our first cooked meal for five days and listened bemusedly to the squinting Afghan, who was telling us a long story. It was, to say the least of it, a sensational story, but at first we found it difficult to fit it into the political and geographical conditions obtaining in these parts. Comprehension dawned slowly; it was a synopsis of M. Jules Verne's *Twenty Thousand Leagues Under the Sea*, which had been translated into Afghan in Kabul.

On the next day, which was July 7th, there occurred a memorable event.

We were eating breakfast in a dense cloud of flies when there ambled up the steps into the garden a small donkey, flying the Union Jack. The bearded, weather-beaten Turki in charge of him bore on his chest the legend BRITISH INDIAN POSTMAN. The mail had come in.

Though we knew there was nothing for us, we watched the padlocked sacks being unloaded not without a thrill. Ponies had carried them up from Kashmir over the Himalayan passes to Kashgar, a journey to be reckoned in weeks; and from Kashgar they had travelled a fortnight on the desert road. And there was more to them than mere glamour; for they contained, besides letters from Indian merchants and consular dispatches, several copies of the weekly edition of *The Times*. These could not, clearly, be much less than three months old; but we had not seen a newspaper of any sort since March, and we were no more particular about the freshness of our news than we were about the freshness of our butter. We eyed the bundles covetously.

They were addressed to 'M. Moldovack, Khotan'. M. Moldovack, we were informed, was an Englishman; but Sinkiang, which if it has heard of London at all imagines it to lie just beyond the Himalayas, draws scant distinction between nationality and race, and we had already been introduced to several Englishmen who disappointingly turned out to be natives of Kabul or Peshawar. So all we knew about M. Moldovack was that he was a British subject.

As such, he could obviously be tracked down; and in the meantime, loose in the postbags, there were several of the coloured *Times* photographs of 'The King at the Microphone'.

'This,' I said to a small crowd which had imperceptibly collected, 'is my Padishah; and this picture was made by my gazette'.

The squinting Afghan, who was clearly a prominent figure in the intellectual life of Khotan, had heard of *The Times* and shook me warmly by the hand, at the same time informing me, through the Chinese-speaking Saduk, that my face was great. Our stock went up all round.

Later in the day we called, at his invitation, on M. Moldovack, who turned out to be an Armenian by birth. He was eighty-five years old and crippled by elephantiasis, but his eyes, though troubled by pain, were bright and kindly. His spotless white ducks contrasted all too favourably with our ragamuffin appearance. In French and English – both a little stilted through disuse – he told us his story in a book-littered room built in the Turki but furnished in the European style.

He had been engaged in the carpet trade, of which Khotan was once a very special and important centre. But the Bolshevik Revolution caught his west-bound caravans at Khokand, across the Russian border, and as his very considerable savings were all in Russian banks he lost everything. So for the last fifteen years or so he had been living modestly in Khotan, a lonely exile in a city lately rife with treachery and bloodshed. Altogether it was twenty-six years since he had left the place. . . . Yes, some of his family, as far as he knew, were still living in Armenia; but things were no doubt difficult there too, and after all these years he did not care to throw himself, a penniless old invalid, on their charity. Besides, it was now impossible for him to make the journey.

We talked politics after that, the politics of Turkistan and of the world; and M. Moldovack was well informed about both. But for my part I could think of nothing but this immaculate and courteous old man, with his tired but still bird-like gestures and his fund of strange knowledge and strange memories; he did not seem ill-contented with his lot, but I was conventional enough to be troubled by the reflection that, when we were gone, M. Moldovack would most probably never see a European face again.

At length we took our leave, bearing away with us an armful of the precious papers and the conviction that we had seen the loneliest of men. (Perhaps Borodishin's exile was starker, more complete; but he did not know it was, with him there was always hope.) A little sobered, we walked back through the bazaar to the aksakal's garden.

Before we broached the papers – the latest of which bore a date in April – we had an argument. Kini said she couldn't understand my lust for news; we had got on very well without it for several months, and the news in any case was just as likely to be bad as good. I said that she was talking nonsense, as indeed she was, and ended by announcing, with irrational conviction, that there would be no bad news for me.

This, I suppose, was Hubris, a very punishable vice in a fatalist. I opened the first weekly edition at a page of photographs and saw instantly among them the well-remembered features of a friend. I had hardly time to wonder in what way he had been distinguishing himself (for he was a person destined for distinction) when I read that he had been fatally injured in a shooting accident in Africa. This seemed to be horribly unfair and made me angry; nor was it easy to believe, for he had always appeared the most indestructible of men. It was several days before I got over this bitter sense of injustice and could remember calmly the things we had done together – the untidy sitting-room at Oxford, blackcock swinging wide against a December sky, an August evening waiting for pigeons among Lowland stooks. I remembered, too, that he had given me, for a journey in Brazil, the light sleeping-bag which I was still using. I could not think of him as dead.

For the rest, the papers showed that the world had been getting on well enough without us. We learnt for the first time that England was celebrating the Jubilee of King George V. Under the aksakal's mulberry trees, with the Tungans' war-songs in our ears, we studied – feeling suddenly and unwontedly forlorn – photographs of familiar streets being tricked out for the processions. An amateur had won the National. Italy's attitude towards Abyssinia was causing grave concern. And here, in an account of a flying accident in Rhodesia, was a passage whose closing words proved that England and *The Times* were still being true to themselves and to each other: 'After walking far in hot sunshine they met a native and wrote an urgent appeal for assistance. Hours later the message reached Mr. Cameron, the locust-ranger, who is an Old Marlburian.' There were also extracts ('World Copyright Reserved') from a number of dispatches which I had sent home from Manchuria and Mongolia. When they were written they had seemed blatantly superficial, but now they struck me as exceedingly profound. I found them, in fact, a little difficult to understand.

CHAPTER XI

THE VANISHED LEADER

A GOOD part of our time in Khotan, where we spent four days, was devoted to official calls. Of these the most important and the most interesting was on General Ma Ho-san, the twenty-two-year-old commander-in-chief of the rebel armies.

Khotan, like most of the big towns in Sinkiang, is divided into the New City and the Old City. The New City, surrounded by a high crenellated wall, was originally a Chinese cantonment and still contains all the official yamens and most of the shops and residences of Chinese traders. The Old City is in effect the native quarter and is not fortified.

The commander-in-chief received us, twice, in a flimsy pavilion behind the yamen of military headquarters. Ma Ho-san is a good-looking young man with a sense of humour and an air of effectiveness. On both occasions he produced an interpreter in the person of a minor official who knew some English; but it was not very much English and the wretched man had bad malaria, so we talked mostly in elementary Chinese.

They were pleasant interviews and resulted in one minor and one major scoop. After some talk about gas and aeroplanes, and the badness of the Russians and of Sheng Shih-tsai, I asked Ma whether the high state of military preparedness which we had marked in all the oases meant that he was going to fight again soon. He would not commit himself to a date, and talked vaguely of expecting help from Nanking; but he did outline to me the strategy of his next campaign, in which (he said), while the main Tungan army marched westwards on Yarkand, a strong force of cavalry would cross the Takla Makan by a little-known route to attack Aksu, thus cutting communications between Kashgar and Urumchi.

Of less academic interest was the partial elucidation of the mystery of Ma Chung-ying. The first time we saw him, Ma Ho-san fought shy of the subject of his half-brother, saying airily that he had gone off somewhere or other on a *yu li*. But if the commander-in-chief would not talk we were resolved that at least he should show us the celebrated Russian photograph of Ma Chung-ying, of which we had heard several rumours, and at the second interview we became subtle and circuitous. We brought our cameras and all the paraphernalia and gadgets we could think of, including a collapsible tripod of Kini's. Ma Ho-san, greatly tickled, changed into his best uniform and posed in a courtyard with four of his personal bodyguard armed with automatic rifles. We took his photograph from every conceivable angle, making a great mumbo-jumbo about it. It was nearly dark, and we knew that none of the photographs could possibly come out; but when we had finished we beamed with delight. How great, we exclaimed, would be our face when we showed our friends these pictures of the great General Ma Ho-san, concerning whose personal appearance there was such widespread curiosity in England and in France! And how splendid it would be if we could only show as well a portrait of his hardly less distinguished half-brother, General Ma Chung-ying. . . .

The dodge worked. An orderly was dispatched and presently returned with a photograph of the exile. It was (to us) a very interesting photograph. Ma Chung-ying was posed in an arresting attitude. His hair was long, like a foreigner's (all the Tungans crop their heads); and he wore the uniform of a cavalry officer in the Soviet Red Army. It appeared that internment on Soviet soil was not without its compensations.

In the twilight we clicked off our cameras at this portrait and departed in high glee.

Another interesting visit was to the mint. In England there is something infinitely respectable about the very word mint. It is otherwise in China. In the civil wars of that country the first sign that a protagonist has arrived (though not necessarily come to stay) is his acquisition or construction of a mint and also, if possible, of an arsenal; but the mint is much the more important of the two. The mint in Khotan was a very primitive one. There was no machinery at all, but in the littered rooms of a ramshackle building no less than 30,000 notes were turned out every day. They were hand-printed in four colours on soggy paper made from the fibre of the mulberry tree, and they were issued without a penny of capital or credit behind them. Their value – even their nominal value – was accordingly very low; but they sufficed to pay the troops, and could be forced on the people with whom the troops did business. The Tungans' currency policy was recommended by a certain straightforward simplicity.

Externally as well as internally, Khotan was dominated by its garrison. All day long, in spite of the oppressive heat, chanting columns of troops marched through the bazaar between their quarters and the various parade-grounds. The officers were all Tungans, but in some of the units the rank and file were Turkis or Turki-Chinese half-castes. For the most part they wore an undress uniform of grubby white, with floppy white sun-hats on their shaven heads; this pastoral and rather feminine headgear consorted oddly with the brutish pock-marked faces, the bloodshot glaring eyes. Often a regiment would pass very slowly through the streets, doing an exaggerated acrobatic goose-step and swinging their arms above their heads; and in the evening, dressed in shorts and a kind of football shirt quartered in red and white, they raced and jumped and played a big-scale variation of Hunt The Slipper under the walls of the new city. Bugles were always blowing some-where, and all day the fierce Moslem songs rolled about the city like the sound of an angry sea. I have never seen troops in China train so hard.

One day we drifted into the arsenal. Like the mint it was neither well housed nor well equipped. In the haphazard workshops men were tinkering away at scrap-iron rifles, and small hand-grenades were being manufactured with as few precautions as if they had been hot-cross-buns. The *pièce de résistance* was fiften or twenty light cannon which had been captured from the Provincial Armies at Urumchi; they were kept in a beautifully spick and span condition, but the supply of ammunition for them was not much more than symbolical.

On July 10th we took the road again. The principal Hindu merchants said good-bye as effusively as they had welcomed us. The aksakal, who had returned to Khotan and proved to be a fat and wheezy Afghan, provided us with an attendant for the journey. This was a Turki-Chinese half-caste called Nyaz. There was something lovable about the oaf. Though neither quick-witted nor resourceful, he was extremely loyal, and his only disadvantage was his firm adherence to the baseless theory that he spoke Chinese. In point of fact his command of this language was limited to two expressions: 'slowly' and 'wait a bit'. These he used impartially to convey various meanings, chief among which were 'quickly, at once', 'not for a long time', 'a little', and 'a very great deal'.

At first, until we got to know him and could read in his face and tone the meaning he was trying to put across, it was a little difficult to get the hang of such conversations as the following:

'How many potai to the next bazaar, Nyaz?'

'*Man man di kelde,*' he would reply, uniting the Chinese for 'slowly' to the Turki for 'come'. On the face of it you would have said he meant that we still had a long way to go; but quite often, we discovered, he meant exactly the opposite. He used to eke out his meaning by closing his eyes, thrusting forward his face, and weaving it blindly to and fro, like a snake in a glass case. It was impossible not to like the gawkish and pathetic dolt.

Saduk, complete with mackintosh, also attached himself to us. He was a sly dog, but a quick and clever Chinese interpreter, and although he spent much of each day and the whole of each night smoking opium in an old Peking cart at the back of the garden we thought he would be useful. But the aksakal warned me against him, and I told him that we had no use for his services; to this he obsequiously replied that he was going to Kashgar anyhow and would render us assistance on the road without remuneration. So we started off together.

Two of the aksakal's underlings escorted us out of Khotan and we turned our back on that lowering, somehow desperate city over which treachery and violence seemed – even to my unfanciful mind – to brood impalpably. A short, hot stage of five hours brought us to a swollen river called the Karakash, across which we and our animals were ferried in flat-bottomed boats. Beyond it we came to a little bazaar standing on a bluff, and in its twisting streets we sought out a caravanserai. The flies were a plague, and when night reprieved us from them other and deadlier insects attacked the hapless Kini; bugs and vermin usually ignored me but found her particularly attractive. But this time I had my own troubles; the night before I had eaten some sour milk which was bad, and it was now fermenting merrily inside me.

On all these stages the custom of the country compelled us to change animals at each bazaar, which meant untold annoyance and delay. Next day we broke our march at Zawa, to rest and scratch and eat some bread; Saduk, who had been too sodden with opium to start with us that morning, caught us up here and was sent back with contumely to Khotan. Then we pushed on towards Pialma, doing a dreary stage across naked desert. In the middle of it we came to a shrine sacred to the memory of a holy man. Here a flock of several hundred pigeons subsist on the pious generosity of travellers, who buy maize to feed them from the warden of the place. There is nothing else there for them to eat, and judging by the alacrity with which the pigeons flew out into the desert to meet us and escort us to the shrine travellers of late had been either rare, impious, or stingy. The birds strutted along beside the track or circled round our heads; and when we duly bought a bowl of maize and scattered it on the ground, they swooped down with a great gusty roaring of wings and flung themselves on the food, until the place was carpeted with two or three layers of struggling birds. They must have been famished.

We were destined not to make Pialma that night. When we went on the evening was overcast and presently the *buran* hit us. It was a plumb head wind; the sand pricked and stung our faces and we had to ride with our eyes shut. In the last of the light we arrived at a great thick-walled post-house, built like a fort, and threw in our hand, spending the night in a cell-like room attended by a friendly and inquisitive old woman.

Next day we went on to Pialma, where Kini cooked a badly needed meal of rice and we gorged ourselves. We changed animals and pushed on, arriving at ten o'clock at a small bazaar which looked dead and derelict in the moonlight. The next day was equally uneventful, but it ended at Guma where, since there was a British aksakal, we were lodged in some comfort.

The aksakal was absent, but a little Hindu doctor with a smattering of English looked after us and, on the following day, helped me in a ticklish affair. It began when the mayor – a fat, perspiring, shifty Turki – called and asked, innocently enough, to see our passports, of which a clerk copied out the particulars. We were promised a change of animals immediately, but they failed to materialize; instead there arrived an orderly from the commandant of the Tungan garrison demanding our passports.

I surrendered them with some misgivings and, sure enough, a message soon came back from the yamen saying that our passports were out of order and why hadn't we got one from Khotan? With a sinking heart I went round to the mayor's office and there interviewed an extremely unsympathetic secretary from Szechwan; he maddeningly but justly pointed out that we had no right to be in the province at all with those papers, and took unconcealed pleasure in prophesying an indefinite delay while the matter was referred back to headquarters at Khotan. The mayor, meanwhile, had disappeared.

So I went, in some trepidation, to the military yamen

and eventually found myself interviewing the commandant himself. He was a stupid, suspicious man, who took a lot of convincing that I was not a Russian spy; but by dint of making cheap jokes with his staff, starting arguments on irrelevant subjects, and generally playing the artless fool I persuaded him to chop the passport.

All this took time, and it was nearly four o'clock before we left for Chulak, which, when we reached it well after dark, turned out to be another fort-like post-house on a bluff. Here our passports were again examined by a man who had formerly commanded a frontier-post at Bash Malghun; we thanked heaven that he had not been there when we arrived in Sinkiang. We were beginning to realize that we had underrated our good luck in meeting complaisant or ignorant officials at Cherchen.

CHAPTER XII

THE LAST OF TUNGAN TERRITORY

NEXT day we rode on through the desert to Khargalik, the last oasis of importance held by the Tungans. We arrived to find bazaar-day in full swing. In the roofed streets crowds of chafferers ebbed and flowed around the booths; among these the hatters' shops stood out decoratively with their tilted ranks of pegs at the end of which little embroidered skull-caps dangled button-like and gay. The British aksakal gave us a particularly kindly welcome, which we appreciated the more because we were both dog-tired and weakened by under-nourishment; it seemed – and was – days since we had had a proper meal.

We needed a change of animals, and the aksakal and I set out in quest of the authorities. Outside the gates of the principal yamen we found the general in command of the garrison. He was a fat man with a cruel but roguish face from which gracefully depended long and villainous mous-taches. He sat squatly on a chair, watching an animated game of netball, while a little boy kept the flies off with a gigantic fan (much bigger than the boy himself) made of eagle's feathers. A large crowd of Turkis and Tungans were also looking on.

A murmur ran through the crowd when I appeared: as well it might, for I looked extremely odd. I presented myself to the general, apologizing for my disreputable appearance, and we indulged for some time in polite conversation, through which I vainly struggled to file an application for our animals. Each attempt was politely brushed aside, and I began to feel aggressive. When the general asked what I thought of netball as a game, I said that in certain countries, and particularly in Russia, it was very popular; but that in England only women played it. He seemed a little nettled by this; nor was he pleased when

I took an old British service rifle from one of his bodyguard, slipped the bolt out, and showed him that the barrel was disgustingly dirty. But he began to treat me less cavalierly and consented to discuss the question of animals.

First he said there were none available. Very well I said, I would walk to Yarkand, even though a man who travelled on foot lost face. The general, who had hitherto found me a disconcerting and incalculable barbarian, was (I suppose) so delighted to discover that my outlook was at least partly Chinese that he capitulated at once and promised the animals for next day. He even, at my request, sent into the yamen for one of the Russian army rifles of which he claimed to have captured large quantities at Urumchi; so far I had seen no Russian rifles of a later date than 1923, but this one was marked 1930, which seemed to bear out his contention that he had taken it from Soviet troops.

Meanwhile there had been two illuminating interludes. From the crowd of spectators watching the netball match an old Turki detached himself, darted forward, and grovelled weeping at the general's feet. He had, it appeared, been wronged by one of his sons, and he poured out an involved domestic grievance. The Tungans roared with laughter and finally shooed him away.

Then there rode up on donkeys two venerable Turki notables, very stately in their long white beards and fine embroidered robes. As they approached to pay their respects the Tungans tittered and made jokes behind their hands; and though they exchanged the needful courtesies they did so perfunctorily, not bothering to conceal their amusement and contempt.

Both incidents reminded me vividly of the Japanese in Manchuria. The Asiatic races can sometimes conquer, but never colonize.

When the match was over the general waddled out on to the ground and with an air of condescension began to hit the ball into the net. When I went up to say good-bye he threw it at me playfully. It was a very light ball and I sent it skyward with a prodigious punt; it fell like a bomb among the astonished crowd, who had never seen a ball

313

kicked before. There was a roar of laughter and I made a creditable exit.

About noon on the next day we passed out of Tungan territory. The troops at the most westerly of their frontier posts halted us peremptorily. At first – like all Chinese when taken by surprise – they were nervous and therefore domineering; but we disarmed them by playing the fool and before long I had them fallen in in the courtyard of their quarters and was marshalling them in a parade-ground voice for photographic purposes. They were almost all armed with old Lee-Enfields (a good many came into the province some years ago from India) and to these forked rests had been attached with strips of tin from Japanese cigarette boxes. A Russian propagandist could have woven a fine fairy-tale of Imperialist intrigue around those weapons.

After we had drunk tea with the commander we were given a cordial send-off by the entire garrison and continued on our way. We crossed a wide, straggling river which for once was spanned by a bridge. It was tremendously hot, so we dismounted and bathed in the thick yellow water; this was delightful at the time but made us feel weak and sleepy afterwards. That evening we reached Posgam, a small bazaar in the centre of a kind of unofficial demilitarized zone which separates the territory controlled by Khotan from that controlled by Urumchi.

The next day we were due to reach Yarkand, and we discussed with some excitement the prospect of meeting our first Europeans, for we knew that there was a Swedish mission station in the city. In the middle of a hot day we came to another river and were ferried across it. On the west bank we ran into the first frontier post of the Provincial Armies.

It was manned by a seedy crew of Turkis. They wore shabby grey uniforms with caps cut in the Russian style; like their enemies, whom we had left the day before, their badges and armlets bore the star of the Kuomintang and thus proclaimed their incorporation in the forces of the Nanking Government. But we were still in Chinese territory, where a trifling incongruity of this sort need occasion no remark.

They were, to put it mildly, surprised to see us. But we adopted a matter-of-fact and airy manner, and it never occurred to them to ask for our passports. They gave us tea and roasted eggs and sent us on to Yarkand with an escort mounted on a fiery horse. Towards dusk the machicolated walls of the New City rose above the tree-tops of the oasis and we heard the faint, discordant mewing of bugles. The escort, a man of unpleasing appearance, insisted that we should go with him to report to military headquarters; but I demurred strongly and after some bickering got my way. We went straight to the aksakal's house. It was July 17th, twenty-eight days since we had left Cherchen; we had been travelling fast, and there were now only five more stages to Kashgar.

We spent a day in Yarkand, which is the biggest city in Southern Sinkiang. It had seen bitter fighting in the civil war. Parts of the bazaar were still in ruins; the bastions of the New City were pockmarked with bullets, and the walls of the houses round it with loop-holes; Chinese inscriptions were defaced. Here a Chinese garrison held out with some gallantry against the fanatical insurgents from Khotan, and after a siege of several weeks were granted a safe-conduct. They marched out of the New City and took the road to Kashgar; in the desert they were massacred almost to a man. The incident is typical of a Province whose whole history stinks with treachery.

Twenty-eight of them escaped, and on one of these men, who now held the position of mayor, we called. He was a pleasant, courteous man from Yunnan, who said that he would like to leave the Province if he could. It seemed a natural wish.

The garrison of Yarkand consisted at that time of one Turki and one Chinese regiment. We paid a visit to the commander of the latter, General Liu, an intelligent and charming young man in an unusually smart uniform. He and his men were North Chinese who had been serving in the armies of the Young Marshal when, in 1932, they were driven out of Manchuria by the Japanese and interned, with their leader Sheng Shih-tsai, by the Russians in Siberia. General Liu, to my relief, did not ask for our passports and seemed to take us very much for granted; but he asked sensible and comprehensive questions about our journey and (as we afterwards heard) forwarded a report on us to Kashgar without delay. We took his photograph and parted very amicably.

Both the Chinese and the Turki troops looked less likely men than the Tungans. Most of their weapons were old Russian army rifles. The Turki troops sang on the march the Communist songs which Moscow had taught to her subjects in Central Asia and which you hear in the streets of Tashkent and Samarkand (a typical one has for refrain 'All about me is mine; now I come to take possession of it'). Here and there you noticed an officer with a mysterious and important air, wearing the Russian equivalent to a Sam Browne – a Tadjik probably or an Andijani from across the Soviet border, who now held a position of more political than military importance on the staff of a Turki unit. Soviet agents were in key positions everywhere.

The Swedish missionaries had, we were told, withdrawn to the mountains for the hot weather, but we were most courteously entertained by the aksakal, a dark handsome Afghan who had recently been awarded the rank of Khan Bahadur by the Government of India for saving the lives of the missionaries during the civil war. He produced Musa Ahun, a Turki who had a fair beard, a clear eye, and a robust physique and who looked altogether like a Viking. Musa Ahun had been with Stein on three of his expeditions, owned a watch with an inscription commemorating his faithful service, and spoke a little Chinese. In his agreeable company we went shopping in the bazaar.

On the way there we passed a professional story-teller who was holding the attention of a large crowd until Kini, sitting down nearby to change a film, provided a counter-attraction. The Turkis here looked a sickly lot; a very large proportion – I believe it is more than half – of the population of Yarkand suffers from goitre. It was evening, and the more prosperous merchants were leaving the bazaar for their houses in the oasis in Peking carts from whose hoods a blue awning was stretched forward to protect the horse from the sun. We pottered about and bought some little skull-caps embroidered with gold thread and also some of the soft leather boots which the women wear and for which Yarkand is famous. As a guide Musa Ahun was both paternal and informative; we felt very much like trippers.

We were both tired and a little enervated by long days in the sun and a diet of tea and bread; and Kini said that she wanted to stay on in Yarkand and rest. But Kashgar was near, I – as usual – was too impatient to be reasonable, and I callously refused to let her have her way. She afterwards told me that this was the only time on the whole journey when she got really angry with me.

CHAPTER XIII

HOBOES ON HORSEBACK

THAT night, at the aksakal's, we rifled a Khotan-bound postbag and borrowed the latest of M. Moldovack's *Times Weekly Editions*. This told us of the death of T. E. Lawrence, and as I sat there in the cool courtyard listening to the evening bugles I remembered the fantastic rumours which had linked him with Sinkiang. They had started, I suppose, in Moscow, but they were firmly believed at Urumchi. A young German engineer who – luckier than his two imprisoned compatriots – had returned from Urumchi to Peking in 1934 had assured us as a fact that Lawrence was active in the British cause among the Tungans; it was well known in Sinkiang, he said, and a friend of his in Srinagar had actually seen this ubiquitous hero start for the Himalayan passes with a force of Sikhs. Not the least fantastic part of the Lawrence legend is this Central Asian footnote.

Breakfast next morning was interrupted by General Liu, who returned our call with such comprehensive reciprocity that he even took our photographs as we had taken his. Then, still accompanied by the foolish and dog-like Nyaz, we said good-bye to the aksakal and faced once more the heat and the dust, not without protests from Kini.

But it was not, as it happened, a very arduous stage. The oasis straggled on along the road and there were only occasional tracts of desert. We halted at a little bazaar to drink tea in the shade. There were half a dozen Turkis doing likewise further down the street, and as I lay on my back dozing and listening to their talk, which had taken a geographical turn, I heard one of them reel off, in a very knowledgeable way, a string of place-names in Russian Central Asia. We fell into conversation and discovered that he spoke Russian. He was not a Turki but an Andijani –

a sly, sophisticated fellow, a kind of sardonic Autolycus, who had escaped from Soviet territory a few years before.

He was full of gossip, and very bitter against the Provincial Government and the Soviet agents who were running it. He told us of property confiscated and of rich men who had disappeared; of the strategic road which was being built from Kashgar to the Soviet frontier; of the redoubtable Tortinjis – levies of Soviet Kirghiz who terrorized the border country; of bribes and betrayals and intrigues. Then, still talking scandal, he took us into a room in the inn to show us the fourteen-year-old girl whom he had recently acquired by purchase; she knelt on the floor kneading dough, a pretty little creature with large dark eyes and a mischievous expression.

'I got her cheap,' said the Andijani complacently. 'The bottom's dropped out of the market. Girls cost twice as much a year ago.'

'And your wife?' asked Kini, who is a relentless catechist.

'Oh, she's waiting for me in Kashgar. Just now I am travelling on business; and I can afford not to travel alone.'

After this stimulating encounter we rode on for four or five hours to Kokrabat, where we camped pleasantly in the courtyard of the headman's house. The flies, like the mosquitoes before them, had now dwindled to a pest of negligible dimensions, and this made a great difference to our lives, for it meant that we could relax completely, and even sleep, during the day-time halts.

The next day's stage, through sheer desert, was long, hot, and uneventful; but on July 21st we were reintroduced to two things which, though widely different in themselves, were alike in that they had long been missing from our lives.

The first thing was the mountains. A still and brilliant morning promised a furnace of a day. We rode out of the dusty hamlet in which we had spent the night and suddenly saw the mountains soaring up on our left – clear-cut, snow-capped, illusorily close at hand. Because of the chronic though often imperceptible dust-haze with which the wind habitually veils the Tarim Basin we had not seen them since we reached Cherchen five weeks before; though I suppose they had been within eye-shot all the time. Now they took our breath away, and the dull slow chronicle of our desert journey acquired a new interest and a new colour, like a bad play redeemed by a splendid setting. But only momentarily; the curtain came down quickly on the transformation scene. Before noon the haze was reinstated, the mountains had vanished like a dream, and we marched once more between flat, smudged, and unprovocative horizons.

It was, we decided, the hottest day yet; but the morning's vision of snow was followed, in the afternoon, by a not less striking phenomenon. It was almost the end of the stage; we were riding into the outskirts of Yangi Hissar, an oasis of some importance. We had just crossed a river, and when we heard, round a corner ahead of us, a kind of roaring sound we put it down to a water-mill. But the noise was not static; it increased in volume; it was drawing nearer. With childish pleasure and childish incredulity we realized that we were about to behold, for the first time since we had left Lanchow, some sort of motor vehicle.

There were two of them – big Russian lorries full of soldiers which came charging round the corner in a cloud of dust and plunged downhill towards the river. They were not quite the white cliffs of Dover, but they made us feel very near to civilization. Later we heard that they were in pursuit of a party of soldiers from Kashgar who had mutinied because their pay was in arrears, wounded the commandant of the garrison, set fire to his yamen, and taken to the hills. We were still, it seemed, some way from Piccadilly.

We put up for the night at the house of the British aksakal in Yangi Hissar. We felt an imperative need to bathe, and this I, but not Kini, was able to gratify in a large public pond unattractively coated with green scum. (In England, I reflected, if one had been by some mischance immersed in such a pond one would have gone home instantly and had a bath.) We learnt that the British Consul-General was away from Kashgar camping in the

320

mountains but that the Vice-Consul would be there when we arrived. There were only two more stages before us, and as these could be done by an unemcumbered horseman in one day we wrote a note to the Consulate announcing our arrival and gave it to a consular messenger who had been travelling with us since Yarkand.

Next day we found the authorities disobligingly disposed to cancel promises they had made about our animals. The mayor was a fat and disagreeable Turki; the commandant was the officer who had been responsible for the massacre of the Yarkand garrison, and he had for his chief of staff and political mentor an Andijani from across the Soviet border. I paid aggressive and outspoken visits to both these officials, and at last the animals turned up. We left at noon, in the worst of the heat.

We had been lucky in all things, all along the road; but to-day Fate was to give us a little admonitory flick, a reminder of how easily, and in how many different ways, our journey could have been made less prosperous. Of all the fronts on which a traveller can be attacked his health is of course the most vulnerable and the most important; but his possessions are, though less important, equally vulnerable. In particular his diaries and his films are a constant source of anxiety, for if they are lost, stolen or damaged he is hard hit indeed.

But Fate let us off with a caution in the form of a practical joke. It came in two instalments. The authorities in Yangi Hissar had given us, for escort, an unprepossessing Turki soldier, and this fool, leading us off the main road on a short cut, attempted to ford a little river at the wrong place. The yellow current, running strongly, came up to the horses' bellies, but all would have been well if we had not struck a patch of quicksands. Kini's horse plunged, floundered, stuck fast, and heeled over on its side. I yelled to her to get her feet out of the stirrups, slid off my saddle into the water, and waded out as quickly as I could. The soldier, who had somehow scrambled across, yelled incomprehensible advice from the safety of the further bank.

The bogged horse had lost his nerve, but after a struggle

we yanked him out and got him ashore. Our own ducking was a luxury in disguise, but Kini's saddlebags and their contents were sodden. We cursed the soldier roundly, then took stock of the damage. Gently we prised apart the pages of her notebooks, in which the ink was already running; with infinite care we unfolded our Chinese passports – huge flimsy sheets of paper which immersion had reduced to wet and flaccid wafers smudged indecipherably with characters. Everything dried quite quickly and no great harm had been done; but we could not help feeling aggrieved that our first accident of this sort should have happened in such a silly way.

Kini, who always complained that I was luckier than she was, revived this theme; she had no cause to do so, though we did not know it at the time. We spent that night in Yapchan, gossiping about Siberia with some of Sheng Shih-tsai's soldiers who had been interned there, and rejoicing that this was to be our last night for some time in the too familiar squalor of an inn. It was really exciting to awake next morning and to remember, as you lay on the hard ground watching the stars fade in a paling sky, that to-day you were due to reach Kashgar, which had once seemed inaccessible and had always seemed remote.

The Consulate's uninvited guests were determined to do their poor best not to disgrace it on their first appearance. Kini put on a clean shirt, and I got out my last razor-blade and shaved. The moment had now come to unpack my suit. I had packed it in Peking against this very occasion; but I had packed it almost furtively, for it had then been a hundred to one that this occasion would never arise and I did not wish, by the arrogance implicit in the act, to provoke Fate into lengthening the odds still further. For five months and more, half-way across Asia, the suit had travelled – an emblem of hopes that were often very faint – at the bottom of my suitcase; it was a thin tropical suit and it took up no room. The creases imparted to it by the admirable Liu were still, I knew, inviolate and symmetrical. Though I care very little about keeping up appearances there are occasions when it is amusing, as well as proper, to do so, and I flattered myself that my entry into Kashgar would be distinguished by a standard of sartorial elegance which was the better worth attaining because its attainment would hardly be expected of me.

I opened my suitcase. Alas for foresight! A plague on vanity! The suitcase was full of water.

And not of water only. Thus diluted, the fine dust of the desert, which habitually found its way through the chinks of all our luggage, had become a thin but ubiquitous paste of mud. One by one I lifted out the soggy garments, noting as I did so that five rolls of film – more than 200 exposures – had also undergone immersion and that the type-written pages of my diary were congealed. The suit, the precious suit, came last of all. Wet it was bound to be, and soiled with mud; what I had not bargained for was that it should turn out to be bright green in colour. The dye from a sash bought in Khotan had run. . . .

I sent for the boy who had been in charge of the donkeys and gave him, to the best of my ability, hell. He explained tearfully that one of the donkeys had lain down in an irrigation channel and that he had been afraid to tell me about it. The other box which had been on the donkey contained, among less important things, our type-writers; these were fast rusting up. We got out some gun-oil and worked on them feverishly, cursing the wretched boy in a variety of languages. It was ironical that we should have brought our belongings safely through so many difficulties only to have them dropped ignominiously in the gutter on the last stage but one.

I had now to decide whether to enter Kashgar disguised as a lettuce, or looking like something that had escaped from Devil's Island. It seemed to me that, if there is one thing worse than wearing bright green clothes, it is wearing bright green clothes which are also soaking wet; I therefore sadly resumed the shorts and shirt of every day and prepared to let down the British Raj.

After rather more than the usual fuss and delay animals were produced, and we rode out of Yapchan for the last lap on the desert road. Gradually the morning's annoyances lost their hold upon our minds. We felt elated and incredulous, and when, in the middle of the afternoon, we sighted the walls of the New City our excitement became almost painful.

But the New City of Kashgar is, as we soon discovered, some six or seven miles from the Old, and with a feeling of anticlimax we settled down to another two hours' ride. We were on a motor road now, a broad dusty avenue between trees, beside which ran the single telegraph wire from Urumchi. We were unattended and wretchedly mounted; our saddles and bridles were tied up with string, and under their coating of dust our faces were far darker than any of the bazaar-folk we passed on the road. We began to have morbid misgivings. The representatives of His Britannic Majesty's Government in the Far East are by no means invariably pleased to see travellers from the interior, who, they fear, will begin by asking for assistance and end by getting into trouble; we wished devoutly that our own appearance was calculated to allay such fears. 'If only we had a topee,' I thought; a topee would have helped a lot.

Then, suddenly, at a turn of the road, we saw a kind of cross between a droshky and a station fly, and in charge of it a turbaned orderly in khaki. This highly reassuring figure galloped up, presented us with a kindly note of welcome, and invited us to dismount and take our places in the vehicle. This, with alacrity, we did, and a moment later we were being whirled at a dizzy speed (we had not travelled so fast since we left the lorries at Lanchow) towards the Old City. Past a huddle of the usual mud houses, past the plumed poles of a graveyard, under the huge curving wall of the citadel, and up an incline towards an outlying group of buildings. . . .

Somebody was riding out to meet us: a tall, immaculate young man (with a topee) on a grey polo pony. We stopped and got out and shook hands.

'I'm Barlow,' said the tall young man. 'The Consul-General's away in the hills on holiday. I'm glad you got here all right. Let's go on up to the house.'

We drove on, exchanging with the young man on the

pony small talk so elaborately casual and conventional that I felt as if I was acting in a skit on something.

'I'm sorry to have dropped out of the blue like this,' I said. 'You see, we couldn't give you more than a day's notice . . .'

'It's not as unexpected as you might think,' said Barlow. 'We've had an inquiry about you from the Secretary of State.'

It was news to us that we had been lost. We had completed the course in bogey or under, and we felt affronted by this governmental solicitude and guilty about the domestic fears which had doubtless inspired it. Still, nothing mattered very much at the moment. The carriage drew up, and we passed, as in a dream, under a gateway above which the Lion and the Unicorn were fighting for the crown.

'I don't know whether you drink beer . . .' Barlow was saying.

He very soon did.

PART SEVEN

THE ROOF OF THE WORLD

CHAPTER I

KASHGAR-LES-BAINS

To most people Kashgar, which is five or six weeks' journey, over 15,000 foot passes, from the nearest railhead in India, must seem a place barbarously remote; but for us its outlandish name spelt Civilization.

The raptures of arrival were unqualified. Discovery is a delightful process, but rediscovery is better; few people can ever have enjoyed a bath more than we did, who had not had one for five and a half months. Usually (it was to happen to us in India) your return from a primitive to a civilized life is an affair of stages – a gradual process of transition, not a sudden step from one mode of existence to another. The last laps take the edge off the contrast, and so many small but valued amenities have accrued by the time you reach your goal that you can hardly remember what it felt like to lack every single one of the blessings that you now enjoy.

But the end of the desert road was not like this for us. One night we slept on the floor, drank tea in mugs, ate doughy bread, argued with officials, were stared at, dreaded the next day's heat; twenty-four hours later we were sitting in comfortable arm-chairs with long drinks and illustrated papers and a gramophone playing, all cares and privations banished. It was a heavenly experience. The most ordinary appurtenances of civilized life took on a curious and charming novelty. It seemed, for instance, delightfully funny to be sitting down to dinner at a table, and the servants who handed round the dishes had something of the glamour of djinns. As for sleeping in a bed, that too was an amusing and eccentric procedure; it felt, indeed, so odd that I hardly slept at all.

We stayed a fortnight in Kashgar, leading a country-house life against an exotic background coloured, in the early John Buchan manner, with international melodrama. Arthur Barlow the Vice-Consul, had seen me act more than once at Oxford; but he was of a forgiving disposition and prepared to let bygones be bygones. He was extraordinarily nice to us and when, after we had been there a few days, Colonel and Mrs. Thomson-Glover returned from the hills I decided that I had never trespassed on better hospitality. The Consulate was a pleasant house with a lovely garden, standing on a little bluff outside the city. From its terrace you looked across the green and chequered valley of a small river towards the too seldom visible mountains.

It was on this terrace that Mrs. Thomson-Glover had been shot the year before. She and the others had been watching Tungan troops advancing on the heels of a Turki-Kirghiz rabble who had just been ousted from their temporary domination of the Old City. The soldiers were streaming across the valley below the Consulate when one of them knelt down and opened fire on the group of white people. He was some 400 yards away, and by the ordinary standards of Chinese marksmanship the consular party were in no great danger. But the man happened to be a good or at any rate a lucky shot, and Mrs. Thomson-Glover, who is a peculiarly indomitable sort of person and who had not even bothered to take cover, got a bullet through the shoulder. The city was in a ferment all that night; there were ugly scenes at the gates of the Consulate, and from the ramparts of the citadel, which dominate it, fire was intermittently poured into the compound. Casualties among the consular staff included the doctor, who received wounds from which he later died. It seems clear that the Tungan leaders were not responsible for this outrage, which was presumably engineered by those elements in the province which have most cause to wish the British ill.

We idled shamelessly in Kashgar, eating and sleeping and playing games and asking interminable questions of our long-suffering hosts. The city is, not without reason, very prone to spy-fever, and the night we arrived the bazaar rumour ran that a British agent had ridden in from Khotan, accompanied by a White Russian disguised as a woman. This was hard on Kini; but the next evening we both played Association Football with the Consulate guard of Hunzas, so that rumour had a longer life than most.

The foreign community in Kashgar is small, and when we were there the Swedish missionaries, who with the British consular staff make up the non-Russian part of it, were absent in the hills. The Russians were a motley and rather incalculable lot. Their Consulate was a large one, and also comprised a heavily staffed trade-agency. Kini and I used to go there a good deal, to bathe in their swimming-pool. They were always charming to us, but appeared to find us disconcerting.

The Russians have long entertained curious and romantic ideas about me. Once, in Siberia, with the help of much vodka, I found out something about my G.P.U. *dossier*, in which it is stated 'This young man is a favourite writer of the capitalist aristocracy and has served as a volunteer in the Japanese Army.' The Soviet Press, equally flattering and equally inaccurate, usually refers to me as 'the veteran journalist'. But what I liked best of all was when the *Daily Worker* published, on my return to England, a series of three articles about me, attacking what I had written in *The Times* about the politics of Central Asia and exposing 'the real motives' behind my journey. Unfortunately I was never quite able to make out what these motives were, for they were not very good articles; and as the number of the *Daily Worker*'s readers who had seen my stuff in *The Times* must have been infinitesimal they had no journalistic justification at all. But they made me out a sinister (though clumsy) agent of Imperialist intrigue, a kind of shady Lawrence; and I could not help feeling pleased that anyone should take me so seriously.

We led a very pleasant life in Kashgar. In the evening we played tennis with the Russians, or football or volley-ball with the Hunza guard, who numbered fifteen. The men – tall, stalwart mountaineers from up the Gilgit road – were a detachment from the Hunza Company of the Gilgit

331

Scouts, and wore in their caps a silver ibex head, the badge of that romantic regiment; they were charming, child-like people, and we took a great liking to them. Twice a week there was polo, organized and led – her bullet-wound notwithstanding – by Mrs. Thomson-Glover, and the Hunzas, whose national game it is, performed with great dash. Ponies apart, the Consulate was well and variously supplied with livestock: dogs, pigeons, wild duck, a young camel, and an eagle, bought from the hawking Kirghiz. There was also a respectable library. It was a delightful house to stay in.

We spent a good deal of our time paying official calls. My memory of these is confused. The whole city was in effect run by the secret police, the Russian advisers, and the Soviet Consulate, and most of the high officials were only figureheads. There was, for instance, Mr. Kung, who was a kind of mayor; we had hardly got through the formalities with him when he was superseded by a Mr. Hsu, from Urumchi, and we had to start all over again. A less impermanent and a more colourful dignitary was General Liu Pin, the commandant of the garrison in the New City: a squat, tough, ribald little man with a plump and cheerful wide. He spoke a few words of English and of Russian, claimed to have been connected with the Y.M.C.A. in China, liked drinking, and had recently been wounded in the foot by mutineers.

Then there was Ma Shao-wu. Ma Shao-wu had held official positions in the Province for thirty years and more, ending up as Taotai of Kashgar. Throughout the crises which that city had with bewildering rapidity undergone during the civil war, Ma had adroitly contrived to keep in with almost all the principal factions; but after things quieted down something in his conduct of affairs had displeased his masters at Urumchi and an attempt had been made to liquidate him. One night, when he was driving back to his house in the oasis with his wife and child, he was ambushed; a gang of unseen assailants, hidden behind a wall, poured a volley into the hooded Peking cart at almost point-blank range. The wounded horses bolted down the road, swerved into a tree, and collapsed. (The dark stains still showed on the tree when we were in Kashgar.) But the assassins had bungled their job; the child was unhurt, the wife was only slightly wounded, and the old man, though terribly shot about the legs, was able to drag himself into the cover of a maize field. Eventually he got home on a donkey, a doctor was summoned, and by the end of the summer he was convalescing. The police, with a cynicism unusual even in Sinkiang, did not even make a pretence of rounding up the men who had shot him. It was a dirty business.

He was a frail and charming old man, very much the old type of official with his long silk robe, his spittoon, and his precise Peking speech. 'I have served the Government of China for many years,' he said, 'first the Emperor, and after that the Republican Government at Nanking. I have always tried to do my best; but I must have committed errors – though I do not know what they were – or this misfortune would not have befallen me. I have lost face.' In his time, no doubt, he had been corrupt and rascally; but I preferred him to the shoddy, specious Kungs and Hsus, and I could not help feeling sorry for him. It was said that they were shortly sending him to Moscow; and months later I read somewhere in a newspaper that Ma Shao-wu, a prominent Sinkiang official, had arrived in Moscow and had refuted, in an interview, the lying allegations of Imperialist powers that the province was under Soviet influence; there were no traces of Soviet influence, Ma Shao-wu had said.

Official interviews apart, we neither had nor needed much to amuse us. There was always, of course, the bazaar. The wares, the architecture, the atmosphere were the same as they had been in Yarkand, Khotan, Keriya; but the crowd was subtly different. Slant-eyed Kirghiz and bearded Tadjiks from the hills moved with a hint of swagger among the self-effacing Turkis. Here and there a stiff black horse-hair veil, a brightly striped robe, betrayed a woman from Andijan or Samarkand. An occasional Russian lorry bumped in from Urumchi, to scatter the knots of philosophers gathered in an open space before the principal

333

mosque. More rarely still a Russian 'adviser' – dressed for the backblocks but not in uniform, admirably mounted – trotted down the street; the bulge in his pocket, his penetrating but evasive stare, his air of furtive consequence conformed splendidly to the standards of discreet melo-drama. You felt, in short, that you were at the end of the dead desert, which had swallowed – but showed no signs of having digested – the outposts of more than one civiliz-ation; you felt the nearness of another Power, of other races, beyond the dust-haze and the mountains.

But the setting was familiar, though the actors and the acting had more of variety and significance than before. From the city walls you saw only a huddle of flat mud roofs, broken here and there by the sweeping and bedevilled eaves of a yamen or a temple. Through the dusty sun-lit streets donkeys trotted, as you had often watched them trot, loaded with grey lumps of salt or with bundles of fodder or of fuel. The same piles of bread and vegetables and fruits attracted, in the open booths, the ubiquitous but no longer overwhelming flies. The same Russian sugar, Russian scent, Russian cigarettes and matches preponder-ated in the wares displayed by more ambitious merchants. Strings of camels stalked through the city westwards, carrying – at a gait and pace well known – bales of wool and other goods to the Russian railhead over the passes, at Osh in Andijan. But here there was a difference; the camels' headropes were fixed not to nose-pegs but to gaily decorated halters. That small thing, more than any other, brought home the fact that we were near a racial frontier.

CHAPTER II

WINGS OVER TURKISTAN

THERE was only one noteworthy incident while we were in Kashgar, and that was the arrival of two Soviet aeroplanes from Tashkent. Shortly before we got there there had been an outbreak of pneumonic plague in the oasis; the infection was supposed to have originated among the marmots in the passes on the Soviet frontier. Both Consulates had put their doctors at the disposal of the municipal authorities, and both had sent for anti-plague serum.

Here I must digress, to describe one of the more amusing decorations of the Kashgar scene. This was the wireless transmitting set in the Soviet Consulate. Its existence was a secret jealously guarded but known to the whole province. The Russians kept, or tried to keep, it dark because, no licence having been obtained for it from the Nanking Government, they had no right to have it on their premises. The whole situation was artificial, and never more delightfully so than when the British met the Russians. The British got their news of the outside world by the trans-Himalayan mail, and the freshest of it was the short Reuter bulletins from the terminus of the Indian telegraph line at Misgar; the Russians, on the other hand, got newspapers from Moscow which were only a fortnight old and sometimes less. Even though the wireless had to be politely ignored, it was therefore justifiable to assume that they were better informed than the British. So we always asked them for news; and it was pathetic to see their faces cloud with concentration, their fingers unconsciously counting back the days, while they sorted out all that they had heard recently on the wireless from what would have been their latest news in papers a fortnight old.

Whether, in these circumstances, they permitted themselves the indiscretion of wirelessing to Moscow for serum

I do not know; but their supply was expected to arrive long before the British which, even after it had been flown up to Gilgit, was still a minimum of fifteen days by mail-runner from Kashgar. It was learnt, moreover, that the Russian serum was coming all the way by air. (The mountain barrier on the Soviet frontier is much lower and narrower than on the Indian; with no landing-place between Gilgit and Kashgar a flight over the Himalayas could only be undertaken at very great risk.)

Days passed, however, and the Russian serum was still on its way. The outbreak of plague, kept under control by the Consulate doctors, had almost run its course when the Soviet planes arrived, only forty-eight hours ahead of the mail-runner with the serum from India.

Three planes, it was rumoured, had started; but only two landed at Kashgar. They circled lengthily over the much astonished city, curious silver innovations against the sempiternal blue, a perhaps prophetic portent in the Central Asian sky. A prominent official went out of his way to assure us that they came from Urumchi; this was typical of the clumsily disingenuous attitude of official circles in Sinkiang, who are morbidly quick to disown any symptoms of Soviet influence. The Soviet Consulate made no attempt to conceal the fact that the planes came from Russia, as indeed they had every right to do.

They brought with them, besides the vaccine, one female and two male doctors. On our last night in Kashgar a banquet was given by the officials, half in their honour and half in ours. The invitations were for seven o'clock, but the party from the British Consulate, who turned up at half-past eight, were among the first to arrive. The tables were laid in an embowered pavilion, once the property of a rich Turki who, like many of his kind, had disappeared from Kashgar society and probably from this world.

We stepped out of our carriages to find that the alley leading to the gateway was lined by the massed bands of the garrison. The musicians were neither numerous nor well-equipped, but as we walked down their ranks they launched at us a point-blank blast of harmony which all but blew our heads off. The garden, when we reached it, bore, in spite of paper lanterns, a martial rather than a festive appearance. You never know what may not happen at a banquet in Kashgar, and each of our official hosts had prudently brought his own bodyguard. Turki and Chinese soldiers lounged everywhere; automatic rifles and executioners' swords were much in evidence, and the Mauser pistols of the waiters knocked ominously against the back of your chair as they leant over you with the dishes.

The food was cooked in the foreign style, and the old English custom of serving benedictine with the soup was punctiliously observed. There was also brandy from the Caucasus, but Kini and I got hold of some coloured vodka (labelled, for some unknown reason, 'English Bitters') and stuck to that, for vodka is a good clean drink. The commandant of the Turki troops was of course an abstainer, but nobody else was anything like one; by the time we got to the speeches the atmosphere was thick with benevolence.

Speeches were made by almost everyone, but General Liu Pin's was the one I liked the best. He spoke, with an air of pugnacity, in hoarse Chinese; and, though he paused every now and then for his remarks to be translated by the widely scattered interpreters into English, Russian, and Turki, he never paused for long. The interpreters, however, stuck to their guns like men, so that very soon four speeches were being made in four languages, simultaneously and at a feverish rate. General Liu, who was dressed in a green suit with a belted jacket and an open collar and whose resemblance to an art student in an operatic chorus was spoilt only by the enormous automatic pistol dangling at his hip, surveyed with complacency the peaceful and prosperous condition of the province, thanked both Consulates for their help in combating the plague, and ended with a peroration about Kini and me. Both the League of Nations (Kini was known to come from Geneva) and the Newspaper - for - the - Enlightened - Apprehension - of - Scholars were complimented with a warmth which might have seemed, even to their most fervent admirers, excessive had not the General brought his speech to an end with the

337

disarming admission that he had not the faintest recollection of what he had been saying or why he had said it. Whereupon, with a loud cry of 'Y.M.C.A.!', he started to dance, uncertainly but with great vigour, and in this impromptu exhibition Kini was soon persuaded to join him. Nobody was assassinated.

CHAPTER III

INTO THE PAMIRS

THE next day, which was August 8th, we took the road for India. For ordinary travellers the journey from Kashgar to Gilgit takes something like thirty days, though the mail-runners do it in much less; from Gilgit it is ten or twelve pony-stages on to Srinagar and the motor-road. Thanks to the Thomson-Glovers' hospitality we felt fat and fresh and quite capable of taking the Himalayas in our stride.

The authorities – with us, as with all British subjects, dilatory and obstructionist behind their parade of affability – had held us up for several days. First it was a matter of our exit visas, then there was the question of passports for the pony-men we had hired, and finally there was some bother over customs formalities. But at last all was ready. Mr. Hsu, the newly installed mayor, sent us a present of a carpet each and provided an escort of two Chinese soldiers. Our inconsiderable luggage was loaded on to four ponies, and the three Turkis in charge of them made to the Consul-General the usual worthless pledges of their devotion to our interests. Mrs. Thomson-Glover, generously unmindful of the fact that her housekeeping had to be done on the basis of one supply-caravan from India *per annum*, pressed on us a large store of delicacies; and her husband lent me a fine grey stallion which I was to present with his compliments to the Mir of Nagar, whose territory borders the Gilgit road.

So we started in fine style though rather sadly, for we felt sorry to be leaving the Consulate and its kind and charming occupants; travellers were never better entertained than we had been. Barlow rode with us through the bazaar, then said good-bye and turned back; we went on through a blazing afternoon towards Yapchan, for we had to retrace our steps to Yangi Hissar before leaving the desert road for good.

It was as hot as we ever remembered it being. We conversed limply with our escort, of whom the elder, Liu, was a kind of corporal; he had a wide mouth and a cheerful disposition and I liked the look of him. Unfortunately he too was riding a stallion, and mine, who was called Cloud, was of a jealous disposition and kicked the other murderously whenever he got a chance. Well after dark we reached Yapchan, where more than a fortnight before the tragedy of the suitcase had been discovered; we slept in the yard of a poor inn on a little raised platform across which, all night long, unaccountably marched an unending procession of toads in single file.

Next morning we discovered that a dog had stolen the Consulate's parting gift of a cold chicken and that two of the tent-poles had been left behind; and Cloud, in a fit of passion, kicked a hole in my suitcase, for which Yapchan was an exceptionally unlucky place. It looked as if we hadn't started in such fine style, after all.

Again it was hot, and at the end of the day's stage we rode into Yangi Hissar with our tongues hanging out. The aksakal welcomed us with sour milk and ice, and I spent the evening thwarting an attempt by the Turkis to delay us for a day. The escort was tickled to death by the discovery that the one miserable Chinese eating place in the bazaar called itself the Peking Restaurant; like many of Sheng Shih-tsai's Manchurian troops they were both Shantung men, and very sophisticated by comparison with the boorish Tungan soldiery to whom we were accustomed.

From Yangi Hissar we branched south off the desert road, and my diary records that the next day was 'perhaps the best march since we hit the gobi'. It brought us to Igiz Yar, a little oasis on a rolling slope of piedmont gravel, and from here, in spite of the dust-haze, you could see the hills. It made a lot of difference.

Early the next morning we left the desert for good, entering the mountains by a narrow valley whose mouth was guarded by a little deserted Chinese fort. The valley floor, between steep jagged hills of loess and rocks, was green and even lush in places; there were a few small clusters of mud houses under poplars and apricot trees. We had to ford the river, and in doing so Wu, the junior member of the escort, dropped his squat German carbine into the torrent. With loud and imperious cries he summoned up some Turki herdsmen and set them to the work of salvage, throwing stones to guide them as one does with a retriever; in the end they fished the weapon out and departed, unthanked.

We did a long stage and camped by an isolated shepherd's house at a place called Aktalla. It felt wonderful to be back in the hills, where the air was cool and the water clear, where there were no flies and no empty horizons. We pitched the tent on good firm ground, and Kini cooked a gigantic meal of eggs and onions. We no longer felt homesick for Kashgar, or indeed for anywhere else.

The next day was the Twelfth of August. But it seemed unreasonable and exorbitant to regret the Highlands when the peaks about you ran to 20,000 feet, and I was not unduly sentimental. It was a grey day. The Turkis pleaded a sick horse and were slow in starting. There were no more trees up here, and the valley had narrowed to a gorge in which the going was often bad. Once Cloud stumbled on a close-shaved ledge and I had a nasty moment; and once, fording the river, one of the loads got dipped. But in Kashgar we had had the sense to seal up our films in watertight tins, so we no longer lived in dread of their immersion.

I was riding, as I had ridden ever since Cherchen, in shorts; towards the end of the stage a small, determined wind blew down the valley and I finished up numb with cold. A little rain fell while we were making camp, and we dined, a thought disconsolately, off half-cooked mutton, the Turkis having annexed a stray sheep which met them on the road. As we were settling down for the night a shot rang out behind the tent, and as its echoes went rolling round the crags above us I thought that perhaps Tartary was going to provide, for once, something more positive than monotony; but it was only Liu, defying imaginary bandits.

Morning came, very cold but brilliant. As we were starting, a mail-runner passed through camp, bringing dark stories of flooded rivers up the road. We rode off, rejoicing in the sunshine and in the stark but friendly background of the Pamirs. We were now entering country whose rare inhabitants were mostly Kirghiz or Tadjiks, and presently we passed a Kirghiz lady almost embarrassingly fraught with local colour; she not only rode a yak but also wore a great white hat shaped like a saucepan and typical of these parts. Later we met the headman from Kashka Su, the next tiny settlement of tents; he and his outlandish train were well-disposed, and he sent back a youth on a more than usually nimble yak to prepare for our reception.

When we got to Kashka Su there were only three yurts, but a cooking fire was at our disposal (in the matter of fuel we were back on the dung standard) and we pitched our tent next door in highly romantic surroundings. It was Liu's ambition to shoot a marmot, and I took him on a punitive expedition against these arrogantly vocal creatures. The expedition was not a great success, but we enjoyed it. Liu pretended to treat the whole thing as a joke but really took it very seriously. Unfortunately his marksmanship suffered from his habit of closing his eyes tightly before pulling the trigger, and although a considerable quantity of the Provincial Government's ammunition was expended there were no casualties among the marmots.

The people of the place killed a sheep for us, and as Kini had gone off to climb the highest available mountain and as I was ravenously hungry I decided to cook dinner myself. I am by nature both clumsy and improvident; and by the time I had set fire to the fat, burnt off my eyelashes, and nearly razed a yurt to the ground I was quite glad when Kini came back and took charge.

We had reached, in this high maze of empty sunlit valleys, the most idyllic stage of the journey. We were well mounted and well provisioned, and from time to time – once in a day, perhaps – we felt (at least I did) a keen, an almost painful stab of excitement at the realization that we were measurably near our goal. For the first time we were entitled to look forward to getting home; and although Kini, for whom the world is much too small, would genuinely have preferred to have gone on travelling indefinitely, and although I had nothing to complain of in our life and knew from experience that for me England had more in common with *ennui* than the first syllable of her name, there *was*, without a doubt, something sharply satisfactory in the thought that we were at last approaching the destination for which with faint hopes we had set out so many months before.

The only fly in our ointment was the Turkis and their ponies. We had hired five ponies, one for Kini to ride and four for the packs; but the Turkis had brought along three of their own, carrying bales of embroidered saddle-bags and similar wares to be sold in the bazaar at Gilgit. Their loads were heavy, ours were light; and as half of the ponies were wretched animals, and as the Turkis, like all Turkis, loaded them carelessly and treated them rough, at least two of the ponies were intermittently unfit for work and most of the others suffered horribly from galls. The result of this was that our picked ponies were given the heavy loads and the crocks were given ours; so that the caravan moved slowly and – what was worse from the point of view of our peace of mind – painfully. There are few worse travelling companions than dishonesty and cruelty; and both, thanks to the Turkis' tactics, were with us all the time.

At Kashka Su, with steep passes ahead of us, we commandeered yaks. We did not want to commandeer them, but the escort were insistent. We imagined that they knew that the three crippling loads were merchandise of the Turkis; but the Turkis saw to it that they knew nothing of the sort. So yaks were called up to carry the foreigners' luggage and when, by stealth, I gave a present of money to the local matriarch Liu found out about it and was furious; his Olympian, plentipotentiary status had been undermined and he had lost face.

He and his comrade-in-arms, who had hitherto been changing animals at every stage, had now to ride on yaks, no horses being available. To the Chinese, as to the English, the yak appears a most barbaric animal; but to the Chinese 'barbarian' is a term provocative rather of contempt than of curiosity, and the yak, being indigenous to a part of what he regards as his dominions, must not be treated with that slightly snobbish respect which Western civilization (very rightly) accords to primitive things. The escort, therefore, sat their shaggy, grumbling mounts with an air of distant but apprehensive condescension: like a duchess on a merry-go-round.

We left Kashka Su and struck up a steep side valley. 'The Gilgit Road', here as elsewhere for much of its length, is a courtesy title; and on the Chinese side of the frontier it indicates no more than the only practicable route for abnormally agile animals. Rough, opportunist tracks zigzagged up to steeply sloping pastures just below the peaks; the early sunlight, falling athwart the long virgin tracts of turf, gave to the red-coated marmots a certain glory and surprise which their peevish sibilation could not altogether kill. Liu bombarded them, violating the turf six feet from the burrows at whose mouths they sat; a mongrel dog who was following us, wise to the game, contented himself with disillusioned and vindictive sniffs at long range and did not jeopardize his dignity.

Up and on we went, riding like gods on the roof of the world; then dropped down steeply into a great valley, at the tail of which we found two yurts. We rested, drank milk, changed yaks, and pushed on, aiming at a double stage. A dry and tortuous gully brought us to another pass which we climbed very slowly, the horses fighting for breath. The descent beyond it was rough going, and as we led our animals clatteringly down a steep stream-bed we marvelled, not for the last time, how the Haardt-Citroen Expedition had ever even pretended to believe that they could get their caterpillar tractors from Gilgit to Kashgar. At dusk, with two stiff stages behind us, we camped at a place called Tohil Bulung, where there were yurts. The escort got in late, ruffled in temper and chary of sitting down after their feats of yakmanship.

CHAPTER IV

THE LAST TOWN IN CHINA

THE next day was August 15th; it was exactly six months since we had left Peking. We did a trying stage, working our way up the valley of a violent river which we had to ford six times. The yaks came through the torrent bluntly and stertorously, like tugs, but the tired sore ponies floundered with an air of helplessness among the submerged rocks. Distraction was provided by a covey of chikkor, on which I opened fire without success. At noon the valley branched in two; we followed the westerly fork which widened as we got higher and led us out at last on to a bare col where three Kirghiz yurts comprised the settlement of Yan Bulak. The Kirghiz, tough and slant-eyed, received us kindly, and Kini, who had lived with their race on the Russian side of the Tien Shan, felt very much at home in their tents. The warmth of our welcome was, it is true, tempered when Liu accidentally discharged the rook rifle through the roof; but they soon got over that.

That night in the little tent we had a great feast of macaroni and vodka to celebrate six months on the road. The scramble of departure – so far off now in time and space – was luxuriously recalled: the fancy dresses and the flashlight on the station platform, the poor Smigunovs' excitement, our own wild guesses into the future . . . It all seemed to belong to another journey, made by other people.

Chichiklik, some 15,000 feet high and the biggest of the Pamir passes, was still before us, and we attacked it the next day. All the morning we rode easily on the turf of a wide, pleasant valley. There were marmots everywhere, and for the first time we saw lammergeyers – huge whitish vultures with something monstrous and prehistoric about their dingy, startling bulk. A donkey belonging to a Turki caravan ahead of us had fallen down and died, and three or four of these great birds were waiting for the human scavengers to finish with the carcase; the Turkis were taking the shoes off it.

At the end of the valley we began to climb less gradually, and soon came to a big stony corrie with a dark green lochan in it. Snow, beaten ice-hard by the wind, armoured the peaks around us. The pass itself was at the top of a steep, forbidding slope of screes, and up this, picking its way awkwardly among the boulders, our caravan began to wind in zigzags. The Turkis stabbed the wretched ponies midway between eye and nostril with long iron skewers which they carried for the purpose; this let a good deal of blood, and though it looked a barbarous and cruel practice it undoubtedly made the animals' breathing easier at high altitudes. Our Turkis always did it on passes and, judging by the amount of blood with which the boulders of the Chichiklik were spattered, it was a universal custom.

At the head of the pass we rested, looking back with complacency at the gashed labyrinth of hills and valleys that now lay behind us. Then we went on, scrambling out of the screes on to easier going, and dropped down to a wide table-land where many yaks were grazing. We rode across this slantwise, plagued a little by the wind, to camp in the evening under another but a lesser pass. For some time there had been strife among the Turkis, and now Tokhta, the idlest, greediest, and most ineffectual of the three, came to me and announced with tears that he went in terror of his life. I called them all together – the dignified one who spoke a little Russian, the tough one who looked like a caricature of a French gendarme, and the abject Tokhta – and abused them in the dregs of three languages; they were tiresome people. We settled down for the night in a bad temper which was not improved by the discovery that our precious Worcester sauce had emptied itself into a bag of Turfan raisins. However, we were slightly mollified by a present of milk brought by some Tadjiks who sprang unaccountably out of the naked plateau. They were bearded, hook-nosed men, wearing hats of a model very

347

similar to that evolved, some years ago, by *The Daily Mail*; they are said to be the racial prototypes of *homo alpinus*.

We made a mildly inauspicious start the next morning. One of Kini's Chinese stirrup-irons had broken, Liu was bucked off his yak and lost face, and there was a good deal of promiscuous shouting at Tokhta. But we climbed the little pass without mishap, and after riding for some time along a high, shallow valley began to descend steeply by a gorge into that great trough of the Pamirs known as Sarikol. This was the worst bit of the road so far. There was no track, and the horses needed the agility of ibex to navigate the broken, boulder-strewn floor of the ravine, down which, to make things worse, a stream ran powerfully.

But we came out at last, unscathed, on to a long bare slope of land where the sun (for we were down to a mere 10,000 feet) struck hotly. From this we descended once more, but easily, through a defile; forded the upper waters of the Yarkand Darya; and saw pleasantly extended before us the green pastures of Sarikol or the Taghdumbash Pamir. We were now not far from Tashkurgan, of which, according to Skrine, 'Ptolemy speaks as having been the extreme western emporium of Serikê (China)'.

Towards evening the town came in sight. Below the bastions of an excessively romantic fort mud roofs and tree-tops huddled. I have a liking for forts, and this one, dominating wide pastures beneath a range of snow-peaks, seemed to be wildly beautiful. The plain round the small bazaar was dotted with horses and camels, many of them with their packsaddles on, and a few clusters of tents supplied the suburbs. We liked the look of Tashkurgan.

The British aksakal was an aged Hindu with a squint. He had a slight and somehow Bunyanesque command of English and described himself, not without pride, as 'failed middle school, A.D. 1902'. We established ourselves in his house and read with interest the testimonials from travellers which he had collected in the course of his long, lonely years of service under the Government of India. He was a charming old man.

In Tsarist days the Russians used to keep a patrol of

Cossacks illicitly garrisoned at Tashkurgan; the subtler Bolsheviks run the place by means of agents, who take their orders from the nearest Soviet frontier post, at Kizil Rabat. We had half expected, for that reason, trouble at Tashkurgan, but the chief local mischief-maker was away hunting mutineers in the hills, and his deputies – a seedy Chinese and a seedy Tadjik – chopped our Kashgar exit-visas without a murmur.

So the next day we were ready to start on the last three stages which would take us out of Chinese territory; but the Turkis were not. As usual they fought, and as usual they lost, a delaying action. They had no grain for the ponies, they said, and no bread for themselves. Both these war-cries had been raised in Yangi Hissar, and in both the note of defiance sounded but hollowly. These matters, I told them, were their own look-out. Grain was procurable in the bazaar, and so was bread; it did not need twenty-four hours to rectify the results of their improvidence. Their resistance crumpled before an imperious and sardonic manner; the Turkis, however plausibly they blustered, were easy people to handle. They speeded the delivery of their grain, had their bread baked quickly, and got under way in the early afternoon.

Tashkurgan was a frontier town if ever there was one. It had, among other things, the air of living on passers-by, on people from outside. The shops, such as they were, sold mainly the things you needed on the road – ropes and boots and fur hats and victuals – leavened with such finery, sweetmeats, and medicines as might attract men to whom the inconsiderable town was what a port is to a sailor. There was little movement in the single street, but the rare loiterer might belong to any one of half a dozen races. Soviet influence had becalmed there several caravans bound for India, and there was also a large party of Afghan merchants camped disconsolately and indefinitely in the best of the poor inns. All these were suffering from trumped-up passport regulations, inspired by aimless malice. We visited the Afghans, and Kini, seeking to ingratiate herself with the embittered monkey who acted as their regimental mascot, was mildly savaged for her pains.

At three o'clock we moved off, under a threatening sky. The Kashgar escort had discharged their mission; we rewarded them liberally with wads of paper money – from now on useless to us and difficult to change in Tashkurgan – and were provided with two local substitutes. One of these was a glib Turki from Turfan, the shoddiest type of the *miles gloriosus*; the other was a tough and slightly less unreliable Tadjik with an oafish, lycanthropic face which suggested a good-natured illustration to the tale of Little Red Riding Hood.

Soon after leaving the town we had to ford the river, here unexpectedly wide and deep; the loads came through all right, but two of the men got a wetting. By the time we reached the further bank dusk was not far off, and we stopped for the night in a house whose kindly people were bullied by our escort. Here we discovered that the Turkis had played their old game of requisitioning horses for their own loads under the pretext that they were part of our baggage; so the usual irritable and inconclusive court-martial was held, the defendants (whose employer had perforce been paid in advance) knowing full well that no penalty could be visited upon them.

We slept uneasily in a room too full and too redolent of humanity and set off again in a grey, dank morning. After the challenging and often lovely landscapes of the last few days the river valley here seemed dull and featureless. But after riding for three hours we saw approaching us three horsemen in whose appearance there was something unforeseen. For months we had been used to watching people ride towards us from a great distance, and we knew instinctively that there was something exceptional about these three; but at first we could not assess or define their oddity, any more than a wild-fowler can always label on sight a duck whose manner of flight brands it, almost imperceptibly, a stranger species to his beat.

Soon, however, we made out that these vaguely anomalous figures had heads which were not only abnormally

350

large but white; and a few minutes later we were conversing with Europeans who wore – uneasily, as for charades – extravagantly wide topees. They were Swedish missionaries – one man and two women – returning to their duties at Kashgar. Their appearance, except for their topees, was dowdy, and they were nice people, with that unsensational outlook which is doubly appreciated when you meet it in the back of beyond. It happened that I knew several of their colleagues and compatriots in Mongolia, and although, like most of the people we encountered on the road, they did not know what to make of us, we had some friendly talk before parting. They said that there was a telegram waiting for me at Gilgit, and this news – for I am a kind of specialist in anticipation – was almost better than receiving the telegram itself. They also said, which was much less heartening, that they had been held up for a day by a Soviet agent at the Chinese frontier post called Mintaka Karaul. Their passports were in order, and there was no excuse, far less a reason, for the delay; but they learnt later that a messenger had been sent to Kizil Rabat, the nearest Soviet frontier post, reporting their arrival and asking for instructions.

By the time we had exchanged grievances and itineraries their caravan had begun to arrive – a long string of ponies bearing opulent, efficient-looking boxes which put to shame our niggardly and nondescript effects. We gave them messages for our friends in Kashgar and went our way.

CHAPTER V

THE RUSSIAN AGENT

In spite of this stimulating interlude the stage was long and dreary. A cold wind had sprung up to underline its bleakness before, in the middle of the afternoon, we sighted Dafdar, an irrigated strip of green, dotted sparsely with yurts and with mud houses, which ran beside the river. It was a very long strip. Dusk was falling, and we were tired, before we reached the end of it, where the headman had his tents.

He and his family received us with off-hand affability. But their yurt was draughty and our bellies were empty; so we spent a cheerless evening, for the ponies with the food and the sleeping bags were not expected until late. We went on expecting them until we fell asleep, inadequately wrapped in the household's spare apparel. A little flour had been kneaded into dough and baked in the cinders; but we were still very hungry, for we had been planning dinner for the last ten miles. We were, however, too weary to be cantankerous.

We woke, as we had both often woken before, to reluctant communal stirrings in the half-light before dawn: to the gradual interruption of snores: to the breaking up of huddled human chrysalids: to the scratchy rumble of dung tipped out of a basket on to the fire. It was a poor family and there was only milk for breakfast; the ponies still had not arrived. One of the escort went in search of them and they turned up at ten o'clock with sad tales of a sick horse, of two sick horses, of Tokhta's belly pains, of being benighted in a biting wind. It was out of the question, they said, to do another stage to-day.

They were at least as hungry as we were and, reserving censure, I told them to cook a meal. We did the same ourselves, and presently I swaggered out with a full stomach to find them, as I had hoped, replete and confident and easily amenable. I gave the whining Tokhta (who had over-eaten at Tashkurgan) a laxative which could have launched him to the moon, and cruelly raised a laugh at his expense, so that the whole caravan, which an hour ago had refused to budge, moved off in good spirits.

It was August 20th. A drab stage brought us to Paik, a day's march short of the Chinese frontier. Here, beside a stream which rumour stocked with trout, there was a ruined house and a yurt, thick with opium smoke, containing eight or ten nondescript guards and officials; their rifles were all either Russian or British. We pitched our tent in the ruins of the house, ate a meal, and tried in vain to understand the soul-destroying grievance which one of the Turki guards did his best to air in a low voice and a medley of languages.

Next morning it was snowing. Not less silent, not less nearly impalpable, not less unprovoked than the flakes themselves, the omens of unpleasantness began to settle round us. Among our men there was a delay – unaccompanied by the usual excuses – in the preparations for starting. Then a tough Tadjik, his coat of Russian cut criss-crossed with equally Russian bandoliers, stumped up from the official yurt and asked, with ill-boding suavity, for our passports. I handed them over and without more ado hid my diary in the recesses of my sleeping bag; I am no alarmist, but the last six months had given me a nose for passport trouble. I also dug out our bar of gold (half of it had been sold for rupees in Kashgar) and dropped it into what was left of the lining of my breeches. Kini also, rather perfunctorily, hid her diary; in matters affecting animals or supplies she scented danger long before I did, but she was comparatively careless of the quicksands (no word is more appropriate) of Oriental bureaucracy.

For an hour nothing happened; and off-hand inquiries from the escort received evasive though sympathetic answers. So at last – very much the innocent foreigner who is perplexed but certain of his rights – I bearded the official conclave in the yurt. Somebody spoke Chinese, somebody else a little Russian; and before long I had them at a technical disadvantage. The Kashgar visas on our passports were in Chinese, which none of them could read; but, since they all unofficially served another Power, there was nothing to which they more readily agreed than the contention that we were still in Chinese territory, where visas issued by Chinese officials were all that could possibly be required. By pressing the point I got the passports back, and all, normally, would have been well. But Russia is a harder taskmaster to her servants than China is, and after some groping the caparisoned Tadjik stumbled on a pretext. He understood, he said, that I had a rifle with me; had I a passport for it?

Oddly enough, I had. At least, I had a passport for the ·44, which I had left behind me in Kashgar; it was an imposing document, made out in Peking, to which my photograph had been affixed, and they were incapable of detecting its irrelevance. Unfortunately I had to leave the yurt to fetch it, and while I was away they had leisure to concert their policy. The rifle pass, triumphantly produced, was scrutinized and rejected. This was no good, they said; I needed a pass made out in Turki. I must accompany them to their superior at the frontier post of Mintaka Karaul.

The rat which I had smelt was there, all right; I remembered the Swedes, and prayed that we might get off with a day's delay, as they had.

The rook rifle was formally – and quite unwarrantably – confiscated, wrapped up in a coat, and tied on behind the saddle of the Tadjik. I had played my cards well, though vainly, and the Tadjik himself was rattled. If there is one thing more disconcerting than to be asked your name and rank by your adversary and to see him write them down, it is to see him write them down at somebody else's dictation; this old trick I had used in childish spite, and it had had its due effect. Relations were strained all round when we started for Mintaka Karaul.

The ride between bare, enclosing hills was uneventful, though once two shots rang out quite close above us and the escort unslung their ancient Russian rifles. Towards the end of the stage the Tadjik passed us at a gallop, wisely bent on getting his story in first. For all our consciousness of rectitude we too quickened our pace, and towards evening, fording a fork in the river, reached Mintaka Karaul, where three or four yurts, standing in good pasture within a few hours' ride of the Russian, Indian, and Afghan frontiers, marked the last inhabited spot in China.

The Chinese rank of the official in charge of this place and of Paik was Lan Fu. The man himself was a sharp-eyed, bearded Tadjik called Zamir, aged between forty and fifty. He spoke excellent Russian and was thereby endowed – as all Orientals who speak a Western language are – with a twofold personality. He received us with the maximum of courtesy in a large yurt, slung about with rifles; a small but interested crowd of Tadjiks, Afghans, Turkis, and Kirghiz was also present.

We avoided the temptation – never stronger than when a *lingua franca* is unexpectedly available – to embark at once on a recital of our grievances; to a Chinese such direct tactics would have seemed unforgivably bad form, and even a Tadjik, I imagine, would have found them oafish and unskilful. Instead we squatted, drank tea, and made conversation: noting the while that, although Zamir expressed the deepest abhorrence for the Soviet regime and attributed his command of Russian to some years of service with Tsarist Russians at Tashkurgan, both the full-skirted cut and the serge material of his black uniform could only have come from across the Soviet border. He also offered me, in an unmistakable packet, some tobacco called Makhorka, formerly common in Russia but now issued only to the fighting forces and the police of the Soviet Union.

After some desultory, polite, and unusually sophisticated talk Zamir suggested that we should move to our quarters; so we left the tent, remounted, and galloped through a snow-storm with him and half a dozen others to two yurts which stood at the mouth of the valley up which ran the Gilgit road. Here we were installed in the yurt which was used by the mail-runners, and when tea had been made and the bustle of arrival had subsided I broached the delicate subject of my rifle.

Zamir was most sympathetic; he apologized for the annoyance we had been caused and said that his subordinate at Paik was an ignorant boor who did not know how to treat foreigners. But he had, Zamir regretted to inform us, acted within his rights; there had recently been promulgated a regulation which required every consignment of arms (poor rook rifle!) in transit on the border to be accompanied by a special pass made out in Turki and Chinese by the provincial authorities. It would be impossible for me to take my weapon out of Sinkiang without such a pass. He was sorry, but there it was.

We argued the point amicably. Why had not the officials in Kashgar, who alone were competent to issue the pass and who knew we had a rifle, told us about this regulation? Could not an exception be made in favour of so puny a weapon? And so on.

It was difficult to make out what kind of game Zamir was playing. With the greatest ease he could have overlooked the alleged regulation; with the greatest ease he could have taken his stand on the letter of this hypothetical law and held us up for days while the matter was referred back to Tashkurgan and perhaps to Kashgar. Very reasonable, but equally conscientious, he hovered irresolutely between these two courses of action, going through all the motions of a man who is waiting to be bribed. But to my oblique hints that the bribe was there if that was what he wanted he responded not at all; it was most mystifying.

Of course he held us in his power: not so much because of the rifle as because of the Turkis, who, like the knaves and fools they were, had failed to declare their three pony-loads of merchandize at Tashkurgan and whose papers were therefore hopelessly out of order. Zamir could quite legitimately have impounded the whole caravan. But he remained affable, charming, and outwardly anxious to help, and somehow we did not feel that there was serious trouble brewing. We celebrated our last night on Chinese soil with a feast of fried potatoes and drank, in vodka, the health of General Chiang Kai-shek.

CHAPTER VI

THE PASS OF A THOUSAND IBEX

THE next day dawned brilliant and frosty; once more the metal on our cameras worked stiffly and was painful to touch, as it had been in the mountains of the Koko Nor. The ponies were loaded up and, at my request, Zamir roundly abused the Turkis before they moved off. Our escort departed, carrying with them our thanks and a more than adequate present of money; they also carried with them (as we discovered later) Kini's gloves and a whip to which I was greatly attached. It was a good whip, with a handle made of orongo antelope horn, and it had cost me a packet of Chinese matches at Bash Malghun, the first place in Sinkiang; to have it stolen at the last place in Sinkiang was an experience whose symmetry hardly condoned its cruelty.

Meanwhile, there was still the question of the rifle: a question which Zamir seemed reluctant to reopen. When at last I obliged him to do so, he put on an 'it-hurts-me-more-than-it-hurts-you' expression and said that he must confiscate it; a practically all-night session with his colleagues had revealed no seemly method to cut the Gordian knot of red tape.

One gets fond of a gun; and although not by nature very sentimental I looked on the rook rifle as something which had given me a lot of fun and contributed materially to the success of the expedition. I was not (I felt almost melodramatic about this) going to hand it over to a rat of a Russian agent.

So I gave Zamir black looks (the ponies were barely out of sight, and I was not in a position to give him anything more) and told him that he had no right to confiscate the rifle. I would send it to my friend the Consul-General as a present. It could go down with the next mail-runner, accompanied by a letter containing an account of my treatment at Mintaka Karaul; and the duplicate of this letter would be sent from Gilgit, in case the original (here more black looks) should go astray. I got out a pad and began to write.

Whether Zamir was rattled or whether he relented I shall never know; but the first vitriolic sentences had hardly been composed when he threw in his hand. He would take the risk, he said; as a personal favour to me he would take the risk. I must leave the Peking pass with him, and write an exculpatory letter; but I could have my rifle ... I galloped after the ponies, dug out the pass, galloped back, handed it over, and said good-bye before he could change his mind.

Horse, foot, and (by a miracle) artillery, the expedition marched on India.

As we followed the ponies up the valley between peaks half covered with snow, very bold and black-and-white against the deep blue sky, we were joined by a man whom I had noticed, during our parleys with Zamir, registering silent disapproval in the background. He was a Hunza man from beyond the passes, who called me 'sahib' and introduced himself as Assa Khan; his clothes and his cap were made of the loose whitish material, not unlike soft Shetland tweed, in which all the Hunza dress, and his face had a Nordic look about it. In Turki – of which by this time I had my usual makeshift smattering – he told us, what we had guessed already, that Zamir was a bad man, in Russian pay, and that his action in the matter of my rifle had been quite illegal. I liked the look of Assa Khan, with his soft speech and his easy stride and his beautiful manners; and he must have liked the look of us, for thenceforward he attached himself to the expedition, acting as our body-servant and showing a genuine reluctance to accept wages. He was one of the nicest people we met in the whole journey.

It was not long before we overtook the ponies. The Turkis had collected a donkey to carry an extra sack of maize, and the donkey, carelessly loaded and carelessly driven, had dropped the maize into the river while the caravan was fording it; the whole circus was enveloped in its habitual atmosphere of obloquy, exhaustion, and ineptitude. We stood by, cursing, until they got under way again. We had started, thanks to Zamir, late, and we had the worst pass on the whole road to cross before nightfall.

A little further on we sighted it: the Mintaka Pass, the Pass of a Thousand Ibex, 15,600 feet above sea-level. A rough zigzag track led up to it, climbing painfully the steep and rock-strewn wall of the valley. We had come at last to the extremest boundary of China.

Snow began to fall as we attacked the pass. The tired ponies came up very slowly, the Turkis stabbing them in the nose and changing the loads repeatedly. I left the sorry hugger-mugger of the caravan and walked on ahead, leading Cloud; the altitude affected me very little and I enjoyed the climb. Here and there beside the track the bones of horses lay whitening, and with a sudden stab of pity I remembered Slalom, standing groggily with his head hanging and his feet apart, just as we had left him; I would have given a lot to know that he was still alive. A flight of snow-partridges swept past and disappeared round a corner; two little birds like redstarts chattered thinly among the rocks. The falling snow made a veil which half shut out the world, the valley sprawling below me and the jagged peaks above; so that small things close at hand took on a kind of intimacy, a new importance. There was no sound at all save the chink of the stallion's hooves on rock and an occasional faint wail of execration from the struggling Turkis beneath me.

About half-way up the track was inexplicably decorated with a fragment of *The Times* newspaper, and I took this for a good omen. Now I could see that the head of the pass was marked by four or five little pillars of close-piled stones. I was suddenly aware that this was an Occasion. In less than an hour our ambitions would be realized; the forlorn hope would have come off. In less than an hour we should be in India.

When I reached the top I found a stone shelter for mail-runners standing in a twisting gully of screes whose turns shut out the prospect ahead of me; the stallion and I were on British-Indian soil, a somewhat metaphorical commodity among these rocks. I sat down on the threshold of the hut and smoked a pipe, feeling sleepy and complacent. Snow was still falling; Cloud shivered and nudged me with his nose, trying to point out that this was a poor sort of place to halt.

Half an hour later, heralded by the raucous objurgations of the Turkis, the caravan came plunging into sight over the lip of the pass; Kini reported a gruelling climb, and most of the ponies were in a bad way. It was getting late and we pushed on without delay – over the screes, into an awkward wilderness of boulders, across a patch of soggy ground, and out on to a little rocky platform whence we looked, for the first time, into India.

The snow had drawn off. Below us a glacier sprawled, grey and white, in the shadowed bottom of a gigantic pit. Opposite, wearing their wisps of cloud superbly, two towering snow-peaks were refulgent in the last of the sunlight. It was a sight to take your breath away.

'So far I like India,' said Kini.

CHAPTER VII

NEWS FROM HOME

THE panorama was cold comfort for the ponies. It was six o'clock already, and we had a bad descent before us. As we started on it one of them, staggering under the Turkis' merchandize, collapsed among the boulders, and two of the others looked to be on their last legs. I lost my temper with the Turkis who, by callous neglect on the one hand and plain dishonesty on the other, had brought the animals to this pass. Furious that they should thus shoddily intrude the sufferings of horses between us and an occasion which we had earned the right to enjoy, I roared at them a polyglot string of oaths and felt a little better. Then, at Assa Khan's suggestion, we left them to meet in their own way this crisis of their own providing and began to pick our way steeply down towards the foot of the glacier.

Dusk fell swiftly. In the uncertain light the skeletons of horses – grisly bric-à-brac to decorate the boulders – seemed to take on solidity and appeared like zebras. Soon we were scrambling in a moonless, starless night; but the excellent Assa Khan knew what passed for the path and at last, two hours after nightfall, a stone hut loomed up out of the broken floor of the valley. We tethered the horses and went in.

We were tired and cold and we had eaten nothing since breakfast, and to crown it all I had lost my box of matches. So we sat shivering in the thick and draughty darkness until cries, as of lost souls, from the grim face above us announced the approach of the Turkis. I went out with a torch to help them and found snow falling fairly heavily; but at last all the animals were collected, unloaded, and given their nose-bags of maize. We made tea and ate some bread, treating the jaded Turkis, who shared the hut, with unsmiling and resigned contempt. It was not long before everyone was asleep on the floor.

It was still snowing at dawn. Before starting, I staged a show-down with the Turkis, with valuable support from Assa Khan. I told them that we were now no longer in China, but in a country belonging to England; that their knavery in breaking down our ponies with their loads would henceforward not go unpunished; and that if I had any more trouble with them they would finish up in jail. At this they looked dejected, if not exactly penitent, and for several days they were less tiresome.

The place of the hut was called Gulkoja, and from there we climbed up out of the rocky pit, whose scenery suggested the nether regions as visualized by those of our ancestors who believed that hell was a cold place. A faint track led us down a deep, narrow valley with a soggy floor, where we passed two cheerful Hunza herdsmen living in a cave. It was a grey day, but still and pleasantly autumnal; at the end of a very short stage we came to the junction of two valleys where there was a straggling grove of silver birch and near it, to our amazement and delight, a little rest-house. To travellers coming from India it would have seemed, perhaps, a bleak and miserable edifice, for it is the meanest as well as the last on the Gilgit road. But to us four wind-proof walls, a roof impervious to the rain which had just begun to fall, a clean, swept floor, and (above all) a fireplace with a real chimney represented the height of luxury. It was true that Cloud, when tethered to one of the posts of the veranda, involuntarily uprooted it with a twitch of his head, it was true that the single chair collapsed almost on sight. But we thought ourselves in heaven, and settled in with that delightful sensation compounded both of snugness and of novelty with which children install themselves in a summer-house and mimic domesticity.

We lay up for the rest of the day. The faithful Assa Khan brought firewood, and we opened one of the two tins, each containing three sausages, which Mrs. Thomson-Glover had given us, and Kini cooked a memorable meal. We blew ourselves out, and I discovered, among the books we had borrowed in Kashgar, an early Wodehouse. It was not the Master at his greatest, and I had read it twice before; but it helped to make the long afternoon at Murkushi (as the place was called) one of the few truly luxurious memories of a journey on which luxuries meant a lot.

The next day, which was August 24th, provided another major landmark. Under grey skies we moved off down a towering glen; the weather, and the little groves of silver birch growing in soggy ground, powerfully suggested Scotland. Between the green patches in the floor of the valley the track wound awkwardly through rocks or ran gingerly athwart steep slopes of screes. In the middle of the morning we met a man with an umbrella, who, as far as we could understand, had been sent out from Misgar to meet us; though who had sent him, and how they had known of our coming, remained a mystery.

At one o'clock we sighted Misgar itself. Cunning irrigation channels had made a kind of oasis on a terraced shelf of rock. Barley was growing thinly in the little fields, and squat mud houses nestled under apricot trees. We beheld the outpost of a curious and frugal civilization.

But the economics and ethnology of Hunza interested us, for the moment, not at all. Misgar was the terminus of the telegraph line from India, and as we rode through the scattered village we heard the wind sing in the single wire. We crossed, by a nasty stone bridge, a clamorous and foaming torrent and came to the rest-house, whose white walls were pleasingly decorated with studies in still life, painted by M. Iacovleff, the artist of the Haardt-Citroen Expedition, three of whose members had spent some time in Misgar. We were welcomed by the official representative of the Mir of Hunza, a stocky, energetic little man who spoke some English, and he led us back across the bridge to the telegraph office.

The Kashmiri clerk in charge cared but little for his desolate and chilly post and was not displeased at meeting strangers. He got in touch with Gilgit and collected the telegrams that were waiting for me there. We watched hungrily while his deliberate pencil interpreted the buzzing Morse into longhand; these were the first communications we had had from the outside world for six and a half months. It was a thrilling moment, spoilt only by the fact that there were no messages for Kini, who before starting had sent home clues to her potential whereabouts which were even more characteristically vague than mine had been.

For all that, we felt that we were very nearly home and sent off jubilant, facetious, and expensive wires to our nearest and dearest. Then we walked back to the rest-house in a state of elation which evaporated suddenly when we reached the stone bridge.

It was the Turkis again. We had outstripped them on the road, but they had arrived while we were in the telegraph office and had started taking the ponies across the bridge to the rest-house. The bridge consisted of two great slabs of rock; it was narrow, and unprotected by anything in the nature of a balustrade. To drive loaded animals across it, instead of leading them one at a time, was the height of folly, but this was what the Turkis had done. The ponies bumped each other with the projecting loads, and one of them lost his balance and left the bridge. In a flash the torrent had swept him a hundred yards downstream, where he stuck against a rock and was with difficulty rescued, miraculously unscathed save for a few cuts. Needless to say, he was the one who carried our suitcases: all our clothes and papers were soaked.

It was the last straw; we cursed the men till we were black in the face and spread out our sodden wardrobes in the sun to dry. Then the Kashmiri from the telegraph office came over and, using him as interpreter, I told the Turkis what I thought of them in greater detail than had hitherto been possible. They had been criminally careless, I said, and I had no further use for them. I selected the four best ponies and announced that to-morrow these animals would carry our loads and our loads only; that they would travel at their own pace, ahead of and separate from the three others with the merchandize; and that I was hiring two men in Misgar to look after them and to see to the safety of our belongings. This was the decisive battle in a long campaign of petty, irritating engagements. From Misgar onwards the Turkis gave us no more trouble.

That night, sitting on chairs in an incongruous atmosphere of firelit domesticity, we gorged ourselves on lapsha and broached the last bottle of brandy, which had been reserved for purposes of celebration. We were only about ten marches from Gilgit; if we flew from Delhi, we would perhaps be home within a month. We could not help feeling excited.

Next morning we packed our damp things, and I gave away my faithful suitcase, now in the final stages of disintegration, to Assa Khan. The Mir, hearing of our arrival, had telephoned his respects from farther down the road, and his representative in Misgar provided us with two men, one of them a mounted orderly attached to the telegraph service. We set off with the four best ponies, the discountenanced Turkis grumbling in the rear.

South of Misgar the road improves, in that it becomes a track built by engineers and well kept up by the Mir of Hunza; but the gorge of the Hunza River grows increasingly spectacular and the going, if less difficult, is much more dangerous than on the reaches above Misgar. Almost as soon as we had started we struck a bad patch, where the track had crumbled on a semi-precipitous slope of screes. The little caravan bunched and got tangled up. Cloud's anti-social instincts, which for some time past had been curbed or modified by fatigue, reasserted themselves and he started kicking. This was neither the time nor the place for such antics. Kini, who was just behind me, was unseated and, although she came to no harm, she very easily might have; it was a nasty place. To the very last, Cloud, whose manners were otherwise perfect, continued to suffer from temperament in places where most horses would have suffered from vertigo; as far as I was concerned, there was nothing monotonous about the Gilgit road.

No lover of the picturesque could have been disappointed in that day's march. The narrow track, just wide enough for a laden pack-horse, wound giddily along the face of cliffs, now dropping down to the river bed, now soaring up the walls of the gorge in the bottom of which the boiling torrent writhed milkily. Often there was a sheer drop of anything up to a thousand feet below us, and I found life more enjoyable on foot than in the saddle.

In the afternoon, after crossing two wooden cantilever bridges supported by steel cables, we descended steeply on the hamlet of Gircha, on whose flat roofs rich golden pools of apricots were drying in the sun. Hunza is economically self-supporting, but only by the narrowest of margins: dried apricots are a staple food during some of the winter months. We went on two or three miles to a little place where there was a rest-house and settled down contentedly beneath great peaks bathed in the delicate and tranquil evening light.

CHAPTER VIII

A THOUSAND WELCOMES

NEXT day we passed through Khaibar, another island of green established by toil and ingenuity in the midst of stern grey desolation, and in the afternoon found ourselves overlooking the Batura Glacier. Huge tumbled ridges of dirty-looking ice swept down a wide gully towards the river bed; the track ended abruptly. Beyond the glacier we could see the few roofs and tree-tops of Passu; they seemed near, but it took us three hours to reach them. The glacier was not easy to negotiate. We struggled in a welter of drab grey gullies, picking our way with circumspection. The horses skidded madly, their hoofs flaying the layer of dust and rubble from the black ice beneath; twice we had to unload and make a portage. There was something unnatural about that tortured, cataclysmic place; it was as though we had invaded the surface of another world, to which the ponies were ill-adapted and anomalous. From time to time strange cracks and groans and rumbles came from underneath our feet.

But at last we were through. We pressed on beyond Passu in a wind that stung our faces with fine grit, climbed up on to a long hog's back, and came to another village. There was no rest-house here, so we pitched our tent on a little terrace. A yellow mongrel bitch had followed us all day; she had the typical curled tail of the pi-dog, but her eyes were golden and her nature affectionate, so we put her on the strength of the expedition and gave her, to her amazement, a meal.

We woke in the morning to find the mountains framed in the doorway of the tent beautifully gilded by the sun. The first half of the march was complicated by a river where the men expected more difficulty than they found; the second was landmarked by an event unprecedented in the history of the expedition – the receipt of a letter. We had passed through Gulmit, a biggish village where the Mir of Hunza spends part of every autumn. The road beyond it was unusually precipitous and on some of its more breathless passages was even equipped with a low wooden balustrade which contributed less to our safety than to our peace of mind. We were on a comparatively unsensational stretch when we were met by a man who turned out to be an orderly from the Political Agent in the Gilgit Agency and who handed me two letters.

With a not more than perfunctory effort at nonchalance I opened them. One was from the Political Agent himself; it welcomed us in the kindest of terms and announced that the writer, together with Colonel Lang, the Resident in Kashmir, was on tour in Hunza and would be reaching the capital, Baltit, next day. As we expected to do the same ourselves this was extremely good news. The other letter was from Mrs. Lorimer, whose husband, Colonel D. L. R. Lorimer, had formerly been Political Agent in Gilgit and was now living in the district for the purpose of completing his study of its language, which comparative philology has hitherto failed to relate definitively to any other language group. Mrs. Lorimer introduced herself as *Times* Correspondent in the Agency, congratulated us on our journey, and said that *The Times* had been worrying about me.

These intimations from another world excited us inordinately. I scribbled a reply to the Political Agent, whom, since his signature gave no clue to his rank, I addressed as 'Dear General Kirkbride'; for China is not the only country where it pays to guess high in these contexts. (He turned out to be a Major, but no harm was done.) Then we went on.

Very soon we came to a place where the wooden beams which shored up the track on a more than usually awkward place had partly collapsed; we had to unload the ponies, lead them across one by one, and make a portage. While Kini and I, waiting for this to be done, lay up in a patch of shade (the river-bed was like an oven that day), Cloud gave a display of eccentrically bad manners by swooping on the donkey and biting it on the back of the neck.

When the horses had been loaded again we rode on, passing a little stone monument which the Mir, many years ago, had caused to be erected in the face of a cliff in honour of Kitchener, who once visited him and for whom he conceived a great admiration. In the evening we reached Sarat, where there was a rest-house, a great many flies, and not much else, but where we were within an easy march of Baltit. It was August 27th, the anniversary of my departure from England. We marked the occasion with a banquet of eggs and brandy, and I remembered the matutinal bowler hats swarming round Liverpool Street, the portly Dutchmen on the Flushing boat, the chequered placidity of the country on the first familiar stage to Moscow. It all seemed much more than a year ago.

At noon next day we reached Altit, a suburb, so to speak, of Baltit. The snows of Rakaposhi, more than 25,000 feet high and adjudged unclimbable by experts, were visible down the valley; against them a little fort stood up bravely, and beneath it a long cool reservoir of water reflected the swimming clouds between ranks of poplars. It was a lovely place.

We rode on, aware of the eyrie-like city we were approaching but unable to see it, for Baltit lies in a westerly inlet in the great valley wall. But presently we came to a kind of gateway on top of a ridge. Beside it stood the inn or caravanserai in which the Turkis were accustomed to lodge, and here Kini and I dismounted. We knew from Kirkbride's letter that the official party was not due to arrive for another hour, and we were a prey to those misgivings which assail you on the door-step of a house when, having rung the bell, you remember that the invitation was for 8.30, not for eight o'clock. But we were no longer the masters of our fate. News of our coming had been noised abroad, and presently an officious but ingratiating man hurried up and insisted on escorting us to the place which was prepared for the reception. This was a kind of terraced park before the Mir of Hunza's guest-house. Some hundreds of the citizens were squatting under the trees and a guard of honour, wearing on their caps the silver ibex of the Gilgit Scouts, was standing easy before the entrance to the lodging of the sahibs. Bunting was much in evidence, and flags; between the trees were stretched great banners bearing the heartening legend (which, as we passed beneath it, made us feel usurpers) 'A 1000 WELCOMES'.

We shambled, as unobtrusively as possible, round the outskirts of the crowd and slipped up a little flight of steps leading to the guest-house. Stuffed ibex (their straddling and ungainly postures took me back to the butter-smeared yaks and tigers at Kumbum) were silhouetted against the dazzling arrogance of Rakaposhi. We found ourselves on a shady lawn. Several large tents – we would have called them marquees – somehow created, in their symmetry and assurance, the atmosphere of a garden party in England. We were ushered into one of them, in which a camp bed and a basin struck a sybaritic note, and we felt – like peasants among chandeliers and flunkeys – that we were getting rapidly out of our depth. We were given books to read, presents from former travellers to the Mir; one by Sir Aurel Stein, and one by Theodore and Kermit Roosevelt, who did a shooting trip in the Tien Shen. I had hardly found, in the latter, the following ethnographical bombshell: 'We saw' (in Yarkand) 'no negroes nor could we make out any trace of negro blood,' when tea – with real jam, real cakes – was served to us.

We were by this time unnerved. We had been marching continuously since we had left Kashgar three weeks before and our clothes were terrible; and, because of the sun, not only did we not look like sahibs but we did not even look like members of one of the white races. While Kini sewed up the most blatant of the rents in my leather wind-jacket we speculated anxiously about the two distinguished servants of the Government of India whom we were about to meet. Their visit to Baltit was after all a state occasion; there would certainly be uniforms, gold braid, at dinner evening dress . . . We waited, while apples plopped agree-

371

ably on the shady lawn; and the longer we waited the more nervous we got.

At last, from down the valley, there came the murmur of distant cheers. Servants and orderlies, sent on ahead, threaded their way through the crowds beneath us and hurried up the steps of the guest-house. The guard of honour was called to attention and clashed through its arms-drill. An unsuspected mountain gun, close by, fired a salute of thirteen shots. When it had finished the sound of music was mingled with the swelling cheers. A Labrador whined excitedly, held by a Ladakhi servant whose high cheek-bones and slit eyes seemed to belong elsewhere in Asia. At the far end of the arena which we overlooked the crowd eddied, bright banners waved, the music squeaked and clanged. A fat spaniel, trailing his leash, bolted up the red carpet and arrived breathless on the lawn. The official party hove in sight.

The Mir, very erect in spite of his age and wearing a dark blue uniform and a turban, walked between the two Englishmen. Both of them, to our infinite relief, were dressed informally in jodhpurs. They inspected the guard of honour and came up to the lawn.

'Hullo! Glad you got here. Come and see the fun.'

It was all charmingly casual; our misgivings were allayed. We went out on to a kind of platform where there was a group of chairs, and watched a short but vehement dance in which men with curved swords and little shields pranced and menaced each other while coloured banners whirled rhythmically. We had the feeling – familiar enough in ordinary life but curiously novel for us then – of being quite irrelevant to our surroundings.

CHAPTER IX

SAHIBS

ASIA is kind to travellers. The hospitality which we received between Peking and Kashmir – though naturally there was not a great deal of it – was the very best kind of hospitality; and no one could have made the last stage but one of a journey which had at times been arduous seem more idyllic than our self-appointed hosts in Baltit. We were given two palatial tents, and we were fed, as it seemed to us, magnificently. Our material comforts perhaps amounted to no more than what a political officer on tour would have regarded as routine equipment; but to two people who had washed in a single frying-pan for several months they seemed luxurious. And in any case our material comforts were not the whole story. We very quickly mastered our tendency to call these two exalted people 'Sir' and discovered the humour of Kirkbride, the charm of Lang, and the wisdom of both. Within two days of meeting them we felt, as you sometimes do after chance encounters, that they were old friends. Our scrambling journey was suddenly promoted to a picnic in the best company, the best of weather, and the best of scenery.

Mir Muhammad Nazim Khan was a remarkable old man. Though over seventy he had but recently become the father of (as far as I can remember) his fifth son. His eyes, behind gold-rimmed spectacles, were alert and shrewd; his broad shoulders did not stoop; his beard, forked and dyed, jutted with an air of determination. For a ruler so remotely situated his grasp of contemporary affairs in Asia and even in Europe was remarkable, and there was no doubting his political acumen. He was installed in office when the people of Hunza, whose addiction to raiding had tried the patience of the Government of India too high, were subjugated by Durand's Hunza-Nagar Expedition in 1891. (The story of this small but spectacular campaign is admirably told in *Where Three Empires Meet* by E. F. Knight, who travelled and wrote in the days when Special Correspondents were not compelled to spend their whole time between the local Foreign Office and a bar.) Ever since 1891 the Mir has ruled his distant valleys sagaciously and well.

The people of Hunza (there are only about 14,000 of them) are a hardy, handsome, cheerful race with a surprisingly European cast of countenance. They belong to the Maulai sect of Moslems, whose earthly head is the Aga Khan; and we observed, not without a sense of incongruity, that small portraits of this potentate, stamped on buttons, were worn by many of them in their hats. I have mentioned before their narrow margin of economic self-sufficiency; pasture is scarce, cultivation is limited by the minute proportion of their country which is irrigable, and the balance maintained between population, herds, water supply, and other factors is accordingly a delicate one. The women and children of the tribe were extremely good-looking, and it was refreshing to find ourselves, for the first time on the journey, among a people who, thanks perhaps to a stable and benevolent administration, were frank and unafraid in their demeanour. It was almost disconcerting to be given honest and informative answers to our questions – to meet, after months of lies and evasions and propaganda, men who meant what they said and said what they meant.

At dusk on the day we arrived in Baltit the hill-tops up and down the valley were linked with a chain of bonfires in honour of the Resident's visit. The flames twinkled tinily, thousands of feet up in the darkening sky, fitly enhancing the savage beauty of the scene. The display was perhaps not great pyrotechnics, but it represented formidable feats of mountaineering.

We dined with the Mir and two of his sons, eating food cooked in the European way and drinking a bottle of champagne – a gift from the Maharajah of Kashmir – and some superb old brandy presented by the Haardt-Citroen Expedition; Kini came in for a lot of badinage from the Mir. After dinner we moved out to seats overlooking a

374

little firelit courtyard where there was dancing and miming to wild music in the light of the flames. The best items in the programme were a dance by four little boys with hobby-horses, made of frames and trailing draperies, strapped round their waists, who wheeled and cavorted in a pretty, medieval way; and a fairly elaborate dumb-show in which tiger, ibex, and eagle were stalked by an excitable sahib and a disobedient dog. It was all done with great spirit and we enjoyed it almost as much as the actors did. When everything was over we retired to the unlooked-for luxury of camp-beds and went to sleep in a silence broken only by the gentle movement of the leaves overhead and the occasional thump of a falling apple.

Next morning we rode four miles down the road to Aliabad for breakfast with Colonel and Mrs. Lorimer, who told us many strange things about the Hunza people and also threw light on the question of our 'disappearance'. Some weeks earlier Mrs. Lorimer had received a cable from *The Times* which began 'Anxious fate special correspondent Peter Failing', and asked her to do what she could to trace me. Soon after this message had been sent the news of our arrival in Kashgar reached the Foreign Office in London, and *The Times* cabled again, telling Mrs. Lorimer that I was all right and that she needn't bother to do anything more. By some mischance, this cable got no farther than the Lost Letter Office in Lahore, and Mrs. Lorimer went on wiring to London that according to rumours current in the Agency a foreigner called Pebbing, or possibly Jenning, was coming over the passes. When at last she learnt the truth, and had clinched the matter with a telegram, she received, the day before we visited her, a wire from *The Times* beginning 'Fleming already in Srinagar . . .' Srinagar was a good fortnight's journey down the road, so this was a little disconcerting; I began to wonder where I really was, or alternatively how many of me there were.

After a delightful and enormous breakfast we galloped back to Baltit, arriving just in time for the official visit to the Mir's palace. To his fort-like and exceedingly romantic

375

edifice, perched high above the little city, we rode ceremoniously on yaks, preceded by indefatigable and merciless musicians. It was a strange place. Steep, ladder-like stairways led up to little chambers and a kind of terrace. The eternal snows towered behind it, and before it the valley stretched superbly southwards towards the glittering and gigantic Rakaposhi. Baltit fell away below us; first the guard of honour, armed with Snyders, erect in the sunlight before the entrance to the palace: a little lower down our yaks and horses and attendants in a courtyard: next the tree-tops, and the nearest of the flat mud roofs on which circles of apricots gleamed like golden coins: and beyond the careful shelves of cultivation the river, crawling to join the Indus between sunlit cliffs.

To the queer, comfortless rooms assorted bric-à-brac lent comfort if not dignity. A chandelier clashed with bows and arrows. Viceroys, Political Agents, Moslem leaders, Kitchener, the youthful Curzon stared portentously from the walls. Ibex horns were much in evidence. The Mir did the honours with bland and twinkling courtesy.

That evening, when it was cool, we watched a display of marksmanship, followed by polo. The polo ground was a hard terrace, some 400 yards long, enclosed by low stone walls. We took our places, to the inevitable harsh music, on a stand, and a presentation of official gifts took place; then the fun began. A silver mark was set up in a little mound of sand, and riders, coming in quick succession at full gallop, leant hard over and shot an arrow at it as they passed; the crowd yelled wildly at a hit. Then a kind of popinjay was hung in the branches of a tree and the horsemen – still at full gallop – fired at it with shotguns, making much poorer practice than they had with bows.

At last we came to the polo. The game, as played in Hunza and Nagar, has certain features which would be regarded as unorthodox elsewhere. Apart from the shape and nature of the ground, six players take part on either side, instead of four; ponies are never changed and the game goes on until one side has scored nine goals. The player who scores a goal immediately picks up the ball and gallops madly down the field, yelling at the top of his voice; midway he throws up the ball and hits it full pitch towards the other goal, which has now become his opponents'. But the most exciting incidents usually occur when a player catches the ball – he is allowed to do this – either in flight or by hitting it against the stone wall so that it rebounds into his hand; as soon as he has caught it he has only to ride through the goal to score, but, since he may legitimately be thwarted by almost any method short of a knife-thrust, this is not as easy as it sounds. It is an exhilarating game to watch.

When we got back to the guest-house we presented the Mir with a bottle of whisky, brought for the purpose from the cellars of the Kashgar Consulate, and he gave us in return a white Hunza cap and a highly decorative whip. At dinner he and his two eldest sons were the guests of the Resident, and after dinner four dancing boys performed with an air of complete detachment. The Hunza dances are an odd shuffling business in which the heel is at least as important as the toe. Two of the boys were dressed in red cloth, and two in green; the red came from Japan, the green from Russia.

CHAPTER X

GILGIT AT LAST

THE next day, the last but one of August, the official party left for Nagar and very kindly took us with them; we put toothbrushes in our saddlebags and sent the Turkis with the ponies on to Gilgit. The little kingdom of Nagar, which has some 15,000 inhabitants, lies across the river from Hunza, and the two tribes are ancient enemies; to-day, under British rule, they live perforce in amity. Our horses were sent round by the bridge, which is several miles downstream, and we rode down to the river on richly caparisoned yaks, escorted by the Mir and his sons, and also by the musicians. (How we wished that they would – as they often seemed about to – burst! But they never did.) Before we left I paid off Assa Khan and we said good-bye with sorrow; we had got very fond of him.

We crossed the Hunza River by an ordinary wooden bridge, at a point just above its confluence with a big tributary which flows out of the Nagar valleys. This was spanned by a rope bridge – a long sagging affair made of three thick strands of plaited twigs; you put your feet on one of them, which was reinforced by a steel cable, and your hands on the other two. In spite of the torrent thrashing beneath you, it was not at all alarming; though the dogs, who had to be taken over in sacks, clearly disliked it.

On the further bank, while crowds fired ragged volleys in salute from the cliff-tops, we were met by the Mir of Nagar and his sons. The Mir was a small, bird-like man, less of a personality than his neighbour in Baltit; but his sons, in well-cut khaki uniforms, were excessively good-looking, and one of them I took to be the handsomest man alive. His face was startlingly un-Asiatic; he looked exactly like the hero of a novel by an Edwardian lady.

A ride of two or three hours brought us to their capital, huddled in a narrow valley at either end of which snow-peaks stood sentinel. Crowds lined the polo ground to welcome us. Again there was a guard of honour, and dances with swords and banners; again, alas, there were musicians. The valleys of Nagar run at right angles to those of Hunza and get much less sun. The people, accordingly, are paler and less stalwart; they also struck me as being less free and easy, surlier, more self-conscious. The place was not quite as idyllic as Baltit had been.

As in Baltit, the Mir's palace dominates the capital; as in Baltit, it contains a chandelier. We stayed there that night and the next, and in the intervening day made an expedition, which was slightly marred by rain, to a nearby glacier. The first evening there was polo; the Royal Family v. the Rest. It was a fiercer game than we had seen in Hunza, and six of the Mir's nine sons (a team out of a fairy-tale) won a popular victory. Then there was shooting from horseback, first with bows and arrows and then with rifles instead of shot-guns; and here again Nagar excelled Hunza. Even the music was slightly more excruciating.

At night no drink was served at dinner, for in this respect Nagar is more faithful than her neighbour to Koranic law. But there were dances and miming in the firelight, and all nine of the Princes – the youngest of them half asleep, poor child – took the floor and easily surpassed the common herd in grace and agility.

At Nagar I parted reluctantly from Cloud, handing him over with Colonel Thomson-Glover's compliments to the Mir. I also gave away the yellow mongrel bitch. I was fond of her, and apart from eating a number of chickens and getting me a reputation for eccentricity (for what sahib cherishes a pi-dog?) she had behaved in an exemplary way; but I should have had to get rid of her later if not sooner and, since the stages now were very hot, it was kinder to leave her here.

On September 1st we left Nagar and rode south in blazing sunshine: past Baltit, under the majestic, unbelievable Rakaposhi, towering inviolable, her peak for ever (it is said) protected by unclimbable walls of ice.

The journey was now, more unmistakably than ever, a picnic; it seemed a long time since I had saddled the horses and helped to load the camels in a snowy dawn, since Kini had gutted hares and braved the bullying winds to cook. We had no work and no worries. What a difference it made, at the end of a long stage, to find lunch ready for you in a rest-house, a syce to take your pony, water to wash in: instead of having to pitch the tent, cart the heavy boxes, fetch dung for the fire. We drank boiled water, brushed our hair, and felt impostors.

It took us three days to reach Gilgit. On the first we slept at Minapin. On the second we rode past the ruined fort at Nilt, in the storming of which no less than three V.C.s were won by the handful of British officers attached to Durand's column. That evening we reached Chalt, and the next day, after a hot double stage of thirty-two miles, we rode over the longest suspension bridge in India into Gilgit.

For more than half the year snow on the Burzil Pass cuts off the headquarters of the Gilgit Agency from Kashmir. Gilgit has an air-field, but the only motor-vehicles which have ever reached it were the caterpillar tractors of the Haardt-Citroen Expedition; and they had to be taken to bits and carried by coolies for a greater part of the way. The British community is a tiny one, and the place is regarded as remote, even by frontier standards. But here again we felt, as we had felt in Kashgar, the keen delight of returning to civilization.

We spent a day there as George Kirkbride's guests. The Turkis came to see us, smiling and obsequious, expecting the usual presents; they got none. We arranged for more ponies to take us on to Srinagar; two Kashmiris were in charge of them, and we also engaged as servant a Hunza man called Wahab. He had worked for the ill-fated German expedition which had met disaster on Nanga Parbat, and he turned out very well. We did the minimum of sight-seeing: the grave of the explorer Hayward, whose murder by tribesmen is resoundingly described in Newbolt's poem; one of the Citroen Expedition's cars, mouldering and forlorn in a backyard: the huge cannon, cast by Chinese in Yarkand and used, not very effectively, against Durand's forces by the defenders of Hunza.

The night before we left George Kirkbride gave a banquet in our honour. It was a great occasion, made doubly memorable by the presence of an officer in the Tank Corps and his wife, who were travelling in the district. They had been up to Leh, with the necessities of life on twenty-four ponies; and the lady, who had been seen in the bazaar in beach pyjamas, arrived for dinner in evening dress. She movingly described the hardships of their journey, and gave some account of the wonders and curiosities of Leh. 'In Ladakh', she said, 'the people all live on stuff called tsamba. It's made of barley meal, and you really ought to see them eat it. They mix it up in tea with the most *awful* rancid butter – with their fingers, of course – and then they simply wolf it down. It really makes you almost sick to watch them.'

I avoided Kini's eye.

CHAPTER XI

LAST LAP

THERE are twelve stages between Gilgit and Srinagar, but the journey can be done in less than twelve days; I believe Curzon, who had special relays of ponies, holds the record with six days. We took eight.

We left Gilgit on September 5th, bidding a sorrowful farewell to Colonel Lang and Kirkbride, who in the last week had become something more than the kindest of hosts. Then we rode through the shady bazaar and out into the naked valley, where the heat was cruel. A dull stage of seventeen miles brought us to Pari, where we lunched off eggs and two heavenly bottles of beer, generously bestowed from Gilgit's slender store. Then we went on, following the west bank of the grey and turbid Indus, which presently we crossed by a wooden bridge. My pony was not up to the forced march, and I had been several hours on foot before we reached, well after dark, the pleasantly named village of Bunji. We did thirty-four miles that day.

Next day I changed my pony and we moved off down the valley, hypnotized by the splendid mass of Nanga Parbat, which stood up gleaming against the deep blue sky. At noon the road left the Indus and turned east into the Astor gorge, zigzagging painfully up the precipitous face called Hattu Pir, and that evening we reached Mushkin, where there was a rest-house in a little patch of vegetation among the rocks.

We slept there, and soon after dawn rode on through lovely fir-trees. The track was good, much better than above Gilgit, and the journey had become almost completely uneventful; although on that day, it is true, we met and talked with four female Swedish missionaries *en route* for Kashgar. They were heavily topeed and veiled, and the two youngest looked fragile creatures to brave the Himalayas.

We spent that night at Astor, the next at Godai, and the next, after a twenty-three-mile stage, at Sadar Khoti, where a cold wind blew and a long bare valley led up to the Burzil Pass. This is less than 14,000 feet high and an easy climb; but in winter the snow drifts so badly on it that a kind of crow's nest on stilts, erected for the benefit of mail-runners at the foot of it, stands in summer some forty feet above the ground. As we rode over the pass marmots whistled at us, for the last time. Beyond it we dropped down into Tyrolean sort of country, where Kashmiri herdsmen camped in grubby tents on rich pasture-land and the hills were clothed becomingly with firs and silver birches. We rode twenty-five miles that day and spent the night in an isolated rest-house at Peshwari.

We were getting very near the end of the journey, and after dinner I promised Wahab my boots. They were splendid boots, boots beyond compare; but in spite of the cobblers of Kashgar they were – I had to admit it – *in extremis*. Next morning, as I drew them on and laced them up (an interminable and irritating process) for the last time but one, I remembered very clearly how they had come into my life. An office on Wall Street; an invitation to shoot quail in Alabama; and then the boots, bought cheaply in a store on Broadway. I remembered how, crashing up Sixth Avenue on the Elevated, I had (almost) caressed the bulky parcel which symbolized a week's reprieve from what I regarded as the intolerable process of being initiated into high finance. Even when new, they had been the best of boots; I had had a lot of fun in them. Baptized in the swamps of Alabama, they had won their spurs on a Guatemalan volcano. They had trodden rabbits out of English brambles, and they were no strangers to the nauseous but snipe-haunted mud of rice-fields of South China. Thus seasoned, they had journeyed to Brazil and bore the scars which boots acquire in the Matto Grosso jungles. They had even been round the world, pausing *en route* to march with a Japanese column on a punitive expedition in Manchuria. They had been a marvel to the ill-shod Caucasus, and a joke (because they were so thin) in wintry Mongolia. On this journey alone I had been asked how much they cost at least a hundred times. They stood for freedom and the backblocks; they stood for the luck which had always dogged me while I wore them. And it is not, after all, every pair of boots in which you can travel, sockless, for several months without discomfort, sometimes doing twenty-mile stages on foot. I gave them to Wahab in Srinagar, though I cannot believe that they are not still somewhere among my possessions, ready for foolish and improbable activities. We shall not look upon their like again.

From Peshwari, on September 11th, we did a stage of twenty-seven miles and broke it at Gurez. Here, I forget why, we visited the Post Office, and in it found a Brigadier-General with a dachshund, in one of whose ears (the dachshund's ears) a trout-fly had just become embedded. The Brigadier-General invited us to the rest-house, where we were made most welcome by a charming Colonel and his charming wife, who were staying there for the fishing. They gave us lunch, and afterwards we sat round a fire, talking pleasantly and reading *The Bystander*, in whose pages the startled, cretinous faces of first-nighters, the simper of hack beauties ('who is, of course, . . .') presaged repulsively the world awaiting us. As a cure for nostalgia, give me an illustrated weekly paper.

When, towards evening, we said good-bye to these well-encountered people, they in their bounty thrust upon us a large trout. We rode on, fast, for eight miles and cooked it at Koraghbal; I suppose it was the first fresh fish we had eaten for nearly half a year. This was our last camp; and although camp was now an affair between inverted commas – so snug were the rest-houses, so commodious the rough bedsteads – we could not help feeling for our sleeping-bags most of those sentiments which the Arab in the poem expressed with reference to his steed.

We were now only twenty-six miles from the head of the motor-road at Bandipur. Next morning, jettisoning – half in glee, half in regret – the jam jar which had carried our butter for 3000 miles and the spare cocoa tin which had solved so many storage problems, we set out in the crisp, gallant Himalayan air on the last stage to Srinagar. The track wound, almost too romantically, down a great valley between fir-trees. The pony caravans which we had passed frequently during the last few days were here more numerous than ever; a faint smell of commerce, the not really perceptible echo of chaffering, seemed to drift over the last mountain barrier between us and the plains. At noon we crossed the Pass of Tragbal, and turned in our saddles to look back as an undecipherable scribble of ridges in the narrow margin between the immediate horizon and the bottom of the sky.

Then we rode a little further on and suddenly, amazingly, there were no more hills before us. Beyond the dark immediate spear-points of the nearest firs there lay – miles distant, thousands of feet below us – a flat vale, half hidden in a haze. Waterish it looked; 'a rather Yangtse Valley landscape', according to my diary. But above all it looked soft – soft and rich and settled and to us (save for its implications) unlovely.

But its implications were after all the main thing: letters from home, a real hotel, and baths. We plunged down the zigzag track. Down and down, to and fro across a tiny section of the Himalayas' southern face. It got hotter and hotter. Presently we could see the clump of buildings that was Bandipur, the long tired ribbon of the motor road. The jaded ponies stumbled. The heat steadily increased. Our heads were full of private speculations, unrelated to the journey and each other.

We had wired to Srinagar for a car and at last we saw it coming – a small toy laboriously dragging its clearly artificial cloud of dust to Bandipur. We rode on, a childish exaltation battled with fatigue. Cherchen, Kashgar, Gilgit – they had all been excellent in their way; but this was the end. In two hours, in one hour, we should no longer have to say 'D.V.' or 'Barring accidents'. The long, improbable journey would be over.

Kini rode ahead, a familiar silhouette. One shoulder slightly hunched, the slung camera dragging at her shirt, her sheepskin sleeping-bag bulging through the thongs which bound it to the saddle and which on the bitter uplands had been so hard to fasten. Getting back meant less to her than to me, who had, paradoxically, at once more ties and more detachment: a greater capacity to enjoy a life to which at frequent intervals I feel myself a stranger, and at the same time more friends and facilities with which to enjoy it. I wished it was not like this. On the road we had, I think, found much the same kind of happiness in much the same kind of things; and I would have liked the end of the road to have given us both an equal pleasure.

But it is foolish to expect life to treat you and your friends fairly; and Kini was at least reasonably excited and proud and curious. We discussed the dinner with which we would celebrate our arrival in Srinagar. It was by no means the first time we had done so, and the arguments over the menu evoked memories which charted our progress across Tartary: the inn at Sining, with its paper windows and its brazier, on the evening when we first learnt that we were going to be given passports: the little tent, its walls bellying to the Tibetan winds, on an evening when optimism ran high or the rice had been burnt: lapping sour milk in a bazaar on the edge of the unluxurious Takla Makan. Time and again we had thrashed out the menu, one arguing that they wouldn't have caviar in Kashmir, the other that smoked salmon was unworthy of the occasion. 'By God, we'll hit India a crack!' had been the war-cry.

CHAPTER XII

TRIUMPHAL ENTRY

THE Vale of Kashmir absorbed us slowly. The track made its last zigzag and flattened out. We rode out of the fir-trees into the edge of the plain. There were maize fields, and children driving humped zebu cattle, and tall thatched houses built with beams and little bricks. There was also a sticky heat. It was seven months all but three days since we had left Peking; we had covered about 3500 miles; and the whole journey had cost us roughly £150 each.

At five o'clock we crossed the bridge which leads into Bandipur. The car was waiting for us; it did not look a very good car and the driver was a specious rogue, but we did not care. We unsaddled and lay down on cool green turf in the shade of a tree, waiting for the pack-ponies to come in. An old man of dignified appearance approached us and rather unexpectedly offered to cut our hair; he always, he said, performed this service for sahibs who came down from the hills, and he produced a number of eulogistic letters in support of this statement. But we said No, we would wait till we got to Srinagar.

At last the ponies arrived and the loads were taken off them and stowed in or lashed on to the car, which looked more inadequate than ever when this had been done. Not without a sentimental pang, we gave away to the Kashmiris a number of things which had figured so long as important necessities that it went against the grain to reduce them to the status of mere junk: things like our faithful kettle, and Kini's red and blue Chinese saddle, which had come all the way from Tangar and was now in the final stages of disintegration. I took my saddle with me to Srinagar, I don't know why.

Then we climbed into the car and it bumped off, roaring, down the road. It was a very bad road, and the engine failed repeatedly on hills. We ran, in the mellow evening light, along the edge of a great marshy lake in which horses and cattle stood knee-deep, lending it a placid, domesticated air. We passed through two or three little villages, crossed a bridge, and came to better going. Night began to fall.

We had, as usual, only the very vaguest idea of what Srinagar was going to be like. We knew that it was often referred to, in the tourist world, as 'the Venice of the East', and we knew the name of the principal hotel. 'Very decent sort of place,' everyone had said; 'they'll make you comfortable there.' We imagined a small dining-room where half a dozen officers on leave propped *Punch* against the cruet.

Presently we struck the main road, metalled and straight. Notices in English flicked past in the headlights. 'Srinagar' said the driver, waving his hand towards the suddenly constellated darkness ahead of us, and soon we honked into crowded streets. 'Escape Me Never' said a hoarding, speaking aptly enough for civilization; the names of Bergner and of Beery figured largely. Srinagar was much bigger than we had imagined it.

So was the hotel. Its imposing portals loomed up and abashed us. Painfully conscious of uncouthness, of dusty clothes and blackened faces, we entered almost surreptitiously; and saw at once that we had chosen a bad moment to do so. People were gathering in the lounge for dinner. Alas for our vision of the little dining-room, the *Punches* propped informally! Everyone was in evening dress. Anglo-India, starched and glossy, stared at us with horror and disgust. A stage clergyman with an Oxford voice started as though he had seen the devil. A hush, through which on all sides could be heard the fell epithet 'jungly', descended on the assembled guests. We were back in Civilization.

There was no question, now, of ordering that special dinner. We would eat what we were given, and whether we should have the courage to eat it in public was by no means sure; we had no clothes in our luggage that were not crumpled and discoloured.

We advanced, through a barrage of shocked looks and muttered disapproval, to the reception desk, and booked rooms. A surly babu answered, curtly and inaccurately, our questions about air-lines and mail (we were about to get our first letters from home for several months). His manner damped what was left of our spirits. 'Will you please register?' he said.

With a last poor attempt at swagger we both wrote, in the 'Where from' column, 'Peking'; but it might have been 'Poona' for all the impression it made on the babu. We turned back to the alien and hostile lounge.

'That's that,' said Kini; and sighed. The journey was over.

FINIS

INDEX

393

All Futura Books are available at your bookshop or newsagent, or can be ordered from the following address:
Futura Books, Cash Sales Department,
P.O. Box 11, Falmouth, Cornwall.

Please send cheque or postal order (no currency), and allow 45p for postage and packing for the first book plus 20p for the second book and 14p for each additional book ordered up to a maximum charge of £1.63 in U.K.

Customers in Eire and B.F.P.O. please allow 45p for the first book, 20p for the second book plus 14p per copy for the next 7 books, thereafter 8p per book.

Overseas customers please allow 75p for postage and packing for the first book and 21p per copy for each additional book.